RESTORATION STUDIES

VOLUME X
2009

RESTORATION STUDIES

T HEOLOGY   AND   C ULTURE
IN   THE   C OMMUNITY   OF   C HRIST
AND THE L ATTER D AY S AINT M OVEMENT

VOLUME X
2009

P ETER   A .   J UDD

EDITOR

John Whitmer
Historical Association

Community of Christ
SEMINARY PRESS

Published by the John Whitmer Historical Association in conjunction with
the Community of Christ Seminary Press.

ISBN-13 978-1-934901-80-9

LCCN 82023375

Restoration Studies is a trademark of Herald Publishing House. *Restoration
Studies* I © 1980, *Restoration Studies* II © 1983, *Restoration Studies* III
© 1986, *Restoration Studies* IV © 1988, *Restoration Studies* V © 1993,
Restoration Studies VI © 1995, *Restoration Studies* VII © 1998, *Restoration
Studies* VIII © 2000, *Restoration Studies* IX © 2005 by Herald Publishing
House. This volume printed under license from Herald Publishing House.

Printed in the United States of America.

Copy editing by Erin Jennings.

Design, typesetting, and cover design by John Hamer.

CONTENTS

Introduction

PETER A. JUDD

THIS VOLUME IS the tenth in the *Restoration Studies* series. The first volume appeared in 1980 to celebrate the sesquicentennial of the founding of the Latter Day Saint movement by Joseph Smith Jr. in April 1830. Successive volumes have been published occasionally since then (every two to five years), with volume IX coming off the press in 2005. These collections of papers have been published by Herald Publishing House, the publication arm of Community of Christ (previously Reorganized Church of Jesus Christ of Latter Day Saints).

This current volume (X) is the first to be published by the John Whitmer Historical Association under a special arrangement with the Community of Christ. Subtitled "Theology and Culture in the Community of Christ and the Latter Day Saint Movement," it contains an assortment of articles (fifteen in all) covering a wide spectrum of topics. Some are scholarly in that they are heavily footnoted; others are testimonial reflecting more the views and opinions of their authors than of others. Some of the articles are historical in that they deal with happenings and people of the early Latter Day Saint period; others draw their focus from the more recent past and from current events.

Many of the articles in this volume were papers delivered at the April 2008 Restoration Studies and Sunstone Midwest Symposium held in Independence, Missouri, sponsored by the John Whitmer Historical Association, Sunstone, and the Community of Christ Seminary. The other articles were either delivered as addresses at various recent events or papers submitted by their authors independent of any specific occasion.

No attempt has been made to organize the articles by subject or chronology. For the most part, the sequence is arbitrary and was established to maintain the reader's interest by creating variety from one entry to the next. The one exception is Community of Christ president emeritus Wallace B. Smith's "Experiences in Growing a Faith: Reflections on a Twenty-year Journey." This is placed first in recognition of the inauguration of the Wallace B. Smith Lectureship at the Restoration Studies and Sunstone Midwest Symposium. It is hoped that this lectureship and the symposium will be held annually from now on.

It is anticipated that *Restoration Studies* will henceforth be an annual publication including many or most of the papers delivered at the annual symposium. It will however be open, as was this volume, to submissions from other sources and writers who wish to address the topic of theology and culture in the Community of Christ and the Latter Day Saint movement. Submissions for volume XI, to be published in 2010, should be sent to the *Restoration Studies* editor: *Editor@RestorationStudies.org*, from whom timeline, length, format, and other specifications can be obtained.

Interest in matters pertaining to "Restoration" churches, people, events, and faith dimensions continues to be widespread and robust. *Restoration Studies* is pleased to be a part of the continuing work of exploring and examining issues related to this important tradition. We trust that readers will find the contents of this volume to make a worthy contribution to this ongoing enterprise.

Experiences in Growing a Faith:
Reflections on a Twenty-year Journey, 1976–1996

WALLACE B. SMITH

Introduction

FIRST, LET ME say how pleased I am to present a paper before the inaugural session of the Restoration Studies symposium. As you know, the periodic volume titled *Restoration Studies* has not been published for some time; however, the scholarly pursuit of themes and issues related to the beliefs, history, polity, and current life of the Restoration Movement is ongoing. Thus, I share the expressed hope of others that this symposium will stimulate the research and produce the essays that will lead to the re-introduction of *Restoration Studies* as a scholarly publication. Admittedly I spent my share of time in the past either defending it or eschewing support for a particular point of view expressed in it. Nonetheless, it is my belief that *Restoration Studies* was and can again be an important and useful lens through which to view our movement.

Additionally, I am honored to be the first presenter in a series I understand will be known as the Wallace B. Smith Lectureship. Let me assure you I am not presumptive enough to think that the scholarship or content of my offering this evening is a worthy contribution to what I hope will become a highly respected lectureship. Let me just say the intent of my presentation is to bring before you the perspective of an active participant in some of the events and circumstances comprising a twenty-year period in the life of the church we now call Community of Christ. I have tried to be accurate and honest in my reflections, but there is an inevitable personal bias that must simply be acknowledged. With that disclaimer, let me begin.

A Summons to Service

THE PHONE CALL came on a Saturday afternoon in the early spring of 1975. It was my father, W. Wallace Smith. He said that if I was not busy he would like to come over and see me for a minute. When he arrived, we talked for a bit about the family, the possibility of going fishing a little later in the spring, and then he got to the point. He said that, at the age of seventy-four, he had been doing a lot of thinking about retirement. And, after much searching, contemplation, and prayer, he felt he had been led by the Spirit to ask me to accept a call to succeed him as prophet and president of the church. For a moment I was literally speechless. Of course, I had thought about such a possibility many times in my life. At the age of almost forty-six, however, and in the midst of a busy medical practice, I believed that the time for such a life-altering decision had somehow passed me by. After taking a few moments to recover, I said as much. Dad said he understood, but asked me to think about it and make it a matter of prayer.

I didn't sleep much in the next few weeks. My concerns were many, but they centered in my lack of preparation and experience as a full-time minister and church administrator. Moreover, I had trained long and hard as a specialist in diseases and surgery of the eye, and I was reluctant to give up a career I loved and in which I felt I had some competence. At the same time, I was loath to ignore Dad's feelings of spiritual guidance and my own desires to respond to a call from God. Being a person of faith I prayed earnestly, expectantly, for guidance—but no definitive answer came. I continued to feel I needed God's help in making a decision, but time was moving on and plans needed to be made. Therefore, using my best judgment, and acting with what flickering light I had at the time, I accepted the call. But still, no unmistakable confirmation came to me.

Preparations were being completed, of course, and finally the time for the 1976 World Conference arrived. I was scheduled to take part in the opening communion service. I lined up with the other participants and proceeded into the conference chamber. As I started up the steps to the rostrum, a light as bright as any I had ever seen seemed to fill the auditorium and a voice of assurance within me said, "You are where you are called to be." From that time forward I was able to assume my responsibilities with the assurance and strong sense of purpose that was to bless me again and again throughout my journey as a spiritual leader in the church.

A Time of Preparation and Study

A T THE TIME my father first spoke to me about becoming "president designate," I indicated I had never heard the term and thought it a bit odd. He assured me it was proper, but I never felt comfortable with it. In fact, I always had the impression that many church members had trouble suppressing a smile when they used the term to introduce me. It just didn't roll off the tongue. The concept, however, was vital to my leadership development.

When I first came into full-time church service in July of 1976, then-apostle Lloyd Hurshman was assigned to supervise my education and training. As we discussed the process, we identified three areas of need: namely, theological education, familiarization with church policies and procedures, and gaining acquaintance with both the domestic and international fields. Of the three areas, the one that seemed to present the greatest challenge was how best to gain a reasonably sound theological understanding in less than two years and in the face of a heavy travel and speaking schedule. My attendance at seminary did not seem advisable, given the climate of suspicion regarding seminary education in many parts of the church at the time. Instead, a plan was devised whereby several of the professors at Saint Paul School of Theology in Kansas City, Missouri, would tutor me privately. Indeed, for almost two years, Dr. Carl Bangs, Dr. Paul Jones, Dr. Charles Baughman, and other faculty members came to my home two or three times a week to instruct me in Christian church history, Old Testament, New Testament, comparative theology, philosophy of religion, and other subjects, almost literally opening up my skull and pouring in a concentrated course of study that could not have been achieved in any other way. I will always be extremely grateful to those good men for their willingness to assist me and the church so unselfishly in this endeavor.

During this period of time I also met frequently with various quorum and council members to review the inner workings of their areas of responsibility. Then, every weekend, I would get on an airplane and travel to a different part of the United States or Canada where the church had a presence. I would meet with a gathering of Saints on Friday or Saturday night, speak at a reception or banquet, usually preach on Sunday morning and afternoon, and then fly home again on Sunday night. This was a rigorous schedule. But it was also an important aspect of my orientation since it gave me an opportunity to meet a large number of church members fairly expeditiously. More importantly, it made it possible for them to see and hear me—this rather unknown quantity who had been designated as their next president.

Amazingly, during this same period, roughly July 1976 to March 1978, I was able to visit many of the jurisdictions in the international church as well, including Japan, Korea, Australia, Tahiti, England, Europe, and Mexico. Indeed, by the early spring of 1978, I felt that, for the most part, I had achieved what I had hoped to accomplish as president designate. I still had many misgivings about my abilities—both my capability and my suitability—for the role I was to assume. But the 1978 World Conference was looming and I needed to prepare.

Faith to Grow

As I began to think about my role as the new president and prophetic leader, I felt it was important to try to assess what the church's present situation was and where, with God's help and direction, we ought to be going. I was aware that the church had undergone a period of relatively rapid growth and expansion in the post-war boom of the late 1950s and early 1960s. In consequence of that expansion, particularly into non-Christian cultures in India, Africa, and the Orient, some re-definition of our missionary message had been introduced. This led to a perception on the part of some that the church was giving up its basic beliefs. There were concerns about such disparate issues as the possible condoning of polygamous marriages among some church members in tribal groups in India and Africa, the introduction of a new Christian education curriculum, and the fostering of closer ties with national and international ecumenical organizations, to name just a few. Also, membership statistics indicated that, while there had been rapid expansion in numerical strength in some of the newer missions abroad, the domestic church had shown little increase in recent years.

In view of these and other forces seemingly pulling the church in different directions, it seemed to me we needed some unifying principle to challenge the people as we entered a new era of leadership. I had discussed this with various persons in leadership roles and there were two areas that particularly seemed to stand out. One was fairly obvious: if we were to remain viable as an organization we needed to expand our membership base. The other reflected the need for the membership to understand and embrace an interpretation of the gospel message that would not only be universal in its application, but also lead to a greater depth of commitment. In other words, we needed to *grow*, both numerically and spiritually. And furthermore, it was going to take a lot of *faith*—in our leaders and in God's guidance—to achieve that growth.

I spoke of having this "faith to grow" in my remarks at the closing service of the 1978 World Conference[1] and it was that phrase that became the central

---

[1] "A Faith to Grow: Excerpts from an Address by President Wallace B. Smith Given on Sunday, April 9," *Saints' Herald* 125, no. 5 (May 1978): 48.

theme of the church's program for the decade of the 1980s. The emphasis was first introduced to a gathering of full-time church ministers and headquarters staff personnel in January of 1979. By means of a series of presentations (later characterized pejoratively by some as the Presidential Papers), the First Presidency sought to lay a groundwork and theological base for the Faith to Grow emphasis. The thinking was that the staff members who would be producing resource materials and the ministerial corps who would be introducing and implementing these concepts in the field should be among the first to hear and discuss the assumptions and rationale undergirding the emphasis.

For the most part, introducing the program in this way proved helpful, in my opinion. It should be noted, however, that a small but vocal minority of staff and appointees saw in these presentations the concretization of what they perceived as a gradual de-emphasis of Restoration fundamentals that had been building since the mid-1960s. The presentation materials, labeled the Presidential Papers and annotated derisively in the margins, were distributed widely by some of these concerned persons; criticisms of the program were mounted before it was ever launched, and I experienced my first taste of the potential hazards of prophetic leadership. It would not be my last.

Leadership Challenges

THE FAITH TO GROW programmatic emphasis was introduced to the church at-large by means of a series of weekend workshops in the fall of 1980. The concepts of growth and expansion were explained and the church was challenged to accept a goal of 5 percent numerical expansion annually during the decade of the 1980s. The commission system of congregational programming was introduced and annual goals and objectives were projected. If a local church achieved these goals they were designated a Faith to Grow congregation.

Many jurisdictions welcomed this new emphasis and saw in it an effort on the part of church leadership to bring about a unified program under the overarching theme of evangelism. The "Theological Foundations" section of the Faith to Grow resource materials laid out quite clearly the basic beliefs on which the program was established. For some, however, these same foundational statements were the very evidence that the church was changing its beliefs and de-emphasizing or abandoning cherished concepts upon which former evangelism programs were based. It was pointed out, for example, that themes such as "the one true church," restoring of the "old Jerusalem gospel," and proofs of the historicity of the Book of Mormon, among others, were all conspicuously absent from the Faith to Grow literature.

In response to these perceived errors and shortcomings of the church's official program, some individual members began organizing counterprogrammatic gatherings to teach and preach what they felt ought to be the church's message. One such group was known as the Restoration Festival. I remember going with then-apostle Roy Schaefer to one of their meetings. Our purpose was to make a gesture of friendship, encourage them to re-join the mainstream of church participation, and invite them to experience the joy and enthusiasm being engendered by the Faith to Grow program. The courteous, but cool, reception we encountered indicated we were probably not going to be successful. Rather, it was likely we were going to continue to contend with such "molehills" of opposition in some places indefinitely. The challenge was to strive to keep them from becoming larger "mountains" of contention as we sought to encourage our membership to develop the faith to grow.

Watershed Decisions

OPPOSITION TO ELEMENTS of the Faith to Grow program was not the only issue that was occupying the interests of the church as I addressed my responsibilities at the start of the decade of the eighties. The question of women's rights had been a topic of much discussion, particularly in the United States, since the early 1970s. This was true within the church as well as in the general population. Indeed, as a member of the Standing High Council, I had participated in the formulation of the church's Statement on Abortion in 1974. And this was just one area in which women had been demanding greater freedom of choice. Questions regarding women's roles in church participation also were increasingly being raised.

Legislation from field jurisdictions seeking either to prohibit or enable the ordination of women had been introduced in every world conference since the mid-1970s. The First Presidency had presented numerous statements from 1976 onward in response to such legislation, including an extensive statement to the world conference in 1982, encouraging the use of women in all ministerial roles not specifically requiring ordination.[2] It was at this same 1982 conference, in fact, that a motion of referral called upon the First Presidency to appoint a taskforce to study the question of the ordination of women, including polling the membership, and report back at the 1984 World Conference. It was in the midst of this intense period of interest in women's roles in the church, including the question of ordination, that I began the discussions, consultations, meditations, and prayerful seeking that culminated in my submitting to the

[2] Reorganized Church of Jesus Christ of Latter Day Saints, *World Conference Bulletin*, 1982, 335.

world conference of 1984 what would become Section 156 of the Book of Doctrine and Covenants.

To undertake a thorough exposition of all the factors influencing that action is beyond the scope of this presentation. I might, however, just make a comment or two. I mentioned the taskforce that was created by 1982 conference legislation to poll the membership on the question of the ordination of women. The results of that survey began to emerge in the fall of 1983. It appeared that a little *over* half of the almost eleven hundred respondents were opposed to the full and equal ordination of men and women and a little *under* half were either supportive or neutral.[3] For me, this presented something of a dilemma. I did not feel that such an important issue as the nature of priesthood calling should be decided by opinion polls. But I also knew the report of the survey would be printed in the conference bulletin and available to all the delegates.

By the early spring of 1984 I was feeling strongly impressed by the spirit of inspiration to recommend that women be ordained; however, the conflict within myself of such a decision was ongoing, particularly in light of the survey evidence of significant opposition. It is one thing to decide on a course of action affecting the whole church when one only supposes there may not be majority support for the action. When one has concrete evidence of that lack of support, but, under a strong sense of spiritual impulsion, still feels the need to pursue the less supported alternative, it is at that point that the burden of prophetic leadership is felt most keenly. It was in that frame of mind, finally, that I presented to the church what I considered to be inspired instructions regarding the ordination of women in April of 1984.[4]

Of course, there were other elements in the provisions of Section 156. The call to begin the construction of the temple in Independence was a fulfillment of the hopes and dreams of countless members of the church. The clear establishment of its purposes, as based on the ministry of Jesus Christ, was important for many to hear. Indeed, it was my feeling that the excitement surrounding the anticipation of the building of the temple helped to temper the feelings of uncertainty, even apprehension, that otherwise seemed to affect the mood of the 1984 conference delegates so profoundly.

In light of the subsequent course of church thought and development, there is no doubt the acceptance of Section 156 by the conference delegates on April 5, 1984, constituted an event of watershed significance. The importance of the action was to be felt in many ways in the years ahead. But the immediacy of that

---

[3] Reorganized Church of Jesus Christ of Latter Day Saints, *World Conference Bulletin*, 1984, 247.

[4] Community of Christ, Doctrine and Covenants 156: 7–10.

impact was most graphically illustrated for me by the fact that, upon leaving the rostrum following the business session that April day, the First Presidency was ushered directly into an adjoining conference room in the auditorium. Awaiting us was a full-blown news conference, complete with microphones and television cameras, with reporters asking pointed questions about what such action meant for the church. I don't think any of us knew just how to answer such a question at that moment. But we sensed the decision was significant and that it would probably be many years before all its implications were fully realized.

New Agendas

WHILE IT WAS true that the full effects of the acceptance of the provisions were still unknown, some were felt almost immediately. Many of those most opposed to the prospects of women being ordained began voicing their objections, threatening to withdraw both their church participation and their financial support. The volume of my mail suddenly increased dramatically and I found it more and more difficult to keep up with the replies. At times I found it helpful to have some assistance in this endeavor and, apart from the other members of the First Presidency, one of the most valuable was Geoff Spencer, serving at that time in the Council of Twelve Apostles. He had a wonderful ability to draft a response to even the most forceful, shall I say, of letters in a gentle and reflective way. I could then take those drafts and adapt them to my personal style without it consuming too much of my time. Although he never seemed to enjoy the assignment much, I was grateful to have his help in this way for a time.

The provisions of Section 156 also called for the establishment of guidelines and instructions dealing with priesthood ordination and function. A taskforce was appointed to begin preparing these guidelines and a target date in November of 1985 was set as the time for the guidelines to be completed and the first ordinations of women to take place. I was privileged to be in Denver, Colorado, on Sunday, November 17, 1985, to participate in one of those first ordination services. Among the ordinands was Sister Bunny Spillman who had been a pillar in the Denver Central congregation for many years. It was my pleasure to assist her son, W. B. (Pat) Spillman, in ordaining her to the office of elder on that happy occasion. Reporters from both the *Denver Post* and the *Rocky Mountain News* were present during the service and in an interview afterward, Sister Spillman and I expressed how pleased we were that the church was finally able to formally recognize through ordination the ministerial gifts and abilities of our membership in a full and equal way.

Discomfort and Joy

UNFORTUNATELY, ONE OF the unforeseen but almost inevitable effects of the church's preoccupation with the provisions of Section 156 was that the focus of the Faith to Grow program began to blur. Even though resource materials continued to make reference to growth and expansion, the reality was, that in many areas—particularly in the domestic field—church membership and participation, rather than increasing, had decreased somewhat. More to the point, much of the energy of many church administrators was being expended in managing the various forms of opposition to church programming. Regrettably, this changing agenda neither left a lot of time nor provided much incentive for an evangelism program inviting prospective members to "come and see," especially if what they were likely to see was considerable internecine strife within some of the congregations of the church.

Although it might have seemed to some in the church that this was a period of unhappiness and turmoil, for others it was a time of great joy. Women who were being ordained brought a sense of enthusiasm and dedication to their ministry that was inspiring to see. I was particularly struck by this thought as I sat on the platform during the communion service on the first Sunday of the 1986 World Conference. This was to be the first communion service at which women would be serving and there was considerable apprehension about just how they would be received. But as they came up onto the platform in company with the men to receive their communion trays and go back down into the congregation, I suddenly knew with a certainty there would be no problems. The sight of their glowing faces was something I will never forget, and if there had ever been a need for a personal confirmation of the rightness of the decision to ordain these good women, I felt I had received it at that moment.

Seashells and Spirals

IN ADDITION TO the adjustments necessitated by a new approach to ordination and priesthood commitment, there was also a great deal of planning and preparation to be done relating to the building of the temple in Independence. In early 1987, a temple project committee met to begin the process of selecting an architect, deciding on a design, identifying a construction firm, and addressing the myriad other details attendant to a project of such major proportions.

One of the first tasks, in fact, was the selection of the architect for the project. After interviewing almost thirty architectural firms, the temple project committee had narrowed the choices to a final three. I and my two counselors in the First Presidency were designated to personally visit the finalists, assess

A scale model of the temple, used in its construction

their work styles and personalities, determine their grasp of the spiritual nature of the endeavor, and make a final recommendation to the project committee. When we met with Mr. Gyo Obata in his office in St. Louis there seemed to be an almost instant rapport established that convinced all three of us that he was the one to design our temple. We never regretted that decision. Amazingly, his preliminary design for the temple complex, incorporating a logarithmic spiral resembling a nautilus shell as the dominant feature, was embraced by the project committee almost immediately. This phenomenon, in itself, seemed to indicate that considerable inspiration was influencing our decisions and for this we were all grateful.

The planning, designing, funding, constructing, and, finally, the completion and dedication of the temple in Independence constitutes a story by itself. Many aspects were reported via articles in the pages of the *Saints' Herald* and later compiled in a booklet by Herald Publishing House.[5] Let me just say, my joy was truly complete at the close of the dedication service on April 17, 1994, as

---

[5] *Preparing for the Temple: A Selection of Herald Articles* (Independence, MO: Herald Publishing House, 1989).

we proceeded up the extension of the worshippers' path and out through the massive bronze doors onto the World Plaza. The congregation was singing "God Be with You Till We Meet Again" and just then a splash of white was reflected off the wings of a flock of doves as they were released into an azure sky. It was an inspiring moment and I offered my own silent prayer of thanksgiving, not only for the many thousands who had given so sacrificially that this magnificent edifice could become a reality but also for the thousands who were yet to be blessed by the ministry of those inspired by its symbolism and beauty.

An Expanded Mission and Vision

I MENTIONED EARLIER THAT the Faith to Grow emphasis seemed to lose momentum as other issues occupied the church's attention in the latter half of the 1980s. Consequently, much thought was being given to a new programmatic emphasis as the decade of the 1990s approached. As part of this effort a Joint Council retreat was held in Estes Park, Colorado, in September of 1988 to develop a new vision and mission statement. We felt we needed to capture the essence of what the church stood for and at the same time re-direct its energies in a positive and forward-looking way. These mission and vision statements were published in the May 1989 *Saints' Herald* and formed the basis of the Outreach '89 evangelism workshops held throughout the church that year. [6]

Subsequently, a shortened mission statement was developed at another Joint Council retreat in 1994. It stated, "We proclaim Jesus Christ and promote communities of joy, hope, love, and peace." It was my feeling that this statement not only continued to emphasize evangelism, but also re-focused the importance of congregational life in an affirmative and hopeful way. I particularly remember the expressions of assurance and optimism among Joint Council members at the close of this retreat, sensing we had been blessed by the Holy Spirit in our deliberations.

It was at this same retreat that discussions about the church's name were also held. For some time my own sense had been that a name more reflective of our contemporary beliefs and less a negative reflection of the LDS Church could be helpful in our evangelism program. In addition, this topic had been a recurring theme for resolutions and debate in general and world conferences since at least 1962, including a resolution in 1992 for the First Presidency to study the question of a new name and make a recommendation to the 1994 World Conference. As our explorations at the retreat proceeded, a general consensus seemed to form around the name Community of Christ. Indeed, as it was later

---

[6] "Official: Planning for the Future," *Saints' Herald* 136, no. 5 (May 1989): 4.

reported in the "Official" column of the *Saints' Herald,* the Joint Council "came to strongly affirm the name ... as one we are prepared to recommend to the church."[7] It is interesting to note, however, that it took another six years of dialogue and study before the 2000 World Conference finally took action to officially adopt the new name.

Succession in Leadership

AT ABOUT THE time the euphoria surrounding the completion and dedication of the temple was subsiding, I began to realize I was approaching the age at which the personnel policies of the church prescribed retirement. Previous presidents had not felt bound by these policies, but it seemed to me that I should at least be considering the possibility of such an action. I had had major surgery in 1991 for prostate cancer, and although I felt I still had the strength and vigor needed to carry out my duties, there were good reasons to begin thinking about a successor.

Throughout my life, of course, I had heard discussions about the relationship of the Smith family to the leadership of the church. These ranged all the way from a conviction that *only* a member of the family could ever hold the prophetic office to the assertion that almost anyone *but* a Smith ought to be chosen. There were, to be sure, a number of descendants of Joseph Smith Jr. available, including several who might well have been candidates for succession to the leadership of the church.

The more I thought about the question, however, the more strongly I was impressed that it was time to move beyond the contributions of one particular family and expand the pool of potential leadership. In a Joint Council seminar several years earlier the question of succession in church leadership had been the topic of considerable discussion. At that time, I presented a review of the statements made and actions taken by former presidents of the church, as well as the precedents cited for their decisions relating to succession in leadership. Included in this discussion was the unprecedented decision of my father, W. Wallace Smith, to retire rather than remain in office for life. I also pointed out again, as had been noted in the "Letter of Instruction" prepared by Joseph Smith III in 1912, church law stipulated only that the incumbent president had the right to name a successor and the designee should be approved by the vote of the conference and ordained by those in authority to do so.[8]

It was with the background of that study and my own reflections that I began to prepare the pastoral letter that was released to the church in November

---

[7] "Official: Our Name and Mission," *Saints' Herald* 141, no. 12 (December 1994): 4.

[8] Joseph Smith III, "A Letter of Instruction," *Saints' Herald* 59, no. 11 (March 13, 1912): 244.

of 1995.[9] In it I reiterated the conditions under which a successor was to be chosen, indicated my intentions to retire in April of 1996, and named W. Grant McMurray as my successor.

At the world conference of 1996, one of my last acts was to relinquish the chair to newly ordained President McMurray. In a brief statement, I thanked a number of people for the help and assistance they had extended to me along the way. And then I took the opportunity to especially thank President Howard Sheehy Jr. for his loyal support of me and my presidency for eighteen years. Among other things, he had presided over all of the business sessions during which the inspired documents I presented had been considered. That was never an easy task and I wanted to particularly recognize him for his steady leadership in that role. I left the platform that day with a sense that the church was in good hands. I believe it still is.

Conclusion

SEVERAL YEARS AGO Paul Edwards conducted a series of oral history interviews with me. As we discussed some of the features of my presidency, I remember commenting that it would be difficult if not impossible to analyze one's own work. And as I stated at the outset of this paper, that has not been my intention here. In my retirement years it has been fascinating to follow subsequent events in the life of the church and try to assess how or to what extent they have been shaped by decisions my colleagues and I made. My medical training many years ago, however, taught me not to rely too heavily on the dictum: *post hoc, ergo propter hoc* (after this, therefore this follows). Too many influences from too many directions affect both diseases and the course of events in social and religious enterprises. So, I will leave the analysis of causes and effects to others. Meanwhile, I will maintain my position as an interested observer, confident that the God who called this people into being will continue to nudge us gently with restoring influences as we labor in the cause of God's kingdom. Most of all, I am grateful for the sense of divine companionship that I felt many times during my tenure, when otherwise I would have felt very much alone. Let me just say this: in all my strivings, I endeavored always to be responsive to the Spirit's leadings in seeking for directions on our way.

As a final word, I want to affirm President Veazey's prophetic call for the church to go deeper in its explorations of what Community of Christ truly means. I am convinced that both our history and our destiny are inseparably linked to a clear understanding of that Divine call.

---

[9] "A Pastoral Letter," *Saints' Herald* 142, no. 11 (November 1995): 3.

Joseph Smith's Conferral of Priesthood on Women: A Reappraisal

I N 1842, MORMONISM's founder Joseph Smith promised the original members of the Female Relief Society he would make them good Masons because Masons knew how to keep secrets. The following year an exclusive group of women within Smith's inner circle began to receive ceremonies known as the temple Endowment. During the feminist movement of the late 1970s, in a period Maxine Hanks terms "fourth wave feminism," several sympathetic scholars began to produce historical studies aimed at refuting the LDS Church's official position that Mormon priesthood has always been exclusively male.[1] D. Michael Quinn, for example, lost his right to membership in the LDS Church for arguing that the bestowal of Mormon temple rites instituted by Smith upon females continues to be a de-facto conferral of priesthood.[2] The argument made by these feminist scholars was that female priesthood was intended by Smith to be an egalitarian blessing to lift up women, a privilege that was lost under the leadership of Brigham Young and his successors in Utah. Ian Barber unfavorably

---

[1] Maxine Hanks, ed., *Women and Authority: Re-emerging Mormon Feminism* (Salt Lake City: Signature Books, 1992), xix.

[2] D. Michael Quinn, "Mormon Women Have Had the Priesthood Since 1843," in Hanks, *Women and Authority*, 366–69. Quinn's article arguing Joseph Smith bestowed priesthood on women followers through temple ceremonies proved so sensitive it resulted in his excommunication from the LDS Church for heresy in September 1993 (Lavina Fielding Anderson, "DNA Mormon: D. Michael Quinn," in *Mormon Mavericks: Essays on Dissenters*, ed. John Sillito and Susan Staker (Salt Lake City: Signature Books, 2002), 329–63.

compared the loss of priesthood for Mormon women in Utah with females who continued to receive the ordinance in schismatic LDS movements led by Alpheus Cutler and Sidney Rigdon.[3] This study does not challenge the assertion that priesthood was conferred on a select group of women by Smith late in his ministry. An alternate theory is proposed, however, that rather than being motivated by egalitarianism, Smith proffered priesthood to a relatively small group of women in exchange for their secretive participation in the clandestine practice of plural marriage with certain church elites, particularly himself. Evidence for this is indicated by Smith's public denials of polygamy and his selective policies that limited the extension of the temple ordinances to the general membership of his church. Yet an equally compelling argument is that Smith's rhetoric was consistent with the antebellum Evangelical agenda of what Paul E. Johnson describes as "free agency, perfectionism, and millennialism,"[4] and more on point, the new sphere of women within the cult of domesticity. When compared in juxtaposition to the era's emerging progressive figures, it will be demonstrated that Smith's attitudes toward gender roles were more consistent with the likes of Finney than with the feminists of his day.

Quinn's controversial 1993 article argues that the esoteric temple rites Smith introduced in Nauvoo included the initiation of women as priesthood holders. In a legalistic sense, Quinn's contention that LDS endowed women are technically the recipients of Mormon priesthood is persuasive.[5] His research does not detail the circumstances that led Smith to alter Mormonism's male only priesthood tradition to include women other than to state its inevitability as "part of the restoration of the gospel."[6] Quinn's argument is based largely on interactions Smith had with members of both the Nauvoo Female Relief Society, a typical antebellum organized women's organization,[7] and the Anointed

---

[3] Ian G. Barber, "The Ecclesiastical Position of Women in Two Mormon Trajectories," *Journal of Mormon History* 14 (1988): 63–68.

[4] Paul E. Johnson, *A Shopkeeper's Millennium: Society and Revivals in Rochester, New York 1815–1837* (New York: Hill and Wang, 1978), 5.

[5] Quinn's thesis is not universally accepted by historians. For example, a recent biography of Joseph Smith states, "The women were not ordained to the priesthood, and the name of the society—The Female Relief Society of Nauvoo—did not imply priesthood, but priesthood was the pattern" (Richard L. Bushman, *Joseph Smith: Rough Stone Rolling* [New York: Alfred A. Knopf, 2005], 447). Quinn, however, does not argue Relief Society membership conferred priesthood on LDS women, but that temple endowment ceremonies did.

[6] Quinn, "Mormon Women," 366.

[7] See the description of the Utica First Presbyterian Church's Female Missionary Society (Mary P. Ryan, "A Women's Awakening: Evangelical Religion and the Families of Utica, New York, 1800–1840," in *Religion and American Culture: A Reader*, ed. David G. Hackett [New York: Routledge, 1995], 161).

Quorum, comprised of both sexes who were the elite beneficiaries of Smith's privately administered temple rituals.

Successive promises were made to these women that they would enjoy the "gifts of the priesthood" and that they were entitled to a "part of the priesthood." It is my contention that these offices constituted tokens offered by Smith to win these women's loyalty and silence as "good Masons" who knew how to keep a secret[8] and not an egalitarian gesture to lift up the status of antebellum females. While it may not have been his only motivation, the benefits Smith received from imparting priesthood to his closest female associates in exchange for their willing and discrete submission to his surreptitious practice of plural marriage was clearly a habitus of imbalanced power between congregants and their spiritual leader.[9] Lawrence Foster describes both Smith's introduction of plural marriage and his attempt to institutionalize its practice as a "risky venture."[10] More difficult, however, is assessing the range of Smith's intentions. Was Smith's gift of female priesthood simply a compulsory erotic manifestation of dominant subordination? On a more practical level, women were involved in temple rituals that included same-sex administration of specific ordinances such as ceremonial washing and anointing of indiscrete body parts required for the sake of propriety.[11] A nuanced anthropological analysis could argue that Smith's gift exchange was an attempt to establish kinship/friendship relationships as a peace-making strategy to bolster solidarity through dynastic marital alliances.[12] Whatever the extent of his personal objectives, the historical context surrounding the explosive exposure Smith faced if his activities with plural wives became widely known necessitated his need to control those involved with a solemn vow of secrecy.

Similar to ceremonial gift giving in some pre-modern cultures was the Mormon temple Endowment in the assigning of a "new name." For those initiated, they become "imbued with supernatural power" which allowed them

---

[8] For the connection between Masonry and Joseph Smith's teachings to the Relief Society, see David John Buerger, *The Mysteries of Godliness: A History of the Mormon Temple Worship* (San Francisco: Smith Research Associates, 1994), 51.

[9] Smith's position of dominance as head of the LDS Church was clearly an unequal "balance of power" with his female followers (Pierre Bourdieu, *Outline of a Theory of Practice*, trans. Richard Nice [Cambridge: Cambridge University Press, 1987], 195).

[10] Lawrence Foster, *Religion and Sexuality: The Shakers, the Mormons, and the Oneida Community* (Urbana: University of Illinois Press, 1984), 150.

[11] Linda King Newell, "The Historical Relationship of Mormon Women and Priesthood," in Hanks, *Women and Authority*, 27.

[12] Ilana Krausman Ben-Amos, "Gifts and Favors: Informal Support in Early Modern England," *The Journal of Modern History* 72, no. 2 (June 2000): 299. Marchall Sahlins, *Stone Age Economics* (New York: Aldine De Gruyter, 1972), 220–22.

to "change from one socially recognized phase of life to another."[13] Joseph Smith held the ultimate spiritual capital; the power to enable a select few of his followers to ultimately become gods themselves would have been appealing to many of the devoted.

In 1976, Mormon historian Jill Mulvay Derr wrote that early LDS women had expanded their domain much further than their contemporaries while noting that "the rights, sphere, and position of Mormon women were determined by the pronouncements of male prophets, seers and revelators." Ironically, Derr goes on to assert, in language reminiscent of Catharine Beecher, that early LDS women did not consider "submission to the priesthood" as being subjected to the "absolute tyranny" of men.[14] However, other Mormon feminist scholars, especially Margaret M. Toscano, began to argue that under Joseph Smith's leadership women shared "equal power with men" to a greater degree than "could be found in any religion."[15] In a 2004 retrospective, Toscano reflected that during her own initiation into LDS temple ceremonies in the 1970s she received a spiritual experience that convinced her she had been "invested or endowed with priesthood." She soon thereafter came to understand Mormon history as affirming an egalitarian position towards nineteenth-century women that was systematically rescinded by the all-male LDS Church leaders during the next hundred years. Toscano's "feminism took the form of developing a broad feminist Mormon theology" that included her new perspectives on LDS history. She became convinced that "LDS women and men could see the sexist problem only if they saw it in the context of their own faith" and her writings would facilitate that goal.[16]

Not much scrutiny is required to refute Derr's and Toscano's broad claims that Mormonism held the most progressive positions in regards to antebellum gender roles. The radical Boston abolitionist and feminist theologian Theodore Parker often shocked his audiences by praying to God as "Mother."[17] In comparison, while Joseph Smith likewise affirmed a female Goddess, he constructed her role within the Godhood to conform to the cult of domesticity's sphere of

[13] Eric R. Wolf, *Envisioning Power: Ideologies of Dominance and Crisis* (Berkeley: University of California Press, 1999), 126–27.

[14] Jill C. Mulvay, "Eliza R. Snow and the Woman Question," *Brigham Young University Studies* 16, no. 2 (1976): 1.

[15] Margaret M. Toscano, "Margaret M. Toscano," in *Transforming the Faiths of Our Fathers: Women Who Changed American Religion*, ed. Ann Braude (New York City: Palgrave Macmillan, 2004), 160–61.

[16] Ibid., 159–62.

[17] Lewis Perry, *Boats Against the Current: American Culture Between Revolution and Modernity, 1820–1860* (New York: Oxford University Press, 1993), 253.

1840s-era married women. Other early abolitionist reformers such as the Grimke sisters and William Lloyd Garrison likewise agitated for equality of the sexes in defiance of popular cult-of-domesticity advocates such as Catharine Beecher, Horace Bushnell, and Sarah Josepha Hale.[18] While both Derr and Toscano find seeds of feminism in Smith's Nauvoo Temple theologies, unfortunately neither pragmatically addresses the context of the historic realities between Mormonism and the prevailing debates emerging within American society.

In defining gender roles, Joseph Smith and his movement mirrored the prevailing cultural attitude toward women that epitomized what Nancy F. Cott terms the very "canon of domesticity."[19] The rise of Mormonism intersected a time of transformation in America's economy that produced a major shift from an agrarian to industrial society. The colonial values formed when men largely farmed land and stayed home were disrupted as men became shop keepers and laborers who increasingly worked away from their families. Evangelical religious leaders preached that a woman should be responsible for maintaining the sanctity of the home in her husband's absence. Her sphere was to rear righteous children and to be a comfort to her spouse in his afflictions after suffering long work days in an outside world full of sin and temptation.

As one married male LDS missionary wrote to the official church newspaper while serving in Ohio, he knew his children were "assisting their lonely mother in arranging the domestic affairs."[20] A member of the LDS Church's ranking

---

[18] Kathryn Kish Sklar, *Catharine Beecher: A Study in American Domesticity* (New York: W. W. Norton & Company, 1976), 151–54. And Anne C. Rose, *Voices of the Marketplace: American Thought and Culture, 1830–1860* (New York: Twayne Publishers, 1995), 19.

[19] Nancy F. Cott, *The Bonds of Womanhood: "Woman's Sphere" in New England, 1780–1835*, 2nd ed. (New Haven: Yale University Press, 1997), 64–67. Also, as Barbara Welter points out, and Joseph Smith would have agreed with, "One reason religion was valued was that it did not take woman away from her 'proper sphere,' her home" (Barbara Welter, "The Cult of True Womanhood: 1820–1860," *American Quarterly* 18, no. 2, pt. 1 [Summer 1966]: 153. For an RLDS feminist perspective see Imogene D. Goodyear, "Women in the Church," in *Restoration Studies* I, ed. Maurice L. Draper (Independence, MO: Herald House, 1980), 243. Joseph Smith was comparatively progressive in some of his theological reforms such as temperance. On the subject of advocating women's rights, however, he was not attempting to re-order the dominant society's views on separate spheres for men and women. The early nineteenth-century discourse Smith echoed while reflecting normative cultural values of his day has largely survived as manifested in the modern era LDS Church. Another of Joseph Smith's innovative theologies in the Nauvoo era was introducing the concept of a Mother in Heaven. Here again, though, this was an anthropomorphic archetype representing what deceased women were expected to aspire to: celestial domesticity (Linda P. Wilcox, "The Mormon Concept of a Mother in Heaven," in *Line Upon Line: Essays on Mormon Doctrine*, ed. Gary James Bergera [Salt Lake City: Signature Books, 1989], 104).

[20] L.[Luman] A. Shirtliff, "To the Editor of the Times and Seasons," *Times and Seasons* 2, no. 23 (Oct. 1, 1841): 556.

Quorum of Twelve, also writing while on a mission abroad, commented that if it were God's will for him he would "gladly [...] retreat from the oppressing heat of public life, and seek repose in the cool and refreshing shades of domestic endearments, and bask in the affections of my own little family circle."[21] Smith instructed his women devotees of the Relief Society to treat their husbands with "mildness and affection" as it was the wife's responsibility to provide "a smile, not an argument" to her troubled and "perplexed" husband. She held the ability to "calm down his soul and sooth his feelings."[22] The broader antebellum society was likewise replete with published accounts of dutiful women tenderly caring for sick males as a means of attaining usefulness along with gaining influence through the effort.[23] Evangelical middle-class men were admonished to curb their "masculine passions through strong character" and "true women" were to be "pious, maternal guardians of virtue."[24] The introduction of polygamy, even on a limited scale, severely strained the discourse of gender roles between Joseph Smith and his legal wife, Emma. Respectively the leader of the church and the president of the Relief Society, they found themselves struggling to define mutually acceptable social norms.[25] Emma and Joseph's dilemma of navigating the boundaries between the praxis of an antebellum religiously motivated female *society* and the larger community where they resided, though extreme, was not unique from the northeastern towns in which they were reared.

Mary P. Ryan asserts that there was tension in the Utica, New York, community (near the birthplace of Mormonism) in the early 1800s regarding the degree to which female charitable societies should exercise their influence as they positioned themselves "precariously on the fragile axis between public and private life."[26] Formed in the early 1830s, Rochester, New York's only relief aid organization was its "Female Charitable Society," comprised of the community's

---

[21] Orson Hyde, "Letter from Elder Hyde, Ratisbon, on the Danube, July 17, 1841," *Times and Seasons* 2, no. 24 (Oct. 15, 1841): 573.

[22] Relief Society Minutes, 6th meeting, April 28, 1842, cited in Linda King Newell and Valeen Tippetts Avery, *Mormon Enigma: Emma Hale Smith, Prophet's Wife, "Elect Lady," Polygamy's Foe, 1804–1879* (New York: Doubleday, 1984), 113.

[23] Welter, "Cult of True Womanhood," 164.

[24] Gail Bederman, *Manliness & Civilization: A Cultural History of Gender and Race in the United States, 1880–1917* (Chicago and London: University of Chicago Press, 1995), 11–12.

[25] A modern LDS Church–published history of the Relief Society ascribes as Emma Smith's "private addenda" to work against all forms of plural marriage practices in Nauvoo by her husband or otherwise (Jill Mulvay Derr, Janath Russell Cannon, and Maureen Ursenbach Beecher, *Women of the Covenant: The Story of Relief Society* [Salt Lake City: Deseret Book Company 1992], 61).

[26] Mary P. Ryan, *Cradle of the Middle Class: The Family in Oneida County, New York, 1790–1865* (Cambridge: Cambridge University Press, 1981), 52–53.

wealthiest Evangelical women. Members of the society went door to door in the poor neighborhoods dispensing help to those they felt most deserving.[27]

In the May 26, 1842, Relief Society meeting, Joseph Smith spoke first and admonished the women's group, a number of whom had already become plural wives,[28] to keep their faith in Mormonism, but added, "as females posses refined feelings and sensitiveness, they are also subject to an overmuch zeal which must ever prove dangerous, and cause them to be rigid in a religious capacity." Looking directly at his wife, Emma, he warned that "the tongue is an unruly member—hold your tongues about things of no moment. A little tale will set the world on fire. At this time the truth on the guilty should not be told openly—Strange as this may seem, yet this is policy." Having experienced Governor Boggs's 1838 "extermination order" that expelled the LDS Church from the state of Missouri, Smith realistically assessed the impact of widespread disclosure of Mormon polygamy.[29] When the Relief Society was formed only two months before, he had charged the organization to "watch over the morals of the community," and now he was reversing that injunction.[30] Smith's admission that his request might seem strange was a tacit acknowledgement he knew what he was asking of them transgressed not only the pervasive Evangelical gender expectations to be society's defenders of virtue, but of his own masculine commission to decisively "protect and direct those weaker than himself."[31]

Following her husband's remarks, Emma Smith proceeded to clarify his message. Gossip should be ignored, but not violations "against the law of God, and the laws of the country." She was determined her organization would weed out and expose any sinners in their midst and those who refused to assist her in this duty would be considered equal offenders. She concluded her comments by emphatically telling the members, "I want none in this society who have

---

[27] Johnson, *A Shopkeeper's Millennium*, 118.

[28] Derr, Cannon, and Beecher, *Women of the Covenant*, 60. At the time the Relief Society was organized in 1842, "at least nine of the twenty women at the first meeting were already, or soon would be, partakers in the newly reinstituted Old Testament practice, five of them as plural wives of the Prophet Joseph himself. Others would become participants during the two years of the Nauvoo Relief Society."

[29] In 1838 Smith faced a similar dilemma in Missouri. See Michael S. Riggs and John E. Thompson, "Joseph Smith, Jr., and 'The Notorious Case of Aaron Lyon': Evidence of Earlier Doctrinal Development of Salvation for the Dead and a Trigger for the Practice of Polyandry?" *John Whitmer Historical Association Journal* 26 (2006): 101–19. This was a valid concern for Joseph Smith as ultimately it was an exposé of his heterodox marital practices that led to his assassination by a mob on June 27, 1844, in Carthage, Illinois.

[30] Newell and Avery, *Mormon Enigma*, 115.

[31] Bederman, *Manliness & Civilization*, 12.

violated the laws of virtue!"[32] Emma Smith briefly acquiesced in her opposition to her husband's involvement with polygamy in the summer and early fall of 1843,[33] and it was during this time that she was initiated into the temple ceremonies as a reward for her loyalty.[34] But soon thereafter she renewed her opposition, using less direct forms of influence. It was found ironic that the Relief Society members in Nauvoo, including the sixteen women in the group Joseph Smith had taken as plural wives, were such staunch defenders of Smith's "public reputation."[35] Given his evolving promises of special ecclesiastical status to be bestowed upon them, however, it would be more contradictory if they did not do whatever was necessary to protect the gift they were to receive.

Mormon women initiated into Nauvoo temple ceremonies received a semblance of priesthood they were told they shared as companions with their husbands. They were not ordained as males were, outside the sacred space of the temple Endowment setting. As part of the temple ceremony, women performed the ordinance of washing and anointing. Early on this became associated with the gift of healing, and Smith sanctioned endowed women to bless one another for health purposes. This practice continued in Utah with increased misgivings by LDS Church leaders until it was discontinued in the early twentieth century.[36] For early followers of Alpheus Cutler (Cutlerites) and many of his flock who later defected to the Reorganized Church of Jesus Christ of Latter Day Saints (RLDS), the legacy of Joseph Smith's Nauvoo female priesthood associated with his temple Endowments further argues the point against its origins being egalitarian.

Following Joseph Smith's death in June 1844, Alpheus Cutler shifted his loyalties to Brigham Young, who, as head of the surviving Quorum of the Twelve Apostles, had positioned himself to become the movement's next spiritual leader. During the December 24, 1845, Nauvoo Stake High Council meeting, Cutler, clothed in the ritual garment and robes of the temple cult, "offered up prayers to God for our prosperity, the preservation of the Twelve [apostles], for

---

[32] Newell and Avery, *Mormon Enigma*, 115.

[33] Conferring priesthood on his wife, Emma Smith, at the end of September 1843 seems to be what temporarily quieted her opposition to Joseph's polygamous activities (George D. Smith, ed., *An Intimate Chronicle: The Journals of William Clayton* (Salt Lake City: Signature Books, 1995), 122.

[34] Andrew F. Ehat, "Joseph Smith's Introduction of the Temple Ordinances and the 1844 Mormon Succession Question" (master's thesis, Brigham Young University, 1982), 89–96.

[35] George D. Smith, *Nauvoo Polygamy: "...but we called it celestial marriage"* (Salt Lake City: Signature Books, 2008), 115.

[36] Newell, "Historical Relationship," 26–44.

means to remove from this place [Nauvoo]."[37] Three weeks later, Cutler married his first plural wife, Luana (*née* Beebe-Rockwell) in the Nauvoo Temple.[38] Less than a month later, he was ceremoniously sealed as husband to an additional five wives.[39]

In the months prior to his death, Joseph Smith had appointed Cutler to serve as a missionary to the American Indians. Cutler reminded Brigham Young of this unfulfilled responsibility following their western exodus from Nauvoo in 1846. Young sanctioned Cutler and his companions, including Lewis Denna, an Oneida Indian convert to the LDS Church, to go on a mission to the Kansas Territory where tribes had been involuntarily removed a decade earlier from the eastern and southern United States. When Cutler left for the Kansas Territory he took with him his family, including his plural wife Henrietta Clarinda Miller who died there.[40] When he and his group returned from their ill-fated mission and resettled in Iowa they openly displayed their disillusionment with polygamy and Brigham Young's leadership.

The antecedents for Cutlerite discontent for polygamy developed gradually over a decade following the death of Joseph Smith. In particular, and especially from the perspective of Cutlerites who later converted to the RLDS Church, skepticism came much sooner. The blame for polygamy and secret ceremonies was popularly shifted from Joseph Smith to Brigham Young, aside from the historical record clearly affirming that Smith was Mormonism's original thinker, visionary, and Young's theological mentor, and not the other way around. The process of contracting plural marriages initiated by Smith was continued and also expanded by Young, which created additional fodder for lurid stories alleging that in the name of religion women were helpless victims of sexual exploitation.

One such story involved a gala held in the Nauvoo Temple the last night the building was used before the majority of Mormons left on their trek west. The occasion celebrated the completion of the edifice and Brigham Young's

---

[37] Devery S. Anderson and Gary James Bergera, eds., *The Nauvoo Endowment Companies, 1845–1846: A Documentary History* (Salt Lake City: Signature Books, 2005), 156.

[38] Ibid., 416.

[39] Ibid., 579.

[40] Emma L. Anderson lists her as "Mrs. Henrietta Cutler" (Emma L. Anderson, "History of the Cutlerite Faction of the Latter Day Saints," *Journal of History* 13, no. 4 [October 1920]: 455). According to Danny Jorgensen, in addition to Cutler losing his youngest plural wife, their child probably died while on the Indian Mission as well (Danny L. Jorgensen, "Building the Kingdom of God: Alpheus Cutler and the Second Mormon Mission to the Indians, 1847–1853," *Kansas History* 15, no. 3 [1992]: 192–209; Danny L. Jorgensen, "Cutler's Camp at the Big Grove on Silver Creek: A Mormon Settlement in Iowa, 1847–1853," *The Nauvoo Journal* 9, no. 2 [Fall 1997]: 49n25).

accomplishment of seeing thousands of the Saints partake in the ceremonies Joseph Smith had previously shared with only a trusted few. During the festivities the following incident transpired that provides some insight on the status of Mormon women involved in plural marriages.

> This Evening [I was] in a social meeting in the Temple[, and after] retiring to a private room[,] Sister Mary Vail Morse was sealed to me by Pres[ident] B[righam]. Young in [the] presence of H[eber]. C. Kimball and Sarah Ann Sanders. Although [there was opposition to this marriage,] Wealthy [Richards] being opposed, yet says Br[other] Kimball[,] don't let a woman take your crown[,] Bro[other]. Richards.[41]

Cutlerite convert to the RLDS Church, Emma L. Anderson, *née* Whiting, was born in 1853, but heard rumors of Nauvoo polygamy similar to the one above that she linked to female priesthood. Her account has elements that are reminiscent of circumstances under which Mary Morse became the plural wife of Phinehas Richards:

> Good people tell me they [Mormons] began to run into light-mindedness and dancing; would open their balls by prayer, and during a cessation of dancing would preach the glories of polygamy. They would (pretend to) bestow the high priesthood upon the young girls, and then get them sealed as (spiritual) wives to the officials.[42]

After Alpheus Cutler "put away" his plural wives and repudiated the practice, the Cutlerites simply pretended it never happened. Within a couple of generations the group was sincerely denying that Cutler had ever been a polygamist. Yet tacit vestiges of the impact it had on the group remained, as illustrated in this confessional account left by a modern Cutlerite historian.

> The first task was to eradicate any taint of plural marriage. Few families had escaped the embarrassment and humility of having daughters espoused as plural wives to leading men of the church, or suffered the shame of seeing sons, brothers, or fathers participate in the practice. Many had been deceived

---

[41] Anderson and Bergera, *The Nauvoo Endowment Companies*, 620. Phinehas Richards, Diary, LDS Church Archives. Mary Vail Morse was Phinehas's first plural wife, but their marriage ended in divorce. His first wife, Wealthy, died in Salt Lake City, Utah, in 1853 (The Winter Quarters Project, "Winter Quarters Ward 11 Residential Area," <http://winterquarters.byu.edu/pages/ward11/pafg22.htm#721>, <http://winterquarters.byu.edu/pages/ward11/pafg17.htm#598> [accessed November 28, 2008]).

[42] E[mma] L. Anderson, "Who Is Abiding in the Vine?" *Saints' Herald* 46, no. 43 (October 25, 1899): 686. For a candid modern RLDS historian's perspective on Joseph Smith's practice of plural marriage and the introduction of the temple ordinances, see Robert Bruce Flanders, *Nauvoo: Kingdom on the Mississippi* (Urbana: University of Illinois Press, 1965), 242–77. Flanders is a descendent of Alpheus Cutler.

into actually believing they were doing God's will. In this manner families became divided and grieving relatives bade their loved ones farewell.[43]

The Cutlerites abandoned their polygamous practices, but by tradition and faith in Father Cutler's teachings continued to retain other Nauvoo-era temple ordinances. Cutler's successor, Chauncey Whiting, spoke to his local historical society in Minnesota and told them that the Cutlerite church built in 1870 was the first in the county. Whiting then explained that "this building has two apartments, an upper and a lower story. The latter is for preaching, praying, exhortation, singing, councils, etc. while the upper room is more particularly for holding our solemn assemblies and secret prayers."[44]

Whiting's description of the log church in Clitherall, Minnesota, is carefully worded so as to not draw too much attention to the distinctiveness of their theology for an audience of outsiders. Hallie Gould became a member of the RLDS Church but was never initiated into the Cutlerite temple ceremonies. The essence of life lived in this distinct community is evident in the information she was able to obtain about the mysterious rituals performed for both men and women in the Cutlerite log church.

> At the right side of the door as one entered was the inclosed [sic] staircase with two low steps outside. The story of what was beyond those steps and the locked door is one that has not been handed down to the younger generations, much as we have curiously or seriously, desired to know. We know merely that only those holding the priesthood (either men or women) were allowed to enter that secret chamber, and we have heard rumors of strange ceremonies, covenants, and endowments, the altar, the tree of life, the ordinance of feet washing, and the peculiar though necessary and significant graveclothes which no one will explain. Even those of the priesthood who later forsook the church organization have been sufficiently true to the binding covenant made there to prevent their satisfying our demands for knowledge.[45]

After nearly fifty years of additional reflection, Gould came to link what she saw as the downfall of the church at Nauvoo in Joseph Smith's day to the

---

[43] Daisy Fletcher, *Alpheus Cutler and The Church of Jesus Christ* (n.p.: privately printed, 1970), 30. A copy of this document can be found at the Community of Christ Archives, UP F632 C1. See also Anderson, "Who Is Abiding," 686–87, for her critical assessment of how Alpheus did not oppose polygamy soon enough. RLDS elder Charles Fry wrote: "Endowments were given to his followers, the authority and pattern for which Cutler claimed to have received in Nauvoo … He was evidently affected by the doctrine of polygamy, and practiced it to some extent, though not publicly, nor did he publicly teach it" (Charles Fry, "History of the Fremont [Iowa] District," *Journal of History* 2, no. 3 [July 1909]: 349).

[44] Chauncey Whiting, 1–12, UP T795, Community of Christ Archives.

[45] Hallie Gould, "Like Sheep That Went Astray," *Autumn Leaves* 34, no. 2 (February 1921): 53.

covert efforts of Brigham Young to infect the church with the "doctrine of the secret order." She believed "it crept in at Nauvoo through so many uniting with the Masonic Lodge. The oaths and covenants of the secret chamber are the same as the Masons, and that is where they originated, not with God or by his command." Significantly, Gould asserted that holding on to the temple rites was to blame for some of the Cutlerites rejecting "the leadership of Young Joseph [Smith III],"[46] president of the RLDS Church and son of the founder of Mormonism. This may partially explain why Lois Cutler, Alpheus Cutler's widow, insisted on being rebaptized when she ultimately defected to the RLDS Church.[47] The potential benefits of the female priesthood were not evident enough to remain Cutlerite for either Hallie Gould or Lois Cutler.

Emma L. Anderson provided the most comprehensive information about the Cutlerite temple experience, short of revealing the actual ceremonies. She and her husband received the Cutlerite endowment before converting to the RLDS Church. Anderson confirms many of Hallie Gould's suspicions about the "Secret Endowment Chamber."[48] From the perspective of a former insider, her practical experience does much to refute Ian Barber's contention that the Cutlerites were less prone to see women "as dependent upon men for their spiritual salvation."[49]

Anderson's parents were Cutlerites; her father, Francis Lewis Whiting, was the brother of church leader Chauncey Whiting. Her husband's family had all joined the RLDS Church ahead of them and actively encouraged their conversion. It was devastating to Anderson's parents when she was baptized a Josephite (RLDS). They considered it worse for her than her sisters, since she and her husband had been initiated into the Cutlerite High Priesthood when they were given their temple endowments, and her parents felt they were throwing away their priesthood. According to Emma, these rituals were

---

[46] Hallie Gould, "The Story of Alpheus Cutler," 1970, p. C3, UP T795, Community of Christ Archives.

[47] Biloine Whiting Young, *Obscure Believers: The Mormon Schism of Alpheus Cutler* (St. Paul, MN: Pogo Press, 2002), 158. Young provides context on the extent of the disappointment Lois Cutler's disaffection held for the Cutlerites; the speculation on her conflicted state of mind relative to abandoning temple Mormonism is mine.

[48] "The Cutlerites had set up their 'Secret Endowment Chamber' and all who were allowed to enter there (as it was supposed by them) were given the Holy Priesthood according to Melchesidek, or it was bestowed upon them. For they claim that those who enter there 'attain to these two Priesthoods,' and thus become the Kingdom and elect of god" (Emma Lucine Anderson, Autobiography, p. EA7, UP T795, Community of Christ Archives).

[49] Barber, "Ecclesiastical Position," 64. Barber's conclusions are based largely on the rhetoric contained in early Cutlerite Pliny Fisher's book of patriarchal blessings recorded during a ten-year time period (1849–1859) and precludes experiences of the group's women.

regarded as the most sacred and secret part of the work of God. Too sacred and secret to be talked about to those who did not belong. [A] vow of secrecy was required by all who entered there, but it was explained to us that we were only permitted to speak of this to others as far as the books speak of it … It was supposed that I had received the Melchisedek priesthood, and I never knew what office I held in the high priesthood. I was never called an elderess or highpriestess or anything, still I held the high priesthood. I had a right to anoint with oil and administer to the sick by lying on my hands and praying to God to heal if no <u>man</u> was present. But if a man was present he never thought of asking a woman to assist, but went ahead alone if there were not two men present who held the priesthood…. it only serves to show how they esteemed a man so much superior to a woman. I never knew them to ask a woman to pray, except once…. or to ask a blessing at the table if a man were present.[50]

The Nauvoo tradition of allowing women to anoint one another and to administer to the sick was understood by Emma Anderson, but was withheld from her by the men in her faith community. As Joseph Smith condoned, endowed women who went to Utah enjoyed this gift somewhat longer, but often were required to engage in it quietly. Barber looked to the Cutlerites to have a more progressive form of female priesthood for women than their Utah counterparts, but on the contrary it was less so.

Neither Joseph Smith nor Alpheus Cutler and his successors produced by design or otherwise a gender equal egalitarian priesthood. For many Cutlerites, maintaining the tradition of receiving temple ceremonies, absent plural marriage, continues to be an important part of their faith. For those who left the Cutlerites and joined the RLDS Church, a movement completely hostile to secret rituals, adherence to temple ceremonies became untenable. Cutlerite women who decided to defect to the RLDS Church were the strongest indictment against the argument that female priesthood was an egalitarian gesture. Women like Emma Anderson knew they would no longer be able to hold their priesthood and yet they left anyway.

While Kierkegaard's assertion that "erotic love loves secrecy"[51] would be too simplistic an explanation for Joseph Smith's involvement in plural marriage, a historical analysis of Smith's language and deeds argues against his conferral of priesthood on a select group of women as a radical act of egalitarianism in the cause of feminism. When compared to the agenda of Evangelical America's cult of domesticity, Mormonism was much closer to that rhetoric than to progressives who were beginning to agitate for equality of the sexes. Social anthropology

---

[50] Anderson, Autobiography, p. EA13.

[51] Søren Kierkegaard, "The Seducer's Diary" in *Either/Or Part I*, ed. Howard V. Hong and Edna H. Hong (New Jersey: Princeton University Press, 1987), 388.

provides an insight that illustrates how female priesthood recipients engaged in a gift exchange with their spiritual leader. Smith's bestowal of the temple Endowment ceremony on an exclusive group of LDS women and men is best understood as a *quid pro quo* exchange of silence for godhood and membership into the most elite inner circle of Joseph's most trusted followers. Finally, using the legacy of Mormon priesthood conferred on women to credit Joseph Smith with egalitarianism is further compromised in the experience of Cutlerite females who readily abandoned all vestiges of esoteric temple ceremonies when they became members of the RLDS Church.

Registered Sex Offenders
and Congregational Life

DAVID N. ANDERSON

A PROCLAMATION ON THE exterior marquee as well as a banner on the wall of the sanctuary of the United Church of Christ in Carlsbad, California, announces confidently that "all are welcome." However, in April 2007, an event occurred that necessitated the pastor, her leadership team, and the congregation to deal with the question, what exactly does the phrase, "all are welcome" mean? Mark Pliska, a new attendee, had declared to the relatively small close-knit congregation a few months previously that he wanted to become a member. He had sought a faith community where he felt welcome. He had enjoyed the worship and fellowship immensely and felt this church to be open and affirming. Mark Pliska wanted to make the Carlsbad church his spiritual home. However, he sent the congregation into turmoil when he freely admitted that he was an ex-convict who was a registered sex offender. He had served time for molesting children.[1]

Congregations in the Community of Christ have struggled with similar, difficult situations. Registered sex offenders and their families have wanted to worship in congregations. The news of these sex offenders worshiping in these congregations has caused much confusion, heartache, and pain within the church body. Many members and friends are grieving, and some feel they

---

[1] Neela Banerjee, "Sex Offenders Test Churches' Core Beliefs," *The New York Times*, April 10, 2007, <http://www.nytimes.com/2007/04/10/us/10pilgrim.html?_r=1&ex=1> (accessed January 16, 2009).

have not had an opportunity to be heard, understood, and respected. Many feel betrayed. Others do not know what to think or how to address their own loss and suffering. After many months of working through principles of reconciliation and restorative justice, these congregations are hoping, to the extent possible, to reach closure on this serious and painful decision.

Churches, mosques, and synagogues are all struggling with such issues. At the crux of the debate is whether these issues expose a conflict in ministries: ministry to registered sex offenders as well as providing healing and spiritual growth and ministry to families and children by providing a secure environment where they feel safe enough to encounter the Divine.

One of the most problematic ethical decisions—and likely one of the most controversial—that congregational leaders can possibly face is whether to welcome a registered sex offender into congregational life. How does the church deal with such a situation? The church is committed to reaching out to those in need and to serve and help the broken hearted. Experts and counselors encourage registered sex offenders to seek out Christian support and fellowship. However, it is also true that providing a safe and protected place for all people, especially children, to learn, to discuss, and to experience the love of the Divine is of the highest priority and concern. Protection of our children is absolutely paramount. In addition, is it ethically proper for Christians to disallow someone to attend church? Do these two ministries conflict to a degree that they are irreconcilable? Can a church really do both—offer pastoral support to sex offenders yet provide a safe and secure environment for our children? What are the ethical factors and the issues that a pastor and her or his leadership team should consider in struggling with such a decision? Do they allow them to participate? If so, what are the restrictions? What are the legal ramifications?

In order to help answer these difficult and potentially explosive questions, this research paper will cover primarily four areas: criminal sex offender behavior, the ethics of restorative justice, the ethics of accountability and protection (e.g., a limited access agreement and covenant between the registered sex offender and the congregation), and the ethic of forgiveness. Finally, the paper will juxtapose Richard B. Hays's three focal images of community, cross, and new creation against this key ethical dilemma.

Surprisingly, ethicists and theologians have not written a great deal on registered sex offenders and congregational life. However, there are a couple of individuals and organizations who appear at the forefront of tackling these issues. One is Reverend Debra W. Haffner, a sexologist and minister. She is director of the Religious Institute on Sexual Morality, Justice, and Healing in Norwalk, Connecticut, and writes extensively on the topics of sexual health, gender diversity, and marriage equality. She has developed an online manual for the Unitarian Universalist Association. This pamphlet has three major principles that present a *balancing act*, as churches struggle with their decision and policies. Her tenets are as follows:

> We have a responsibility to assure that children and youth will be safe in our congregations from sexual abuse, sexual assault and harassment even or perhaps especially when we do not know if there is an offender in our congregation. Indeed, we have a responsibility to see that our congregations are sexually healthy congregations and free of sexual harassment, abuse, and exploitation for all of our members—children, youth and adults—as well as visitor and staff.
>
> We are called to treat every person with worth and dignity, and to offer a congregational home to all who are seeking one like ours, while honoring that in the case of an individual with a history of sex offenses, there must be limitations to congregational involvement. That commitment means that only in rare cases will a person be denied access to ministry and fellowship. In the words of one congregation's policy, we must provide "compassion, support, affirmation, and protection against further harm."
>
> We have a responsibility to educate ourselves about child sexual abuse and healthy childhood sexuality, to be well informed about sexual offenses and offenders and to develop processes that will help us make good decisions about the actions that we are called to take. We must be willing to listen, to use a democratic process, and to be humble about our own certitudes in creating these policies.[2]

Another organization, Keeping Kids Safe Ministries, founded by Gregory Sporer and Steven Vann, encourages a sex offender management team that helps church leaders remain accountable to ensure protection of youth from sexual offenders. The organizers argue that sex offenders need to be held accountable and to grow in their relationship with God. There are three aspects critical to the church: verification, covenant and commitments, and spiritual growth and accountability. Church leaders need to ensure that the registered sex offenders are meeting conditions of their probation as well as all expectations of their treatment. Additionally, the church and the registered sex offender have an upfront and honest list of expectations that provide guidance and support. Lastly, each offender is expected to have an ongoing spiritual accountability program with an assigned spiritual advisor.[3]

In order to make appropriate decisions about the dilemma of incorporating registered sex offenders in congregational life, one needs to understand the

---

[2] Debra W. Haffner, *Religious Institute on Sexual Morality, Justice and Healing*, <http//www. religiousinstitute.org/abuse.html> (accessed March 18, 2008).

[3] *Keeping Kids Safe Ministries*, <http://www.faithwebsites.com/sysfiles/member/worshipservices/ worshipservice.cfm/> (accessed March 19, 2008).

characteristics of child sex offenders, to focus on an ethical framework concerning restorative justice and forgiveness, and to develop a process of accountability and protection.

Criminal Sex Offender Behavior

URRENTLY, THERE APPEARS to be a lack of informed public debate regarding sex offenders and their re-entry. Much of the discussion is emotionally charged using assumptions that are not supported by scientific evidence. According to one source, the public continues to believe that the threat from sex offenders is greater than what it actually is.[4] Advocates continue to fuel the public perception. Due to this lack of dialogue and inaccuracy, many lawmakers are enacting many fear-based laws around the country that impact negatively on successful re-entry.[5] The fact is that of those children who have been abused, 60 percent of the boys and 80 percent of the girls are actually sexually abused by someone they know.[6] These perpetrators are parents, stepparents, grandparents, other relatives, teachers, coaches, ministers, babysitters, etc. Other statistics show that more than eight in ten sexual abusers are never reported. Additionally, many believe that sex offenders will likely re-offend. However, the Center for Sex Offender Management, US Department of Justice, states that all treated sex offenders had a re-offense rate for another sexual crime of less than 13 percent.[7] According to another study, "With specialized treatment, a person with a history of having sexually offended who accepts full accountability for his or her crime can learn to control his or her abusive behavior. Without treatment, the sexual recidivism rate for sex offenders is 17 percent. With treatment, sexual recidivism among sex offenders drops to 12 percent."[8] However, these statistics should not mollify the importance of vigilance.

Identifying a sexual predator, whether registered or not, is difficult. According to statistics from the National Center for Missing and Exploited Children, there are over 500,000 registered sex offenders in the United States.

[4] Anne-Marie McAlinden, *The Shaming of Sexual Offenders* (Portland, OR: Hart Publishing, 2007), 78.

[5] Deborah Donovan Rice, "Community Re-entry Recast as Primary Prevention," *Sex Offender Law Report* 7, no. 5 (August/September 2006): 65.

[6] Rice, "Community Re-entry," 65.

[7] Center for Sex Offender Management, *Recidivism of Sex Offenders* (Washington, DC: US Department of Justice, 2001), 12.

[8] R. K. Hanson, et. al., "First Report of the Collaborative Outcome Data Project on the Effectiveness of Psychological Treatment for Sex Offenders," *Sexual Abuse: A Journal of Research and Treatment* 14, no. 2 (2002): 169–97, <http://sax.sagepub.com/cgi/content/abstract/14/2/169> (accessed January 16, 2009).

In England and Wales there are 28,994 registered sex offenders.[9] Most sex offenders are not in prison. Those who are in prison normally don't serve lengthy sentences. A study sponsored by the University of New Hampshire indicates that it is difficult to create a profile of who will perpetuate sexual crimes against children.[10] However, Dr. Leigh Baker lists the ten most common characteristics of a sexual predator:

- Refusal to take responsibility for his or her actions and blames others or circumstances for failures
- A sense of entitlement
- Low self esteem
- A need for power and control
- A lack of empathy
- An inability to form intimate relationships with adults
- A history of abuse
- A troubled childhood
- Deviant sexual behaviors and attitudes
- Drug and/or alcohol abuse[11]

Sexual abuse is a horrendous crime. To protect the church from such sexual predators requires attentiveness from all congregants, including members, priesthood, and pastors. Additionally, regardless of the statistics and probability of re-offense, the congregation needs to remain vigilant.

Restorative Justice

A CRITICAL ASPECT OF an ethical framework for a congregation to deal with a registered sex offender is to advocate the concept of restorative justice. This process is more transformative and healing. The key to the restoration process is the offender taking responsibility for repairing the harm. As Lorraine Amstutz states, "Restorative justice, by dealing with crime and harm in a holistic way, promises to sew together the pieces of torn lives into a fabric of justice that is meaningful."[12]

---

[9] Reid J. Home, "Sex Offender," in *House of Commons held in London, 4 September 2006*, <http://www.publications.parliament.uk/pa/cm200506/cmhansrd/cm060904/test/60904w2295.thm>.

[10] Emily M. Douglas and David Finkelhor, "Childhood Sexual Abuse Fact Sheet," University of New Hampshire, <http://www.unh.edu/ccrc/factsheet/pdf/csa-fs20.pdf>, 8.

[11] Leigh Baker, *Protecting Your Children from Sexual Predators* (New York: St. Martin's Press, 2002), 16.

[12] Lorraine S. Amstutz, "Restorative Justice," *Center for Christian Ethics at Baylor University*, 2004, <http://www.baylor.edu/christianethics/> (accessed March 17, 2008).

Amstutz uses Micah 6:8b to encourage the importance and ethics of restorative justice: "And what does the Lord require of you, but to do justice, and to love kindness, and to walk humbly with your God?" Furthermore, she states that God calls us to actively engage in restoring God's love to the world. Doing what Micah wisely states is recognition that we are God's family. As such, we need to advocate strongly for restorative justice when we work on the ethical issues involved with decisions on whether to allow sex offenders in congregational life.

Specifically, restorative justice is the process involving, to the extent possible, those who are affected by a specific offense. Collectively, they identify and address the harms, needs, and obligations. This discussion and dialogue heals and puts things as "right as possible."[13] Signposts of restorative justice focus on the harms rather than rules broken. They empower the survivors and respond to their needs. At the same time, they support offenders, while encouraging them to accept their obligations. Research shows that supportive and nurturing relationships are paramount to assist and to help prevent sex offenders in relapsing.[14] Primarily, restorative justice demonstrates respect to all, including the survivor, the community, and the offender. Paul provides in II Corinthians 2 the framework of restoration, which includes forgiveness. Congregations must grapple with the issues of forgiveness and reinstatement in creating an environment of respect, safety, and comfort in congregational life for all persons impacted by the offense. Accountability and guidelines are paramount.

Accountability and Protection

CONCERNING THE INTEGRATION of a registered sex offender into the congregation, one must acknowledge the difference between forgiveness and trust. Forgiveness is a Christian ethical and moral imperative. However, trust is another matter. Given how the nature of the crime and the health and safety of our children is so critical, the congregation cannot afford to minimize the danger. There is no stated cure of a sex offender and the congregation must take every effort to keep the sex offender accountable to the congregation and to create a safe space for youth. Leaders must develop and implement procedures for keeping youth safe from sexual abuse, for educating youth and adults alike about sexual abuse and prevention, and for responding to a person who is convicted or accused of sexual abuse. Key components of those responsibilities include a limited access agreement for the registered sex offender, a robust youth

---

[13] Howard Zehr, *The Little Book of Restorative Justice* (Intercourse, PA: Good Books, 2002), 37.

[14] Baker, *Protecting Your Children*, 247.

worker registration and training program, and continuous education of both youth and adults in the congregation for prevention of child abuse.

The registered sex offender, as a child of God, in many ways has the same needs for the community of believers as those who have not committed a crime. In fact, one might even argue that he or she has more of a need for fellowship. However, there are two critical elements that need to occur before he or she returns: (1) the individual must reassure the congregation that her or his involvement does not pose a danger to the youth; and (2) strict policies are in place to assure the congregation that the registered sex offender does not have an opportunity in the church to re-offend again. The core response to these two requirements is a *limited access agreement*. This agreement or covenant allows the offender's participation in certain aspects of congregational life, sets clear boundaries including what he or she can and cannot do, and strictly restricts his or her contact with youth. The "primary message to the sex offender should be that they are welcome to participate in adult worship, adult social, and adult educational activities and that they must covenant with the congregation to avoid all contact with children."[15]

Every congregation should take seriously the church's youth registration program, including youth worker training. Although such procedures will not guarantee that a problem will not occur, it will help reduce the risk of child abuse in a church ministry. Additionally, such policies will help build a foundation for dealing with a registered sex offender as a member of the congregation. Paramount to the youth ministry registration is to screen, select, and register all people who work with the youth. The over-arching safeguard is that only registered youth workers be used in the youth programs of the church. Two-deep leadership is absolutely necessary. All youth programs, activities, and outings need to have at least two registered youth workers present. If activities are coed, then the workers should be coed. Another critical safeguard is that all contact with youth needs to be in full view of other adults and young people.

Youth worker training should occur regularly. Church leaders need to encourage youth and adults alike to report improper behavior and determine a proactive status regarding reporting and cooperation. Train youth to recognize situations that place them at risk of abuse and how abusers operate. Create a safe and vigilant congregation for youth. In fact, Glover argues that congregations should

> create an environment in the church that is decidedly hostile to sexual predators. Make it known that there are watchful eyes. Take an aggressive,

---

[15] Debra W. Haffner, "Balancing Acts—Keeping Children Safe in Congregations," <http://www.uua.org/cde/ethics/balancing/balancingact.pdf>, 3.

no-nonsense stance. Do not be afraid to assert your position in the congregation and firmly establish the position of the church. Urge everyone to be aware of these issues. Bring in experts to address your congregation on the subjects of child abuse and sexual predation....By creating a hostile environment, you will discourage any sexual predators.[16]

Educating adults in the congregation is another essential element in helping churches handle sex offenders. Leaders should offer workshops on boundary issues such as power and vulnerability, dating, friendships, dual relationships, personal needs, and red flags.[17] Haffner outlines methods that include "discussing the prevalence of child sexual abuse, developing programs that help adults educate their children about sexuality and prevention of sexual abuse, and ensuring that all know how to handle correctly a suspected case of child abuse or child sexual abuse. Prevention is paramount."[18]

Forgiveness

THE ETHIC OF forgiveness is critical in making a moral decision. However, it is far too easy to concentrate on an instant forgiveness and expect those who suffer to easily forgive and forget. This attitude is an easy temptation as the Christian ethic to reconcile and forgive is so strong. Those in leadership must acknowledge that there needs to be a "serious recognition that forgiveness and reconciliation are a long process and, in the end, a gift from God, not something which we can easily manipulate."[19]

Eugene Duffy acknowledges that urging someone to forgive quickly could be a sign of one's own discomfort with the grief and anger of sexual abuse. Possibly, it's a type of denial and a method of suppression of our own feelings or an attempt out of our aversion to deal with those feelings. Authentic forgiveness permits truth to come forward—with all the suffering, pain, anger, and grief. The process of healing and forgiveness cannot be short circuited. It can take a great deal of time, patience, and effort to work through the process.

When deciding whether a registered sex offender should be a member of the congregation, one needs awareness that there will likely be members and friends who were abused sexually as children. National surveys suggest that

---

[16] Voyle A. Glover, *Protecting Your Church Against Sexual Predators* (Grand Rapids, MI: Kegel Publications, 2005), 64.

[17] Nancy W. Poling, *A Sacred Trust: Boundary Issues for Clergy and Spiritual Teachers*, DVD (Seattle: Faith Trust Institute, 2003).

[18] Haffner, "Balancing Acts," 18

[19] Eugene Duffy, *The Church and Child Sexual Abuse*, ed. Eamonn Conway, Eugene Duffy, and Attracta Shields (Dublin: Colour Books, Ltd., 1999), 69.

between 5 and 10 percent of adult men and between 9 and 32 percent of adult women report that they were survivors of sexual abuse.[20] For many, this abuse has lifelong ramifications. The process of healing is a painful and slow journey. Often they have difficulty talking about such pain. They have several needs that the church should acknowledge:

- To be heard
- To receive understanding by the church
- To know that officials will not downplay the issue
- To not be labeled as unforgiving
- To be considered as more than victims or their victimization
- To hear an apology
- To be considered courageous, not troublemakers
- To heal
- To be accepted within the community and know they are loved.

These people have tremendous hurt, as well as insights. Dealing with this issue may reopen the wounds. The pastor, leadership, and congregants must acknowledge these peoples' pain and experience and have courage to help in the healing process.

Another extremely difficult and divisive situation is when a former priesthood member who is now a registered sex offender wishes to rejoin the congregation. Nothing tests our resolve more than to forgive a leader who has violated her or his sacred trust with the congregation.

Richard Irons and Katherine Roberts call these fallen leaders "the unhealed wounders." They argue that he or she has a potent blend of both woundedness and power. "Over 80% of sexually exploitive professionals experienced psychological wounding in their formational environments."[21] They themselves were survivors of emotional, physical, or even sexual abuse as youth. The process toward their reconciliation and healing helps with an honest assessment of their spirituality. The objective is to help them see the God-given gifts of grace, hope, and faith. Normally, these individuals are in a high state of denial. However, through the painful process the individual can begin an acknowledgment of guilt and remorse resulting in a spiritual awakening.

When the fallen leader repents and asks for forgiveness, Paul's counsel in Colossians 3:12–13 provides insight on the community's response to these fallen leaders: "Forgive each other; just as the Lord has forgiven you, so you must also forgive." Reading these words doesn't make it easier. To carry each

---

[20] Douglas and Finkelhor, "Child Sexual Abuse Fact Sheet," 5.

[21] Richard Irons and Katherine Roberts, *Restoring the Soul of a Church: Healing Congregations Wounded By Clergy Sexual Misconduct*, ed. Nancy M. Hopkins and Mark Lanser (Collegeville, MN: The Liturgical Press, 1995), 49.

other's burdens is difficult amidst the atmosphere of corporate embarrassment and feelings of betrayal. "Even if we manage to forgive abusive leaders, to restore them makes us very uneasy...restoration does not mean 'going back to what was.'" Rather, forgiveness, healing, and restoration mean a new norm and "bringing about what should be."[22] Furthermore, Robert Kruschwitz argues that it is inconsistent with the spirit of forgiveness to hold truly restored members in a "state of perennial disgrace...it is inconsistent with forgiveness to make them 'pay' with continued humiliation or to put them on any other probation."[23] The church needs to treat a fully restored individual with the same grace extended to all. However, this grace does not mean that the individual is restored to a previously held leadership position.

Hays's Three Focal Images

RICHARD B. HAYS, in his book *The Moral Vision of the New Testament*, outlines three images: *community*, *cross*, and *new creation*. He argues that these three key images cover the moral unity and ethical sense of the New Testament (NT) canon. To Hays these three images clarify the coherence of the NT because they show a textual basis represented across the entire scriptures in the NT, support the ethical teachings of the NT witnesses, and provide a "sufficiently broad view of the New Testament's image of moral concern."[24] He posits that no single image can appropriately cover the intertwined and complicated unity of the NT. He argues these three focal images come out of the text and uses them as sign posts for reflections about the moral vision of the NT. In this section of the paper, we will peer through these three focal lenses to seek clarity of the NT moral vision in regard to our ethical and moral dilemma. Our understanding of the scriptures is brought into focus by these three images: community, cross, and new creation.

Community

HAYS INDICATES THAT "the church is a countercultural community of discipleship, and this community is the primary addressee of God's imperatives."[25] This image focuses on God's plan to form a covenant people. Rather than concentrating on just the individual, the primary concentration of

---

[22] Robert B. Kruschwitz, "Failing Leaders," *Center for Christian Ethics at Baylor University*, 2001, <http://www.baylor.edu/christianethics/> (accessed March 17, 2008), 73.

[23] Kruschwitz, "Failing Leaders," 74.

[24] Richard B. Hays, *The Moral Vision of the New Testament: A Contemporary Introduction to New Testament Ethics* (New York: Harper One, 1996), 195.

[25] Hays, *Moral Vision*, 196.

the community is the obedience of the body of Christ. It is not a concept but an expression of the people of God. What Hays means by community is ecclesial. "We seek God's will not by asking first, 'what should I do' but 'what should we do?'" In examining the scriptures, we must acknowledge that the church is a community called to live in discipleship and to exemplify forgiveness and love of all. Paul's call to embody reconciliation and Matthew's message to be the light of the world are key elements of the church's identity. Actions and behaviors of individuals are important but what are more important are the purity, health, and wholeness of the community. As Hays declares, according to Paul, everything we do as Christians impacts the whole body of Christ.

In regard to dealing with registered sex offenders, as a community of believers, Christians should forgive the sex offender and work toward healing. We are required to forgive when forgiveness is sought—this is grace. However, total reconciliation for all may never occur. The community should also ensure that provisions are in place to allow for the health and wholeness of the entire community. The development of a limited access agreement between the congregation and the registered sex offender would be appropriate to protect the body.

Cross

ACCORDING TO HAYS, "Jesus' death on a cross is the paradigm for faithfulness to God in this world."[26] He argues that the church engages in building the kingdom of God by participating in Jesus' suffering. His death is an act of self-giving love. As a community of believers, we are constantly called to take up the cross and follow in the way of his death. Furthermore, our actions are not necessarily governed by producing success but more by their congruity with the example of Jesus. Those with wealth and power ought to surrender it or use it for the sake of the weak and downtrodden. Here, Jesus provides an extraordinary example of normative behavior. Jesus had fellowship with sinners and the scum of society. He called them to a better life and service. As a community called to suffer in the name of Jesus, we too must "be the source of hope, healing and wholeness for the suffering...all over the world."[27] The cross is the paradigm for living. As such, we forgive, for the sake of Christ. In the case of the registered sex offender, this focal point provides clarity that the congregation should allow the registered sex offender to attend. Trust is another issue. It can only be rebuilt over time and depends on circumstances (e.g., was there confession without

[26] Hays, *Moral Vision*, 197.

[27] Conquest Offender Reintegration Ministry, *Equipping Your Church to Minister to Ex-Offenders* (Washington DC: Conquest House, Inc., 2000), preface.

coercion? was there confession after disclosure? was there any attempt to deny?). If the offender is totally committed to the cross, he or she will be willing to suffer the consequences of their actions, serve the community, and seek for wholeness and healing for all.

New Creation

HAYS CONTINUES: "The church embodies the power of the resurrection in the midst of a not-yet-redeemed world."[28] New creation is a sense of optimism amidst the pain and suffering in an imperfect world. It is the hope of transformation to a new life. We are to struggle to live in faith at our place and time. We have the promise of the future even though we recognize the destructive parts of nature and that the actions of humans are broken. The grace of God trumps all. The image of new creation provides clarity in the decision of fellowship for the registered sex offender as well as all members of the congregation. Amidst the guilt, pain, and remorse of all of our broken relationships, we have the promise of transformation in becoming whole. As a community of God, the church is called to assist the individual to live between the consequences of actions and the "not yet to be." New creation gives all of us—members, friends, youth, registered sex offenders, survivors of sexual abuse—a powerful sense of hope and optimism for the future and meaning to our lives.

In Case of a Crisis

NO ONE KNOWS for sure if or when it may happen. Perhaps a person who is a registered sex offender wants to become a member. Perhaps a member of the congregation was recently placed on the sex offender list. What's paramount is to be prepared for such an event. History shows that congregations can be divisively at odds over whether the offender should worship in the congregation. Many congregants are alarmed and fear for their children. Others, who have survived sexual abuse in their childhood, struggle with the pain and fear, and revisit horrible trauma as they deal with the past. Not all will heal at the same time. Congregational leaders need to acknowledge that the issue will likely be painful, controversial, and difficult. They need to allow people to share their feelings before a decision is made and to offer them pastoral care. Additionally, leaders must communicate, communicate, communicate. They must keep the congregation informed as they work to develop procedures and implement the decision. Another critical and important element is to allow sufficient time. The process is lengthy, messy, laborious, and emotional. Even more challenging

---

[28] Hays, *Moral Vision*, 198.

and difficult is a situation where the offender seeks re-entry into their home congregation. A nearly impossible situation is where an offender seeks to return to the congregation in which their offense occurred. Not all members and friends will be happy with any decision. In fact, the congregation will likely lose members either way. If the decision is to allow the registered sex offender to worship, some members will leave because of the possible danger to their children. If the sex offender is not welcome, others will leave because of their belief that Christians are to forgive. They believe that all are sinners. Additionally, they argue that as long as the congregation takes reasonable precautions, the sex offender should be allowed to worship.

The ethical issue of whether a registered sex offender should be allowed to worship in a congregation is difficult and extremely problematic. As a moral authority, the church must honor competing callings. The church has a commitment to provide a secure and safe environment for its children, youth, and adults to worship, have fellowship, and to draw close to the Divine. On the other hand, Christians are called to serve humanity, including modern-day tax collectors and prostitutes. All of us fall under God's grace. All of us are sinners. The research in this paper demonstrates the need for key leadership to understand that this ethical dilemma facing a congregation puts leadership into a crisis situation. As such, there is a huge danger but also a rich opportunity for growth. Leaders need to face squarely the issue, to ensure communication, and to allow for healing. As in any huge ethical dilemma, the solution is not entirely clear. The key is to follow the correct process. Paramount to this process is to uphold an enduring value of the church: the worth of each person. "God loves each of us equally and unconditionally. All persons have great worth and should be respected as creations of God with basic human rights. The willingness to love and accept others is essential to faithfulness to the gospel of Christ."[29] We are called to protect those who are vulnerable yet offer a profound ministry and provide a spiritual home to all. The church's actions should be directed toward the healing of the victims and survivors of sexual abuse, prevention of future offenses, and treatment of the sex offender. As Reverend Debra W. Haffner states so adequately: "We can honor our most basic principle that every person has inherent dignity and worth, and balance justice, compassion, accountability and safety. We are called to do no less."[30]

---

[29] www.cofchrist.org/ourfaith/faith-beliefs.asp

[30] Haffner, "Balancing Acts," 41.

Does Beelzebub Have a Body?
The Corporeal Nature of Satan in Early
Restoration Experience and Thought

ALONZO L. GASKILL

THE PROPHET JOSEPH is purported to have said:

> We came to this earth that we might have a body and present it pure before God in the Celestial Kingdom. The great principle of happiness consists in having a body. *The Devil has no body*, and herein is his punishment. He is pleased when he can obtain the tabernacle of man and when cast out by the Savior he asked to go into the herd of swine showing that he would prefer a swine's body to having none.[1]

The vast majority of the faiths that trace their origins back to the prophet Joseph hold that Satan is merely a spirit—havening a noncorporeal nature.[2]

---

[1] William Clayton's Private Book, January 5, 1841, cited in *The Words of Joseph Smith: The Contemporary Accounts of the Nauvoo Discourses of the Prophet Joseph*, Religious Studies Monograph Series 6, comp. and ed. Andrew F. Ehat and Lyndon W. Cook (Provo, UT: Religious Studies Center, Brigham Young University, 1980), 60 (emphasis added).

[2] Of any of the various faiths who trace their origins back to the Restoration through the prophet Joseph Smith, the Mormons have the most developed doctrines of a personal devil and the ministry of angels. Nevertheless, the Utah church is not alone in its belief in both the reality of Satan and also the existence of angels that have the power to interact with humankind. One Community of Christ source states: "From its inception, the Restoration movement has experienced angelic ministry" (Alecia M. Cripps, "Historical Development of Angelology" [unpublished manuscript, Community of Christ Archives, 1996], 90). In another Community of Christ document we find this: "The ministering of angels is very widely known in our

However, in the early days of the Restoration numerous figures experienced physical attacks at the hands of the devil—Joseph Smith, Newel Knight, Sidney Rigdon, and Harvey Whitlock, to name a few. These various encounters require us, as students of Restoration theology, to query as to what exactly the prophet Joseph meant when he said, "The devil has no body."

---

early church history. Angelic visitations is one of our basic foundations" (Dennis E. Sharier, "The Ministering of Angels: A Key of the Aaronic Priesthood," rev. ed., ed. Wilbur Sartwell [unpublished manuscript, Community of Christ Archives, September 23, 1991], 33). Elsewhere we read: "Some of our literature, and the testimony of a number of people, describes experiences people have had with what they understand to be spiritual beings, sometimes identified as angels" (Presiding Bishopric, "Report on Ministry of Angels," in *Aaronic Foundational Ministries*, ed. Paul M. Edwards [Independence, MO: Herald Publishing House, 1995], 155). In the *Saints' Herald* we find this statement: "The belief of the church about the devil is difficult to describe. Since the World Conference has never dealt with this matter, we have no official statement to refer to. Likewise it is not possible to give a consensus of the belief of the membership. At one end of the range there are those who believe that Satan is a person, that he actually led a rebellion in heaven and was cast out from the presence of God (see Genesis 3:4, 5, I.V. and Doctrine and Covenants 28:10) ... At the other end of the range are those who believe that the devil is not a person but the personification of evil.... This is one of those questions which all of us must answer for ourselves after we have prayerfully read and studied the scriptures" (Fred L. Young, "Question Time," *Saints' Herald* 118, no. 1 [January 1971]: 47). While serving as assistant to the RLDS First Presidency, Cecil Ettinger wrote: "Very often questions are asked about what the church believes. The church expresses itself in World Conference assembly. Sometimes this is accepting the words of the prophet as expressing the mind and will of God and on other occasions in the form of General Conference resolutions. Other than this we can only surmise what the general feeling of members of the church is about a certain subject. Very often it is felt that the church expresses itself, when in reality what is expressed is merely the opinion of a prominent minister" (Cecil R. Ettinger, "Question Time," *Saints' Herald* 127, no. 3 [February 1, 1980]: 85). Thus, the official position of the Community of Christ regarding the nature of angles or the devil is hard to ascertain. Nevertheless, in the October 13, 1888, *Saints' Herald* the following appears under the heading of "Questions and Answers," "Joseph the Seer said ... 'There are two kinds of beings in heaven—viz., angels who are resurrected personages, having bodies of flesh and bones. For instance, Jesus said, "Handle me and see, for a spirit hath not flesh and bones, as ye see me have." The spirits of just men made perfect—they who are not resurrected, but inherit the same glory. When a messenger comes, saying he has a message from God, offer him your hand, and request him to shake hands with you. If he be an angel, he will do so, and you will feel his hand. If he be the spirit of a just man made perfect, he will come in his glory; for that is the only way he can appear. Ask him to shake hands with you, but he will not move, because it is contrary to the order of heaven for a just man to deceive: but he will still deliver his message. If he be the Devil as an angel of light, when you ask him to shake hands, he will offer you his hand, and you will not feel anything: you may therefore detect him. These are three grand keys whereby you may know whether any administration is from God'" ("Questions and Answers," *Saints' Herald* 35, no. 41 [October 13, 1888]: 653). See also Cripps, "Historical Development of Angelology" (1996), 104, 123.

This paper will examine a handful of physical demonic attacks[3] that took place in the early history of the church, and the implications of these experiences on our understanding of the nature of Satan's body in Restoration theology.

The Prophet Joseph Smith

O F COURSE, THE reader will be familiar with the first and most sacred of events tied to the Restoration—namely the appearance of the Father and Son to the prophet Joseph Smith. That spring morning of 1820 Joseph had a very physical encounter with the adversary that left him with no doubts as to Satan's power in the physical realm. I quote:

> I kneeled down and began to offer up the desires of my heart to God. I had scarcely done so, when immediately I was seized upon by some power which entirely overcame me, and had such an astonishing influence over me as to bind my tongue so that I could not speak. Thick darkness gathered around me, and it seemed to me for a time as if I were doomed to sudden destruction ... and at the very moment when I was ready to sink into despair and abandon myself to destruction—not to an imaginary ruin, but to the power of some actual being from the unseen world, who had such marvelous power as I had never before felt in any being—just at this moment of great alarm, I saw a pillar of light....[4]

Joseph describes here what must have been a terrifying and unimaginable encounter. Among other things, he notes that he was "seized upon" and "entirely overcome" by Satan. He states that Lucifer bound his tongue so that he could not speak or cry out. Elsewhere Joseph noted that during this experience the devil caused his tongue to physically swell up and cleave to the roof of his mouth.[5] He also spoke of hearing distinct footsteps walking toward him, as he began his prayer; but he could not see Satan's person.[6] In one account of the experience the prophet noted that throughout the ordeal he was "severely tempted" with

---

[3] Not demonic possessions, but physical attacks.

[4] "Joseph Smith—History: Extracts from the History of Joseph Smith the Prophet," 1:15–16 in Pearl of Great Price. See also Dean C. Jessee, *Personal Writings of Joseph Smith*, rev. ed. (Salt Lake City: Deseret Book, 2002), 230; Milton V. Backman Jr., *Joseph Smith's First Vision* (Salt Lake City: Bookcraft, 1971), 162–63.

[5] Joseph Smith, Journal, November 9, 1835, quoted in Jessee, *Personal Writings* (2002), 104–05; Backman, *First Vision* (1971), 159; Alexander Neibaur, Journal, cited in Backman, *First Vision* (1971), 177.

[6] Ibid.

"improper pictures" and his mind was "darkened" and "filled with doubts"—all via the devil's influence.[7]

This was certainly not the prophet's only encounter with the adversary. Although we do not know all of the details surrounding each of these experiences, we do know that Joseph confided to at least one member of the early church that Satan had made repeated attempts to physically destroy him. Heber C. Kimball—one of the first men to be called as an apostle in this dispensation—stated: "Brother Joseph ... told me that he had contests with the devil, face to face. He also told me how he was handled and afflicted by the devil."[8] Heber did take the occasion to share the details of one of the many demonic encounters the prophet had suffered. We read:

> I will relate one circumstance that took place at Far West, in a house that Joseph had purchased, which had been formerly occupied as a public house by some wicked people. A short time after he got into it, one of his children was taken very sick; he laid his hands upon the child, when it got better; as soon as he went out of doors, the child was taken sick again; he again laid his hands upon it, so that it again recovered. This occurred several times, when Joseph inquired of the Lord what it all meant; then he had an open vision, and saw the devil in person, who contended with Joseph face to face, for some time. He said it was his house, it belonged to him, and Joseph had no right there. Then Joseph rebuked Satan in the name of the Lord, and he departed and touched the child no more.[9]

Thus, the record shows that Joseph experienced Satan in a very real and tangible way. This was not isolated to the very strange encounter in the "Sacred Grove." On the contrary, the devil—apparently on multiple occasions—physically and violently accosted the prophet "face to face."

---

[7] Orson Pratt, *An Interesting Account of Several Remarkable Visions*, 1840, quoted in Backman, *First Vision* (1971), 171. Orson Hyde, *A Cry From the Wilderness, A Voice From the Dust of the Earth*, 1842, quoted in Backman, *First Vision* (1971), 174–75.

[8] Heber C. Kimball, "Elders Called to Go on Missions," March 2, 1856, in *Journal of Discourses*, 26 vols. (Liverpool and London: Latter-day Saints' Book Depot, 1854–56), 3:229–30. See also Kimball, "The Saints Should Prepare for Future Emergencies," June 29, 1856, in *Journal of Discourses*, 4:2.

[9] See Orson F. Whitney, *Life of Heber C. Kimball*, 4th ed. (Salt Lake City: Bookcraft, 1973), 258–59. See also Alma P. Burton, comp., *Discourses of the Prophet Joseph Smith* (Salt Lake City: Deseret Book, 1974), 177. I express appreciation to Dr. Scott Esplin (of Brigham Young University) for bringing this experience to my attention.

Heber C. Kimball

I T SHOULD NOT be surprising to learn that the prophet Joseph was not the only member of the early church to be attacked by Lucifer. Indeed, Elder Kimball's aforementioned conversation with Joseph regarding physical satanic attacks did not come up in a random "chewing of the fat." Rather, the conversation was provoked by an encounter Heber had while serving a mission to the British Isles. Brother Kimball spoke of this experience on numerous occasions, each time sharing additional and/or different details. As space will not allow us to provide each of Brother Kimball's many descriptions, what follows is an amalgamation of the salient points of what happened.

In 1837 Elders Heber C. Kimball, Willard Richards, Orson Hyde, and Isaac Russell had been laboring as missionaries in the vicinity of Preston, England.[10] They were sharing a three-story flat on Wilford Street when the unthinkable happened. On Sunday, July 30—somewhere around daybreak—Elder Russell rushed into the room of Elders Kimball and Hyde, waking them, and claiming that he was so afflicted with evil spirits that he would not live long if someone did not cast them out. The two brethren administered to him; rebuking the devil, and petitioning the Lord for relief from the enemy that held Isaac bound. Elder Kimball was voice during the blessing. Near the end of the administration his voice began to falter, and then his tongue was bound so that he could no longer speak. Suddenly he began to tremble and reel back and forth. At that moment some invisible force threw him forward onto the floor. As he hit the ground he let out a deep groan, then lay there prostrate as though he were a dead man. Brother Hyde, with the assistance of Brother Russell, immediately laid hands on Elder Kimball, blessing him and rebuking Satan; at which point Heber regained consciousness, but had only partial strength. He noted that, as he regained his senses, sweat began to roll from him so profusely that it was as though he had just stepped out of a river. Elders Hyde and Russell lifted Elder Kimball, and placed him on his bed. However, his physical agony was so intense that he pulled himself back onto the floor, and reaching his knees he began to plead with the Lord for intervention.

At some point during these bizarre happenings, Elder Willard Richards awoke and made his way up to the third floor where the events were unfolding. Elder Kimball noted that, having finished his prayer, he sat on his bed and, to the surprise of all present, they were wrapped in a vision of the "infernal world." The four brethren said that they saw "legions" of evil spirits—company after company

---

[10] Laboring with these four brethren in Preston were John Snider, Joseph Fielding, and John Goodson. However, these three brethren were not present during the satanic encounter we are about to relate.

of them. According to Heber, these demonic hosts "struggled" to attack the elders, and "exerted all their power and influence" to destroy them. These spirits were in the shape of men; with fully formed bodies, hands, eyes, hair, ears, and every feature of a human—though some had hideous distortions in their face and body. With knives, they "rushed" upon the brethren "as an army going to battle." Elders Kimball and Hyde testified that they saw them as plainly as one would see a person standing in front of them. These demonic assailants came toward them, foaming at the mouth, and "gnashing their teeth upon" the elders. Orson Hyde noted that there were also numerous snakes accompanying the satanic hosts, hissing, writhing, and crawling over each other. Willard Richards, who had his watch on his person, noted that these "foul spirits" remained in the room threatening the brethren for an hour and a half.[11] Elder Kimball indicated that the following day he was so weak from the physical attack that he could scarcely stand.

Years later Heber spoke in detail of the encounter, and then added, I "cannot even now look back on the scene without feelings of horror; yet, by it I learned the power of the adversary, his enmity against the servants of God, and got some understanding of the invisible world."[12] Similarly, nearly two decades after the experience Elder Hyde wrote: "Every circumstance that occurred at that scene of devils is just as fresh in my recollection at this moment as it was at the moment of its occurrence, and will ever remain so."[13] Although much of the foregoing account was visionary, rather than tangible, Heber was quite clear that he was physically assaulted with a force that felt akin to being punched in the face by the fist of a strong man—to say nothing of the faltering voice, bound tongue, and physical weakness encountered.

---

[11] For the actual accounts of this experience, as told in the words of those present, see Kimball, *Journal of Discourses*, 3:229–30; see also Kimball, *Journal of Discourses*, 4:2; Journal History of the Church of Jesus Christ of Latter-day Saints, December 1860, 16:4, LDS Church Archives; Heber C. Kimball, *Journal of Heber C. Kimball* (Nauvoo, IL: Robinson and Smith, 1840), 18–19. Kimball, "Men Ought to Practice What They Teach," February 19, 1865, in *Journal of Discourses*, 11:84. See also Whitney, *Life of Heber C. Kimball* (1973), 129–32; Stanley B. Kimball, ed., *On The Potter's Wheel: The Diaries of Heber C. Kimball* (Salt Lake City: Signature Books, 1987), 9–10; *Elders' Journal* 1, no. 1 (October 1837): 4–5; Wilford Woodruff, March 3, 1889, in *Collected Discourses*, 5 vols., ed. Brian H. Stuy (n.p.: B.H.S. Publishing, 1999), 1:217–18; Myrtle Stevens Hyde, *Orson Hyde: The Olive Branch of Israel* (Salt Lake City: Agreka Books, 2000), 86–87; Joseph Fielding, *Diary of Joseph Fielding* (1963; Provo, UT: Brigham Young University Special Collections), 21–24; Heber C. Kimball, "A Letter From Heber C. Kimball to His Wife, Vilate Kimball," *Elders' Journal* 1, no. 1 (October 1837): 4–5.

[12] Kimball, *Journal* (1840), 19.

[13] Ibid., 101–102. See also Whitney, *Life of Heber C. Kimball* (1973), 131.

Wilford Woodruff

N OT UNLIKE THE experiences of Joseph, Heber, Orson, Willard, and Isaac, during the winter of 1840, Elders Wilford Woodruff[14] and George A. Smith[15] were also physically attacked by the devil, as they labored in the city of London. Elder Woodruff spoke of this assault on numerous occasions. On October 18, 1840, he wrote the following in his journal:

> We [meaning Wilford and George A. Smith] retired to rest in good season and I felt well in my mind and slept until 12 at night. I awoke and meditated upon the things of God until near 3 o'clock and while forming a determination to warn the people in London and overcome the powers of darkness by the assistance of God; A person appeared unto me which I considered was the Prince of Darkness or the Devil. He made war with me and attempted to take my life. He caught me by the throat and choked me nearly to death. He wounded me in my forehead. I also wounded him in a number of places in the head.[16] As he was about to overcome me I prayed to the father in the name of Jesus for help. I then had power over him and he left me though much wounded. Three personage dressed in white came to me and prayed with me and I was immediately healed and [they] delivered me from all my troubles.[17]

Although he doesn't mention it in the forgoing account, on later occasions Wilford indicated that Satan did physical harm to *both* he and George A. Smith—and had it not been for "three holy messengers" who gave them each a priesthood blessing, both of them would have been killed by Satan on that occasion.[18]

---

[14] Wilford was called to the Quorum of the Twelve Apostles April 26, 1839.

[15] George A. Smith was also called to the Quorum of the Twelve Apostles April 16, 1839.

[16] The sentence "He wounded me in my forehead. I also wounded him in a number of places in the head" is written in the original, but has been struck through with pencil by someone at a later date.

[17] Scott G. Kenney, ed., *Wilford Woodruff's Journal*, 9 vols. (Midvale, UT: Signature Books, 1983), 1:532. Spelling has been standardized.

[18] Wilford Woodruff, March 3, 1889, in Stuy, *Collected Discourses* (1999), 1:218; Wilford Woodruff, *Leaves from My Journal* (Salt Lake City: Juvenile Instructor Office, 1881), 109–10; Wilford Woodruff, discourse, October 19, 1896, in Stuy, *Collected Discourses* (1999), 5:236–37. For some reason no reference to this event by George A. Smith has survived. However, Elder Woodruff stated that he and Elder Smith were sleeping on cots some three feet apart when Satan appeared to them that night. Thus, there can be no doubt that he was aware of what happened, and was left with indelible impressions, as his companion was.

Newel Knight

THE PROPHET AND the early missionaries were not the only individuals to suffer physical attacks at the hands of the adversary. In what some have called the "first miracle of the church," Newel Knight[19] had a rather strange physical encounter with Lucifer. In the LDS *History of the Church* we find the following reference to the event:

> Amongst those who attended our meetings regularly [in April of 1830], was Newel Knight…. Newel had said that he would try and take up his cross, and pray vocally during meeting; but when we again met together, he rather excused himself…. Accordingly, he deferred praying until next morning, when he retired into the woods; where, according to his own account afterwards, he made several attempts to pray, but could scarcely do so…. He began to feel uneasy, and continued to feel worse both in mind and body, until, upon reaching his own house, his appearance was such as to alarm his wife very much. He requested her to go and bring me to him. I went and found him suffering very much in his mind, and his body acted upon in a very strange manner; his visage and limbs distorted and twisted in every shape and appearance possible to imagine; and finally he was caught up off the floor of the apartment, and tossed about most fearfully. His situation was soon made known to his neighbors and relatives and in a short time as many as eight or nine grown persons had got together to witness the scene. After he had thus suffered for a time, I succeeded in getting hold of him by the hand, when almost immediately he spoke to me, and with great earnestness requested me to cast the devil out of him, saying that he knew he was in him, and that he also knew that I could cast him out. I replied, "If you know that I can, it shall be done," and then almost unconsciously I rebuked the devil, and commanded him in the name of Jesus Christ to depart from him; when immediately Newel spoke out and said that he saw the devil leave him and vanish from his sight…. This scene was now entirely changed, for as soon as the devil had departed from our friend his countenance became natural, his distortions of body ceased, and almost immediately the Spirit of the Lord descended upon him, and the visions of eternity were opened to his view…. All this was witnessed by many, to their great astonishment and satisfaction.[20]

Knight confirms the details of this aforementioned account in his autobiography, where he both acknowledges that the event took place, but also

---

[19] Newel Knight was a member of the first High Council in Missouri, being called in July of 1834.

[20] Joseph Smith, *History of The Church of Jesus Christ of Latter-day Saints,* 7 vols., ed. B. H. Roberts (Salt Lake City: The Church of Jesus Christ of Latter-day Saints, 1978), 1:82–83. See also B. H. Roberts, *A Comprehensive History of The Church of Jesus Christ of Latter-day Saints,* 6 vols. (Orem, UT: Sonos Publishing, 1991), 1:199–202.

speaks in detail of the subsequent June 29, 1830, trial in which he was called as a witness, and interrogated regarding the aforementioned luciferic encounter.[21] Although Newel Knight's experience may seem more like demonic possession than satanic attack, clearly he was being physically accosted. Not only was his body actually distorted and disabled by the experience, but he notes that Satan physically lifted him off of the floor and "tossed" him about the room as if he were a rag doll.

Sidney Rigdon

LESS KNOWN THAN the aforementioned experiences is an event that took place in September of 1831. The prophet Joseph decided to take his family, then dwelling in Kirtland, and move to Hiram, Ohio, where he could continue the work of translating the Bible. Sidney Rigdon was left to preside over the Saints in Kirtland. On one occasion (during Joseph's absence) Sidney informed a body of Saints that the "keys of the kingdom" had been taken from the church.[22] Those present were confused and dismayed by the announcement. Joseph was immediately sent for, and upon his return declared that the things Sidney had taught were false. The prophet added that, because of the things Elder Rigdon had said and done, "the devil [would] handle him as one man handles another."[23] In fulfillment of Joseph's words, "a few weeks after this, Sidney was lying in bed alone, and suddenly 'an unseen power lifted him from his bed ... and tossed him from one side of the room to the other.' His family heard the noises coming from the room and rushed in 'and found him going from one side of the room to the other.'"[24] This happened some three times over

---

[21] See Newel Knight, *Newel Knight Autobiography*, L. Tom Perry Special Collections, Harold B. Lee Library, Brigham Young University, Provo, Utah, 3–4, 8–9, 13. See also Smith, *History of the Church* (1978), 1:91–3; Roberts, *Comprehensive History* (1991), 1:207.

[22] See Lucy Mack Smith, *The History of Joseph Smith by His Mother* (Salt Lake City: Bookcraft, 1958), 221; Lavina Fielding Anderson, *Lucy's Book: A Critical Edition of Lucy Mack Smith's Family Memoir* (Salt Lake City: Signature Books, 2001), 561. Richard Bushman conjectures that the reason for Rigdon's claim that the "keys of the kingdom [had been] rent from the church" was a concern he had about property. Bushman writes: "Rigdon had long been deprived of a home for his large family and perhaps was suffering mentally" (Richard Bushman, *Joseph Smith: Rough Stone Rolling* [New York: Alfred A. Knopf, 2005], 186).

[23] Philo Dibble, "Philo Dibble's Narrative," in *Early Scenes in Church History*, Faith-Promoting Series, 8 bks. (Salt Lake City: Juvenile Instructors Office, 1882), 8:80; reprinted under the same title (Salt Lake City: Bookcraft, 1968), 80, cited in LeMar E. Garrard, "A Study of the Problem of a Personal Devil and its Relationship to Latter-day Saint Beliefs" (master's thesis, Brigham Young University, 1955), 121, 247.

[24] Ibid., 121.

the course of the night.[25] Sidney was physically "laid up" from the effects of the experience some five or six weeks. Thus, having spoken under the influence of the devil, Sidney was then turned over to the physical buffetings of Lucifer.

Benjamin Brown

ALTHOUGH EACH OF the aforementioned stories involves high-profile members of the early church, nevertheless, a number of less-known believers in the restored gospel had similar encounters. For example, one early Saint by the name of Benjamin Brown had spent the years prior to his discovery of Mormonism looking for "the ancient gospel" of New Testament Christianity. In the process he is said to have had a number of visions. However, when Brown shared these experiences with a local minister, he was told that both his visions and his desires to find "the ancient" church of the Bible were "of the Devil."[26]

On one occasion after his conversion, Brother Brown and two friends were called upon to cast an evil spirit out of a possessed sister. While attempting to exercise the priesthood, Brown and one of his companions learned, from direct experience, Satan's ability to physically interact with mortals.[27] Among other things, he noted:

> The evil spirit … came out full of fury, and, as he passed by one of the brethren, seized him by both arms and gripped them violently. Passing towards me, something, which by the feel appeared like a man's hand, grasped me by both sides of the face, and attempted to pull me sideways to the ground but the hold appearing to slip, I recovered my balance immediately. My face was sore for some days after this. The other brother that was seized was lame for a week afterwards.[28]

Like so many others, Brother Brown and his companion learned firsthand that Satan's hands *can* be felt!

---

[25] See Kimball, *Journal of Discourses*, 3:229–30; Kimball, *Journal of Discourses*, 4:2; Anderson, *Lucy's Book* (2001), 563–64.

[26] Mark R. Grandstaff and Milton V. Backman Jr., "The Social Origins of the Kirtland Mormons," *BYU Studies* 30, no. 2 (Spring 1990): 61.

[27] As noted, although Benjamin Brown is not a well-known figure in church history, his experience seems consistent with those heretofore noted, and thus seems germane to our discussion.

[28] Benjamin Brown, "Benjamin Brown Autobiography," in *Testimonies For The Truth* (Liverpool: S. W. Richards, 1853), ch. 2; Benjamin Brown, in "Testimonies for the Truth," in *Gems For The Young Folks*, Faith-Promoting Series, 8 bks (Salt Lake City: Juvenile Instructors Office, 1881), 4:72.

Harvey Whitlock

ONE FINAL EXPERIENCE is worth sharing here. It involves the ordination of Harvey Whitlock to the office of high priest. Brother Whitlock was an on-again, off-again believer in the Restoration who was baptized into the LDS Church some three times, before finally becoming a member of the RLDS Church (or Community of Christ).[29] Brother Whitlock's experience with Satan was recorded by a number of individuals, some of whom actually witnessed it. For example, Levi Hancock[30] wrote:

> The Fourth of June [1831] came and we all met ... near Isaac Morley's in Kirtland, Geauga County, Ohio.... Joseph put his hands on Harvey Whitlock and ordained him to the high priesthood. He turned as black as Lyman was white. His fingers were set like claws. He went around the room and showed his hands and tried to speak; his eyes were in the shape of oval O's. Hyrum Smith said, "Joseph, that is not of God." Joseph ... bowed his head, and in a short time got up and commanded Satan to leave Harvey, laying his hands upon his head at the same time. At that very instant an old man said to weigh two hundred and fourteen pounds sitting in the window turned a complete summersault in the house and [landed on] his back across a bench and lay helpless. Joseph told Lyman to cast Satan out. He did. The man's name was Leanon Coply [Leman Copley], formally a Quaker [Shaker]. The evil spirit left him and as quick [as] lightning Harvey Green fell bound and screamed like a panther. Satan was cast out of him. But immediately entered someone else. This continued all day and the greater part of the night.... After this we ... heard Harvey Whitlock say when Hyrum Smith said it was not [of] God, he disdained him in his heart and when the Devil was cast out he was convinced it was Satan that was in him and he knew ... it. I also heard Harvey Green say that he could not describe the awful feeling he experienced while in the hands of Satan.[31]

Lucy Mack Smith also referred to the Harvey Whitlock experience in her 1844–45 preliminary manuscript that would become her *History of Joseph Smith by His Mother*. While she confirms Levi Hancock's account of the events, she adds a couple of additional insights that Hancock did not include. Mother Smith stated that Whitlock convulsed when under the physical influence of Satan, and was left physically weak after the devil was cast out of him. She also noted that Copley had his tongue bound during the episode, so as to prevent

---

[29] See Susan Easton Black, *Who's Who in the Doctrine and Covenants* (Salt Lake City: Deseret Book, 1997), 326–27. In 1866 Whitlock served a mission for the RLDS Church.

[30] Levi Hancock was a member of the original seven presidents of the Seventy (LDS D&C 124:138/ RLDS D&C 107:44a).

[31] Levi Hancock, Autobiography, L. Tom Perry Special Collections, Harold B. Lee Library, Brigham Young University, Provo, Utah, 33–34.

him from speaking.[32] Both of these "symptoms," if we can call them such, are comparable to the experiences of Joseph Smith, Heber C. Kimball, and Newel Knight. Philo Dibble, who was a firsthand witness to this experience, confirms Lucy Mack Smith's additions to the story. Dibble wrote:

> Harvey Whitlock stepped into the middle of the room with his arms crossed, bound by the power of Satan, and his mouth twisted unshapely. Hyrum Smith arose and declared that there was an evil spirit in the room.... Shortly Hyrum rose the second time, saying, "I know my duty and will do it," and stepping to Harvey, commanded the evil spirits to leave him, but the spirits did not obey. Joseph then approached Harvey and asked him if he believed in God. Then we saw a change in Harvey. He also bore record of the opening of the heavens and of the coming of the Son of Man, precisely as Lyman Wight had done. Next a man by the name of Harvey Green was thrown upon his back on the floor by an unseen power. Some of the brethren wanted to administer to him by laying on of hands, but Joseph forbade it. Harvey looked to me like a man in a fit. He groaned and frothed at the mouth. Finally he got upon his knees and came out of it. Next thing I saw a man came flying through the window from outside. He was straight as a man's arm as he sailed into the room over two rows of seats filled with men, and fell on the floor between the seats and was pulled out by the brethren. He trembled all over like a leaf in the wind. He was soon ... calm and natural. His name was Lemon Copley. He weighed over two hundred pounds. This I saw with my own eyes and know it is all true, and bear testimony to it.[33]

What seems significant here—at least as it relates to our discussion—is not so much the fact that Harvey Whitlock was possessed by the devil, as apparently were others. Rather, what seems noteworthy are the physical attacks on Leman Copley and Harvey Green. Whereas Whitlock was clearly possessed, these other

---

[32] She wrote: "When [Joseph] came to Kirtland he found ... the Devil had been deceiving them with a specious appearance of power manifested by strange contortions of the visage and unnatural Motions which they supposed as being occasioned by an operation of the power of God.... He called upon one of the brethren who had been deceived by an evil spirit to speak[.] [W]hen he arose he was immediately convulsed in the most singular manner[;] his face[,] his arms[,] and his fingers being drawn like a person in [a] spasm[.] Joseph turned to Hyrum and said will you go and lay hands on that brother[?] [W]hen Hyrum did so the man fell back into his chair as weak as though he had exhausted himself by excessive hard labor[.] [H]e then called upon another who was standing on the outside of the house leaning in the window[.] [T]his man pitched forward into the house and[,] after trying sometime to speak without being able to do so[,] was administer to by the laing on of hands which affected him the same as the one who had preceeded him" (Lucy Mack Smith, Manuscript, 1844–45, p. 193, LDS Church Archives. A copy of this manuscript is available in Anderson, *Lucy's Book* [2001], 506–08).

[33] Philo Dibble, "Recollections of the Prophet Joseph Smith," *Juvenile Instructor*, May 1882, 303.

two brothers exhibited behavior that implied they were also being physically (not just spiritually) harassed by the adversary.

The Nature of Heavenly Angels

A S A PARENTHETIC note, the material nature of spirits is not isolated to luciferic angels. The physical makeup of righteous spirits is apparently also material. David Patten Kimball, son of Heber C. Kimball (mentioned above), had an experience where he had physical contact with the spirits of his deceased parents, who visited him from the spirit world. He noted that he had gotten lost in the desert of Arizona, and was near death for want of water. His father and mother appeared to him and gave him a drink of water that sustained his life until he could be found.[34]

Elder Parley P. Pratt—a member of the original Quorum of the Twelve Apostles—had a similar experience to that of David Kimball. Pratt was unjustly incarcerated in Richmond, Missouri, and had been fasting and pleading with the Lord to know if he would ever be freed from that "gloomy, dark, cold and filthy dungeon." In response to his prayer, his wife—who had been deceased for nearly two years—appeared to him. She held his hand, and laid her cheek against his. Pratt noted the warmth of her face as she pressed it against him. She

---

[34] See David P. Kimball to Helen Mar Whitney, January 8, 1882, cited in Orson F. Whitney, "A Terrible Ordeal," in *Helpful Visions*, Faith-Promoting Series (Salt Lake City: Juvenile Instructors Office, 1887), 14:9. In a somewhat related vein, according to history, when Joseph and Oliver went to Cumorah to return the plates to Moroni, the hill opened up, and inside of it was a room some sixteen feet square. (Some accounts only mention Joseph and Oliver. However, when the various accounts of the experience are combined, the list of those present include Joseph and Oliver, but also Hyrum Smith, David Whitmer, and Joseph Smith Sr.) The room was said to be filled with plates—"wagon loads" of them—lining the walls. There was light in the cave, a table in the center of the room, and the "Sword of Laban" hanging upon the wall (See Brigham Young, "Trying to be Saints," June 17, 1877, in *Journal of Discourses* 19:38; Kenney (1983), December 11, 1869, in 6:508; Edward L. Stevens, *Reminiscences of Joseph, the Prophet, and the Coming Forth of the Book of Mormon* (Salt Lake City: Edward Stephens, 1893), 14–15; Jerry C. Roundy, "Joseph and Moroni" (unpublished manuscript, author's possession, 1982), 50–51; H. Donl Peterson, *Moroni: Ancient Prophet—Modern Messenger* (Salt Lake City: Deseret Book, 2000), 135–37. Joseph and Oliver handled items in the room, and yet it is said that Joseph believed that these "wagon loads" of plates were not deposited in the hill in New York (from which he acquired the Book of Mormon). Rather, historical sources suggest that Joseph believed that the room he and Oliver entered—the room in which they touched items pertaining to the Nephite nation—was somewhere in Central America (see H. Donl Peterson, "Moroni, the Last of the Nephite Prophets," in *The Book of Mormon: Fourth Nephi Through Moroni—From Zion to Destruction*, ed. Monte S. Nyman and Charles D. Tate Jr. [Provo, UT: Brigham Young University Religious Studies Center, 1995], 243–47). Thus, Joseph and Oliver had a physical encounter with items they were seeing with their "spiritual eyes," per se.

had come in answer to his pleadings, and informed him that he would again see the light of day.[35]

On a related note, in the Gospel of Matthew we're informed that it was an angel that rolled back the stone that covered the opening of the sepulcher in which Jesus had been placed (Matthew 28:2).[36]

Each of these encounters implies that the spirits of the righteous retain a materiality even once they are separated from their mortal bodies.

Conclusion

WHAT HAS BEEN shared is only a sampling of the numerous examples of demonic attacks recorded in the diaries and journals of the early Saints, and in the historical records of the church. Were space not an issue, many more could be offered as evidence of the point we sought to make by sharing these—namely that Lucifer is capable of having physical contact with mortals. One 1840 British convert to the church, George Q. Cannon,[37] spoke to this subject on more than one occasion, cautioning the Saints:

> I have come to the conclusion that if our eyes were open to see the spirit world around us, we ... would not be so unguarded and careless, and so indifferent whether we had the spirit and power of God with us or not; but we would be continually watchful and prayerful to our heavenly Father for His Holy Spirit and His holy angels to be around about us to strengthen us to overcome every evil influence.[38]

Of course, all of this begs the question: How is it possible that the devil and his minions—beings traditionally understood to be void of physical bodies—are able to attack human beings in such a physical manner? Are we to be dismissive

---

[35] Parley P. Pratt Jr., ed., *The Autobiography of Parley Parker Pratt*, 5th ed. (Salt Lake City: Deseret Book, 1961), 238. I express appreciation to Paul E. Damron, who directed me to this source.

[36] While it is possible that this angel was a resurrected being—having been one of those who obtained his resurrection with Christ (Matthew 27:52–53)—Greek scholar Joseph Thayer suggests that the "angel" in Matthew 28:2 is a spirit, rather than a resurrected personage. See Joseph H. Thayer, *Thayer's Greek-English Lexicon of the New Testament* (Peabody, MA: Hendrickson Publishers, 1999), 5. There certainly doesn't appear to be a glory associated with this angel, as one might expect if he were a resurrected being. Indeed, Mark speaks of him as looking like "a young man" in appearance (see Mark 16:5), rather than one having the glory and look of a resurrected being. Of course we cannot rule out the possibility that this was a translated being either.

[37] Canon joined the church in England when he was thirteen years old. He eventually became an LDS apostle and counselor to three presidents of the Mormon Church.

[38] George Q. Cannon, "Blessings of the People of God," November 13, 1864, in *Journal of Discourses*, 11:30. See also George Q. Cannon, "Travelling Through the Settlements," September 2, 1883, in *Journal of Discourses*, 24:375–76.

of these historical narratives as simple misunderstandings on the part of those who experienced the events described? Such does not appear to be a viable solution. Not only are a number of these brethren known to be men of character, righteousness, and trustworthiness; but each seems quite certain about what he saw, experienced, and described. Beyond this, there is a consistency in their experiences that suggests that they are describing events that actually happened (e.g., being left weak; having one's tongue bound; acts of physical violence, such as being pinned to the floor, thrown to the floor, or tossed about the room, etc.). Finally, each of the aforementioned experiences had witnesses present who watched or experienced firsthand the demonic attacks. Thus, reason would suggest that these events happened as described.

Perhaps one explanation of these happenings is to be found in the nature of Satan's body. As we noted at the beginning of this article, the prophet Joseph is purported to have taught:

> We came to this earth that we might have a body and present it pure before God in the celestial kingdom. The great principle of happiness consists in having a body. The devil has no body, and herein is his punishment. He is pleased when he can obtain the tabernacle of man and when cast out by the Savior he asked to go into the herd of swine showing that he would prefer a swine's body to having none.[39]

Accurately, this statement points out that Satan's premortal rebellion or fall stripped him of the right to have a mortal body. However, the tendency is to assume that Joseph is here saying that Lucifer's "spirit body" is therefore void of any physical properties. Yet this is clearly not what the prophet is claiming. Regarding the physical nature of the "spirit body," the prophet noted: "the body is supposed to be organized matter, and the spirit by many is thought to be immaterial, without substance. With this latter statement we should beg leave to differ—and state that spirit is a substance; that it is material, but that it is more pure, elastic, and refined matter than the body."[40] Similarly, approximately a year later Joseph stated: "There is no such thing as immaterial matter. All spirit is matter but it is more fine or pure and can only be discerned by purer eyes. We cant see it but when our bodies are purified we shall see that it is all matter."[41] LDS scholars Stephen E. Robinson and H. Dean Garrett wrote: "Spirits are made of matter. Just as matter can change form from matter to

---

[39] William Clayton's Private Book, January 5, 1841, cited in Ehat and Cook, *Words of Joseph Smith* (1980), 60.

[40] Joseph Smith Jr., "Try the Spirits," *Times and Seasons* III, no. 11 (April 1, 1842): 745.

[41] William Clayton Diary, May 17, 1843, cited in Ehat and Cook, *Words of Joseph Smith* (1980), 203.

energy, so, apparently, matter can be refined and purified to the point where it is normally discernible only to bodies that have been similarly refined and purified. The universe is not composed of two mutually exclusive entities, matter and spirit, but of only one—matter in one or another stage of refinement."[42] Thus, the notion that Satan's spirit body—or for that matter the spirit body of any being—is immaterial, and thus intangible, appears to be incorrect. The devil's spirit body is made of matter, just as our physical bodies are made of matter. And the aforementioned luciferic encounters strongly suggest that spirit matter and mortal matter can interact.

---

[42] Stephen E. Robinson and H. Dean Garrett, *A Commentary on the Doctrine and Covenants,* 4 vols. (Salt Lake City: Deseret Book, 2000–05), 4:239.

Pentecost and All Things Common: Acts 2 and 4:31–33 as Template for Community in Kirtland, Ohio, 1830–1837

ANDREW BOLTON

The Birth of the Early Church—Acts Chapter 2

THE EARLY CHURCH community was *conceived* by the calling of individual disciples by the Rabbi Jesus who formed them into a wandering band gathered around him. They kept a *common purse* to meet the needs of the poor (John 12:6, 13:28–29). Together the disciples went through the devastation of the crucifixion of Jesus and were surprised by his resurrection. According to Acts chapter 2, their birthing as a community is complete, after the ascension of Jesus, by the pouring out of the Holy Spirit on the disciples. This happens at the Jewish feast of Pentecost that comes fifty days after the feast of Passover and traditionally celebrates the giving of the Torah at Mount Sinai. Devout Jews from every nation in Jerusalem gather for the Pentecost festival, understand what the disciples are saying in this spirit-filled event, and are amazed.

This is the reverse of the story of the Tower of Babel. Here there is no imposed totalitarian unity and single language implied in the Tower of Babel story. Instead, difference of language and culture means diversity is irreducible, but people can be in harmony with the Holy Spirit and one another.[1] Like the

---

[1] For a brilliant analysis of the difference between the Tower of Babel and Pentecost see Miroslav Volf, *Exclusion and Embrace—A Theological Exploration of Identity, Otherness, and Reconciliation*

creation account in Genesis, this story thus begins with the dramatic, powerful, yet gentle movement of the Holy Spirit. Peter then explains that the giving of the Holy Spirit is the fulfillment of the words of the Prophet Joel: "In the last days it will be, God declares, that I will pour out my Spirit upon all flesh, and your sons and your daughters shall prophesy" (Acts 2:17).

Here both female and male are equally presenced by the Holy Spirit, again suggesting that the community being formed is to be different from that of a surrounding Roman colonized culture.

Peter then preaches to the crowd about the crucifixion of Jesus and how his resurrection is the fulfillment of prophecy. He ends with this challenge to a Jerusalem crowd that seven weeks earlier had included those who yelled for the crucifixion of Jesus: "Therefore let the entire house of Israel know with certainty that God has made him both Lord and Messiah, this Jesus whom you crucified" (Acts 2:36). Cut to the heart, members of the crowd ask what they should do. Peter tells them: "Repent, and be baptized every one of you in the name of Jesus Christ so that your sins may be forgiven; and you will receive the gift of the Holy. For the promise is for you, and your children and for all who are far away" (Acts 2:38–39).

Already those from different nations are blessed by understanding the disciples. They and their children, both male and female, are also promised the Holy Spirit. Now forgiveness equalizes and draws in even those who participated in the victimization of Jesus and shouted for his execution. The promise of the Holy Spirit is also extended to their children so they are blessed by grace, not cursed for the sins of their parents. Three thousand are baptized and join the community of the 120, devoting "themselves to the apostles' teaching and fellowship, to the breaking of bread and prayers" (Acts 2:41–42).

The birth of this remarkable community continues with the believers living together, with all things in common, meeting the needs of all (Acts 2:44–45). Here we have expressed not only the Exodus liberation from slavery and Hebrew prophetic vision of the end of poverty, but also the Greek ideal of sharing friendship in a form of spirit-inspired communal living.[2] Finally, these

---

(Nashville, TN: Abingdon Press, 1996), 226–31.

[2] "The Holy Spirit liberates from the bourgeois quest for material security (cf. Luke 12:16–21) and he liberates for a community that expresses the Greek ideal of friendship, in which friends have all things in common (cf. Plato, Republic 4.42a), as well as the Hebrew hope for a community free from poverty (Deut. 15:4–5). Luke's picture of the community of goods is a criticism of the indifference of all well-to-do Christians toward their needy brothers and sisters and is a call to find creative ways to overcome the gulf between the rich and poor in the church, which is the eschatological alternative to the communities of the world, including unrepentant Israel" (Gerhard A. Krodel, *Augsburg Commentary on the New Testament, Acts* [Minneapolis:

early disciples continue daily to spend much time in the temple living virtuous lives, having the praise of the people, and seeing continuing baptisms.

This spirit-led communal living and concern for the poor is to be found again later in the story of Acts; especially Acts 4:31–35, which in many ways is a summary and restatement of Acts 2. The teaching of Jesus to remember the poor is faithfully continued in the life of the early church (see also Acts 6:1–6, Galatians 2:10, I Corinthians 16:1–2, Romans 15:25–27, II Corinthians 8, 9:1–3, Acts 24:17, James 1:26, 2:14–17, 5:1–6).

Briefly told above is the account of the birth of this radical former-day-saint community inspired by Jesus that could also be described as utopian, in the sense of being a good (eu) place (topia), with a mission to transform not only Jerusalem and Israel, but the world. The story of the early Christian community described in Acts 2:42–45 and 4:32–35 has influenced serious Christians and prophetic radicals down through the centuries. I will give just three examples.

The Benedictine monastic system, now sixteen hundred years old, is a very famous example of men and women living lives of prayer, work, and all things common. St. Benedict's rule makes an explicit connection to references in Acts 2:42–47 and 4:35 to all things common.[3]

Anabaptism, the radical reformation movement begun in 1525 that includes twenty-first-century Mennonites, Amish, and Hutterites as descendents, has links to Benedictine monasticism through, for example, the early leader Michael Sattler, a former prior of a Benedictine monastery and principal author of the 1527 Schleitheim Confession.[4] The Hutterians were, and still are, explicitly communal and their descendents still hold all things in common as they farm the prairie states and provinces of the U.S. and Canada today. The *Hutterian Chronicle* describes the connection made to communal living described in Acts 2:42–45 and Acts 4:32–35 at their beginning.[5]

Augsburg, 1986], 95; see also David L. Mealand, "Community of Goods and Utopian Allusions in Acts II-IV," *Journal of Theological Studies* 28 [April 1977]: 96–99).

[3] The Holy Rule of St Benedict, "Chapters 33, 34, 55," <http://www.kansasmonks.org/RuleOfStBenedict.html> (accessed January 10, 2009); see also "Expressing their unity in community of goods, monks strengthen their common bonds through their prayer and work together and by their mutual support and compassion" with reference to Acts 2:42–47 and Acts 4:32–35 (A Declaration on Benedictine Monastic Life for the Monasteries of the Swiss-American Benedictine Congregation, "Part II: Life in the monastery D13," <http://www.osb.org/swissam/declaration/IIA.html> (accessed January 10, 2009).

[4] C. Arnold Snyder, *Anabaptist History and Theology—An Introduction* (Kitchener, ON: Pandora Press, 1995), 60–62. For the influence of monasticism on early Anabaptism, see also John H. Yoder, ed. and trans., *The Schleitheim Confession* (Scottdale, PA: Herald Press, 1977), 227.

[5] For the beginning of the Hutterian movement see Hutterian Brethren, ed. and trans., *The Chronicle of the Hutterian Brethren* (Rifton, NY: Plough Publishing House, 1987), 1:78, 81.

Radical Gerald Winstanley, during the English Revolution 1640–59, was an advocate for the Diggers, the True Levellers that wanted to have common ownership of the land and abolish the privileges of the rich and the aristocracy. In 1649, he and others occupied land on St George's Hill in Surrey, England, and started digging it as their own. For Winstanley, Jesus was the head Leveller,[6] and he quoted Acts 4:32, among many other biblical passages, to justify all things common.[7]

It can be argued that the early Christians' later radical movements and the early Latter Day Saint movement are examples of what political scientist James C. Scott calls "little traditions" that subvert the "great tradition" of a religion held by the nobility, educated, priestly classes (and serving their interests), in favor of those at the bottom of society.[8] The poor have thus heard with gladness biblical support, especially in Acts 2:42–45 and Acts 4:31–35, for the injustice of their condition. Acts has inspired left-wing, nonconformist, dissenting, little-tradition Christianity down through the centuries. I want to argue in this paper that the early Latter Day Saints belong to this stream of radical Christian traditions and were powerfully influenced by passages in Acts 2 and Acts 4 that describe holding all things common. So how did Acts 2 and 4:31–35 inspire the early Saints in Kirtland, Ohio, in the 1830s?

Acts 2 and 4:31–35 as Template for the Church in Kirtland

THE EARLY Latter Day Saints can also be called a utopian movement because they were likewise a community with a mission—that of changing and transforming the world into a good place.[9] They had a vision of the kingdom of God on earth in this life and began by gathering to demonstrate or model the change they felt God was calling the world to make—the project of bringing about the kingdom of heaven on earth, what they called Zion. The time was now. It was the latter days.

Their template, the model of what they were trying to do, was taken from Acts 2 and Acts 4:31–33 in the New Testament. The Latter Day Saints were a

---

[6] Christopher Hill, *The World Turned Upside Down—Radical Ideas during the English Revolution* (Harmondsworth: Penguin Books, 1972), 132.

[7] Gerald Winstanley, *The True Levellers Standard ADVANCED: OR, The State of Community opened, and Presented to the Sons of Men* (London, 1649), <http://darkwing.uoregon.edu/~rbear/digger.html> (accessed January 10, 2009).

[8] James C. Scott "Protest and Profanation: Agrarian Revolt and the Little Tradition, Part 1," *Theory and Society* 4 (1977): 1–38, 211–46.

[9] Utopia is a Greek word that means good (eu) place (topia). See discussion by Michael Tyldesley, *No Heavenly Delusion?—A Comparative Study of Three Communal Movements* (Liverpool: Liverpool University Press, 2003), 2–4.

restoration or restitutional movement seeking to recover in radical faithfulness the life of the early Christians. These passages from Acts inspired their imagination as a utopian movement, particularly with the promises for the latter days in Acts 2:17.

Evidence for Asserting the Influence of Acts on the Early Latter Day Saints

Textual Development

FIRST OF ALL we find the textual development of Acts 4:31–33 in IV Nephi 1:2–6 and Doctrine and Covenants 36:2g–i. Chapter 4 of Acts begins by describing opposition by Jewish authorities to the healing ministry of Peter and John, whose courageous preaching and witnessing, arrest and imprisonment, and then victorious release is a powerful vindication of the Gospel. Acts 4:31–33 is a recapitulation of the day of Pentecost with the Holy Spirit coming in power with an all-things-in-common lifestyle in the Christian community, which has now grown to over five thousand baptized members (Acts 4:4).

In the table on the next page, Acts 4:31–33 in the King James Version is compared with Doctrine and Covenants 36:2g–i and IV Nephi 1:2–6. There clearly are parallels of language suggesting that Joseph Smith Jr. was basing Doctrine and Covenants 36 and IV Nephi passages on the Acts 4 passage.

The reworking of Acts 4:31–33 in IV Nephi 1:2–6 occurred before the formal organization of the church. We probably cannot be sure when this particular passage in IV Nephi was composed by Joseph Smith Jr., although perhaps in 1829. Fourth Nephi goes on to describe the *golden age* of the Nephites and can be called the spiritual and literal climax of the book. The gift of the Holy Spirit follows repentance and baptism and the converted become disciples of Jesus and live all things in common. There is peace and everyone deals justly with one another. It lasts two hundred years, suggesting this pattern is normal, faithful Christianity. It also is set in an ancient American past with the implication that it is thus possible in America in the latter days; so any nineteenth-century seeker who reads the whole Book of Mormon could be inspired by the IV Nephi account and conclude that the pattern of all things common found in Acts 2 and 4 was not an exception but the intended norm for Christians.

Thus Acts 2 and 4 are reworked in fresh, but faithful ways in the emerging Nephite and Enoch sagas/myths of the early Latter Day Saints. It becomes their *DNA* expressed as the cause of Zion.

Acts 4 *(King James Version)*	Doctrine and Covenants 36 *(December 1830)*	IV Nephi 1 *(1829?)*
31. And when they had prayed, the place was shaken where they were assembled together; and they were all filled with the Holy Ghost, and they spoke the word of God with boldness.	2g. And the fear of the Lord was upon all nations, so great was the glory of the Lord which was upon his people.	2. And as many as came to them and truly repented of their sins were baptized in the name of Jesus; and they also received the Holy Ghost.
32. And the multitude of them that believed	2h. And the Lord called his people Zion because they	
were of one heart and of one soul:	were of one heart and one mind	3. And there were no contentions and disputations among them,
neither said any of them that ought of the things which he possessed was his own;	and dwelt in righteousness	and every man dealt justly one with another.
but they had all things common.	2i. and there was no poor among them;	4. And they had all things common among them, therefore they were not rich and poor, bond and free.
33. And with great power gave the apostles witness of the resurrection of the Lord Jesus; and great grace was upon them all.	and Enoch continued his preaching in righteousness unto the people of God.	6. And there were great and marvelous works wrought by the disciples of Jesus, in as much as they healed the sick, and raised the dead.

Acts 4 compared with Section 36 of the Doctrine and Covenants and IV Nephi 1.

Sidney Rigdon's Acts 2 Communal Family

SECOND, SIDNEY RIGDON was a Campbellite preacher who lived in Mentor, about two miles from Kirtland. He had earlier heard the debate between his colleague Alexander Campbell and the Scottish industrialist and reformer Robert Owen in Cincinnati in April 1829. Owen had been seeking to build a communist utopia without religion at New Harmony, Indiana. Rigdon returned to his congregation in Mentor after the debate, enthused by Owen's system of *family commonwealths* to foster a religiously inspired communal life after the example of the early Christians. By February 1830, Rigdon had persuaded Lyman Wight and Isaac Morley, among others, to start implementing a common stock commune or *family* after the pattern of Acts 2:44–45 on Morley's farm near Kirtland. By October 1830, the group numbered more than a hundred persons.

Parley P. Pratt was a former Campbellite preacher and associate of Rigdon. When Pratt was converted to Mormonism, he visited his old friend Rigdon and succeeded in baptizing him into the young movement in November 1830. Over a hundred others were also baptized, including all the members of the Kirtland communal *family*.[10]

This was momentous for the development of the church in Kirtland. A month later, in December 1830, Joseph Smith Jr. received a revelation about the prophecy of Enoch that later became part of Genesis 7:1–78 of the Inspired Version. Included are these words: "And the Lord called his people Zion, because they were of one heart and one mind, and dwelt in righteousness; and there was no poor among them; and Enoch continued his preaching in righteousness to the people of God" (Doctrine and Covenants 36:2h–i).

This is a reworking of the early Christian community described in Acts 4:31–33 as shown in the table above. This righteous community is now called Zion. Later, Smith's resetting of this Doctrine and Covenants 36:h–i passage in Genesis in the Inspired Version implies that Zion existed at the dawn of biblical history and only waits to be restored to earth through a faithful people. It could be argued that the preacher of righteousness, Enoch, echoes not only the apostle Peter in Acts 2, but possibly the contemporary prophetic role of Joseph Smith Jr. In the same month of December 1830, Joseph received a revelation directing that the Saints should move from New York and gather in Kirtland,

---

[10] Richard S. Van Wagoner, *Sidney Rigdon—A Portrait of Religious Excess* (Salt Lake City: Signature Books, 1994), 49–53. At the 1830 meeting of the Mahoning Baptist Association, Rigdon argued "that our pretensions to follow the apostles in all their New Testament teachings, required a community of goods; that as they established their order in the model church at Jerusalem, we were bound to imitate their example" (53). Alexander Campbell disagreed, and this among other differences caused their separation.

Ohio (Doctrine and Covenants 37). This was the first direction given to gather in one place. So, in Kirtland, the Acts 2 pattern already being attempted on the Morley farm was joined by a people with a living prophet from the state of New York who had additional scripture in the IV Nephi reworking of Acts 4:31–33. In the hybridization of Smith's and Rigdon's movements, Acts 2 and 4 arguably became the template of the early Latter Day Saints seeking restoration of the early Christian pattern.

Kirtland Expressions of Acts

THIRDLY, MANY OF the major themes of Acts 2 are expressed in some way in the life of the Kirtland church from 1831 to 1837: gathering (Acts 2:1), Pentecostal endowment of the Holy Spirit (Acts 2:2–15), the promise of the latter days (Acts 2:16–18), signs of the coming end times (Acts 2:19–21), preaching the Gospel (Acts 2:36–41), attempts to live all things common through the law of consecration (Acts 2:44–45), and the building of a temple in which to worship and learn (Acts 2:42, 46). This is described in more detail in the table in the appendix at the end of this paper. The whole book of Acts is about inclusion of those who were excluded. Those who felt excluded because of their poverty are drawn to the emerging Latter Day Saint movement.

What is interesting is that in Acts 2 the chapter begins with the Pentecostal outpouring of the Holy Spirit and ends with all things in common—first grace then works. This is reversed in Kirtland. It is the economic arrangements that are tackled first, yet continue to haunt perilously the early Latter Day Saint community. Tragically, not too long after the season of Pentecostal endowment associated with the dedication of the Kirtland Temple in March 1836, the Kirtland bank fails and Rigdon and Smith have to flee at night.

Economics, Education, and Aspirations among Early
Latter Day Saints

THE LATTER DAY SAINT movement is a movement first of all of the poor and the uneducated. Historian Robert Flanders describes the Smith family belonging "to the large company of Americans who were beyond the edge of successful genteel society and the institutional Establishments of their time. And they were generally inclined to distrust the Establishment whether its manifestations be theological, ecclesiological, political or economical."[11]

---

[11] Robert Flanders, "To Transform History: Early Mormon Culture and the Concept of Time and Space," *American Society of Church History* (March 1971): 110.

Former University of Notre Dame scholar Nathan Hatch describes the economic and social status of some of Smith's earliest disciples: Brigham and Lorenzo Dow Young, Orson and Parley Pratt, Heber C. Kimball, Jedediah Morgan Grant, and Thomas B. Marsh, all of whom were involved in the Kirtland era. Hatch states,

> None of these seven young men cut an impressive figure in a culture that deferred to wealth and idealized upward mobility. When they heard the call of the prophet Joseph Smith, these semiliterate young men—a painter and a glazier, two blacksmiths, a potter, a farm hand, a shinglemaker, and a waiter— had virtually no stake in society. Their formative years gave them every reason to forego worldly ambition and throw their considerable energy into building a spiritual kingdom in opposition to the competitive and capitalist mores of Jacksonian America.... Severing ties of place and, when necessary, of family, they pursued relentlessly the cause of a church that had returned power—as in apostolic days—to illiterate men such as themselves.[12]

To this end Hatch argues that the Book of Mormon spoke to their condition: "The Book of Mormon is a document of profound social protest, an impassioned manifesto by a hostile outsider against the smug complacency of those in power and the reality of social distinctions based on wealth, class, and education."[13]

The average annual income of a farming family at this time was perhaps four hundred to five hundred dollars. A laborer, depending on his skill, might earn twelve to forty dollars a month—that is from fifty cents a day to perhaps one dollar sixty cents a day.[14] Truman Coe, a Presbyterian minister who lived in Kirtland among the Saints for four years, describes the Saints' poverty in 1836, the year the temple was dedicated, in these terms: "Many of them live in extreme indigence. They suffer accumulated evils by crowding a multitude of poor people together.... A grotesque assemblage of hovels and shanties and small houses have been thrown up wherever they could find a footing; but very few of all these cabins would be accounted fit for human habitation."[15]

One can perhaps compare the poverty of the early Saints at this time to the poverty of people today living in the Third World in terms of life expectancy and infant mortality rates.[16] The reading of Acts 2 and 4 by the early Latter

---

[12] Nathan O. Hatch, *The Democratization of American Christianity* (Newhaven, CT: Yale University Press, 1989), 121–22.

[13] Hatch, *Democratization*, 115–16.

[14] Conversation with Lachlan Mackay at the Kirtland Temple, July 2003.

[15] Milton V. Backman Jr., "Truman Coe's 1836 Description of Mormonism," *Brigham Young University Studies* 17, no. 3 (Spring 1977): 352.

[16] Third World Nations are also called Developing Nations. However, that assumes a Western paradigm of what is developed. The Two Thirds World (since the poorer nations make up two

Day Saints offered them a pattern for exodus from poverty—salvation both spiritually and materially from their marginalization and destitution. They read it from *below*, from the perspective of the marginalized, and read it seeing all the hope and glory of its promise for the poor and forgotten.

In addition the Saints were not learned. Their poverty limited their opportunities for education. Joseph himself could read but he needed others to write for him. Sidney Rigdon, in Missouri shortly after the Kirtland period, said the Saints felt taken advantage of because of their lack of learning.[17] Yet, although poor, they had aspirations. They were passionate about learning and this found expression in educational functions of the temple.

It is a pity after a season of great spiritual blessings around the dedication of the temple in the first half of 1836, that economic disaster happened within the next year. The church-run Kirtland Safety Society bank collapsed amid other banking failures in the panic of 1837, and Smith and Rigdon were blamed by angry church members. The Kirtland era effectively ended when Joseph Smith Jr. and Sidney Rigdon fled for their lives at night to Missouri in early January 1838. Other Saints followed. In Missouri the nightmare only got worse.[18] Within ten months the Mormon war in northern Missouri had happened and Governor Boggs had issued his infamous order: "The Mormons must be treated as enemies and must be exterminated or driven from the state."[19]

Smith had adapted Acts 2:44–45 and Acts 4:31–35 in the development of the law of consecration found in Doctrine and Covenants 42. In the end, the practice of this failed in Kirtland, Independence, and Far West, and was also abandoned in Nauvoo. It could be argued that it failed because those baptized were not fully converted and had not undergone the training and preparation that, for example, monks undergo in an *all things common* economic system that is already functioning. Nevertheless, it can be argued that economic justice of the poor is a central thrust of the Community of Christ from its earliest days.

---

thirds of the world's population) or the South (since most rich nations are in the northern hemisphere and most poorer nations are to the south) are better terms but less familiar to the general reader. I use Third World because most people know it refers to the poorer nations of the world.

[17] Sidney Rigdon, *Oration Delivered by Mr. S. Rigdon on the 4th of July, 1838* (Far West, MO: Journal Office, 1838), 10 (Community of Christ Library-Archives).

[18] For a full account of the Kirtland Safety Society bank see Marvin S. Hill, C. Keith Rooker, and Larry T. Wimmer, "The Kirtland Economy Revisited: A Market Critique of Sectarian Economics," *Brigham Young University Studies* 17, no. 4 (Summer 1977): 391–475.

[19] Cited in Alexander Baugh, "The Haun's Mill Massacre and the Extermination Order of Missouri Governor Lilburn W. Boggs," *Religious Studies Newsletter* 12 (September 1997): 2.

Historians of Early Latter Day Saint History and the Importance of Acts 2 and 4:31–35

WHAT IS SURPRISING to me is that good historians of early Latter Day Saint history have missed the impact on the development on the early Restoration of Acts 2 and Acts 4:31–35 through IV Nephi 2:2–6 and Doctrine and Covenants 36:2g–i. Richard Howard, whose methodology of textual development in Restoration scripture I have borrowed in this paper, does not mention the Acts connection in his book *The Church Through the Years*, volume 1 (Independence, MO: Herald Publishing House, 1992). Neither does Paul Edwards in *Our Legacy of Faith* (Independence, MO: Herald Publishing House, 1991), although this is perhaps understandable given that he is more of a philosopher than a student of the Bible. Lyndon W. Cook, in his book *Joseph Smith and the Law of Consecration* (Provo, UT: Grandin Book Company, 1985), mentions an Acts 2 connection for Sidney Rigdon's community, but not with the work of Joseph Smith. Leonard J. Arrington, Feramorz Y. Fox, and Dean L. May, in their book *Building the City of God: Community & Cooperation among the Mormons* (Salt Lake City: Deseret Book Co., 1976), do not make any connection between early Latter Day Saintism and Acts 2. Neither does Milton V. Backman Jr. in *The Heavens Resound—A History of the Latter-day Saints in Ohio 1830–1838* (Salt Lake City: Deseret Book Co., 1983). Only Ronald E. Romig, Community of Christ archivist, makes a brief mention of Acts 2 as the source of inspiration for Joseph Smith Jr. in the first years of the Latter Day Saint movement in *Stewardship Concepts and Practices* (Independence, MO: Herald Publishing House, 1992), 6.

What I want to suggest to my more learned scholarly colleagues is that the Acts 2 and 4:31–35 as *a template for the early Latter Day Saints theory* explains so much of what the early movement was about. Even if Acts is later abandoned, the impact of those early years still reverberates today in the movement, including canonized scripture like IV Nephi and Doctrine and Covenants 36. The Acts template theory has the potential to expand our self-understanding as a movement. It can build a bridge for us with Christians for whom the Bible is the only scripture. It can also be the source of our renewal. It is time to give more in-depth consideration to the contemporary implications of the Acts template theory for early Latter Day Saints.

Implications of the Acts Template Theory for the Mission of the Community of Christ

I F ACTS 2 AND 4:31–35 were normative for the early church communities in Kirtland and Jackson County, Missouri, what are the implications of this for the contemporary mission of the Community of Christ?

1. The Reorganization has traditionally identified with the Kirtland rather than the late Nauvoo period. In the early to mid twentieth century, the slogan of the church was, "Evangelize the world and zionize the church." Today the mission statement of the Community of Christ is, "We proclaim Jesus Christ and promote communities of joy, hope, love and peace." It could be argued that both mission statements summarize Acts 2 and 4:31–35. To read Acts 2 and 4:31–35 in the larger Acts story more diligently may help us find both renewal and clarity of mission for the Community of Christ today.

2. The poor are organizing themselves. The early Latter Day Saints were the poor who were self-organizing to do something about their poverty. Richer churches did not reach out to them and create patronizing dependency. The participatory human development process used by Outreach International, the church's development agency, is in this tradition of the poor organizing themselves, although it is a secularized process.

3. Pentecost begins with believers gathered in prayer. The Acts 2 story begins with a congregation of men and women that had been formed by being in fellowship with Jesus. Endowment by the Holy Spirit for mission and just community begins in meeting to pray. The Holy Spirit comes in power to break down barriers between ethnic groups, cultures, and nations. Indeed the voices of all are heard, including the voices of the poor. The promise of the Holy Spirit is for all, including male and female. The Holy Spirit brings together, in gentle unity, a diverse world. Notwithstanding the intellectual and rationalistic bias of many of us, we still need to humbly pray for spiritual endowment.

4. Proclaiming the cross. The proclamation of Jesus, his death and his resurrection, is central to Peter's sermon on the day of Pentecost. Peter ends with a challenge to the crowd: "Therefore let the entire house of Israel know with certainty that God has made him both Lord and Messiah, this Jesus whom you crucified" (Acts 2:36). The crowd, that seven weeks earlier had participated in yelling for the execution of Jesus, now realizes their sin in creating an innocent victim.

The early Latter Saints often felt themselves victims of violence and then turned in violent retaliation to also create victims. They were, first of all, Americans who believed in using guns to defend their rights rather than

Christians who followed Peter's repudiation of violence in Acts 2. As Steven LeSueur has said: "The failure of past military ventures had not persuaded Smith of the inefficiency of force, rather, each failure served to convince him that greater military force was needed to protect the Saints."[20] Smith's belief in violence as a solution to violence came from being locked into the logic of what Rene Girard calls the "victim mechanism" and Walter Wink calls the "myth of redemptive violence." The work of French anthropologist Rene Girard on how societies and groups create victims is very illuminating, particularly in light of his argument that the Hebrew prophetic tradition and the Gospels expose and reveal the victim mechanism to stop it.[21] New Testament scholar Walter Wink can also be very helpful when his concept of the myth of redemptive violence is used.[22] The myth of redemptive violence is a world view that reality is inherently violent and we can only be saved by the use of violence. This myth, that violence will save us, is very strong in the myths of Americans, particularly in the myths of the righteous revolution in 1776—the most sacred event in U.S. history. Wink argues that salvation comes in the Christian story, not through military might, but through Jesus as a victim. From the underside, Jesus exposes and judges the powers of Rome and the Jewish elite and the myth of redemptive violence that guides them.

The early Latter Day Saints, in seeking to use violence or the threat of violence, forgot the Sermon on the Mount, even though it is given again in III Nephi in the Book of Mormon and is lived out in the golden age of peace in IV Nephi. Their theology either forgot or did not understand the cross as the revelation that God loves God's enemies and calls us to do the same. In the contemporary proclamation of the Gospel by the members of the Community of Christ, we often show the same terrible weakness of not understanding the cross as the judgment of all violence and the ways of violence. Taking off the cultural lens that justifies violence and rereading the Bible in the light of the New Testament, especially Jesus' crucifixion, is key to our salvation and faithfulness as a movement.

5. Missionary movement. The Acts of the Apostles is gloriously missionary. Three thousand are baptized in one day by a group of 120 in Acts 2:41. The church has grown to five thousand in Acts 4:4. Baptism is not, however, sectarian or proselytizing, rather it is conversion from division, violence, and greed to Spirit-inspired unity, learning, and generous sharing. Early Latter Day Saint times

---

[20] Stephen C. LeSueur, *The 1838 Mormon War in Missouri* (Columbia: University of Missouri, 1987), 48.

[21] Rene Girard, *I See Satan Fall Like Lightning* (Maryknoll, NY: Orbis, 2001).

[22] Walter Wink, *The Powers That Be—Theology for a New Millennium* (New York: Doubleday, 1998).

and the first sixty years of the Reorganization were years of many baptisms and vibrant church growth. We need to recover the missionary spirit today in the Community of Christ in the affluent West.

6. *Economic justice.* Acts 2 and 4:31–35 describe Spirit-inspired economic sharing among the believers according to human need. This is not the only time this is portrayed in the Bible. The burning bush experience of Moses issued in his call to go to Pharaoh to release Hebrew slaves from their bondage. Jesus read, "The Spirit of the Lord is upon me … to preach good news to the poor," from Isaiah 61:1 in his home synagogue at the beginning of his public ministry (Luke 4:18). The early Latter Day Saints were counseled in Kirtland and Missouri to "remember the poor, and consecrate of thy properties for their support" (Doctrine and Covenants 42:8b–c). To adapt an insight of Joseph Smith Jr., "Spirit inseparably connected with economic justice experiences a fullness of joy."[23]

The need for communities that witness another kind of economic life is sorely needed in our day. Boss pay in the U.S. was forty-two times that of the average worker pay in 1982. In a 2007 report it was 364 times greater.[24] The U.S. has the greatest gap between the rich and poor of the developed nations. Its middle class is the smallest and the U.S. suffers the greatest concentration of both income and wealth in the hands of the few when compared with other affluent democracies.[25] Income inequality has significantly increased in the last thirty years in the U.S.[26] Recent tax cuts in the U.S. overwhelmingly benefit the rich and increase further inequality.[27] The extent of poverty in a nation is measured by the United Nations Development Program using the poverty index. Among the developed nations for which statistics are available, the U.S. has the worst poverty and ranks seventeenth.[28]

Looking at our world as a whole, the gap between rich and poor is even more startling. The World Bank reports that "of the world's 6 billion people, 2.8

---

[23] This is an adaptation of Doctrine and Covenants 90:5e.

[24] Sarah Anderson and others, *Executive Excess 2007—The Staggering Social Cost of U.S. Business Leadership* (Boston: United for a Fair Economy/Washington, DC: Institute for Policy Studies, 2007), 5.

[25] "Inequality in America: The rich, the poor and the growing gap between them," *Economist*, June 17, 2006, 28–30; Sylvia Allegretto, "Dow's All-Time High Inconsequential for Most Americans," *Dollars & Sense*, Spring 2007, 37.

[26] Harlan Beckley, "Mind the gap—Facing up to inequalities," *Christian Century*, June 14, 2003, 24.

[27] Chris Hartman and David Martin, "Bush Tax Cut Unfair, Won't Help Economy," *United for a Fair Economy*, rev. June 6, 2003, 1–3.

[28] United Nations Development Programme, Human Development Report 2003 (New York: Oxford University Press, 2003), 248.

billion—almost half—live on less than $2 a day and 1.2 billion—a fifth—live on less than $1 a day."[29] Economic well-being is central to a peaceful world. Poverty is the worst form of violence. A people of God, informed by Acts 2, will want to work to abolish poverty among themselves and in the wider world.

7. *Temple.* As Jesus cleansed the Jerusalem temple he quoted Isaiah 56:7 and Jeremiah 7:11 asking: "Is it not written, 'My house shall be called a house of prayer for all nations?' But you have made it a den of robbers" (Mark 11:17). Again the theme of economic justice is affirmed and the system that ripped off the pious poor was condemned. For this the chief priests and scribes want to kill him (Mark 11:18). For the temple to be a house of prayer for all nations, suggests that all nations are invited to come and worship in it. Furthermore it suggests that in the sacred space of the temple, war is ended; for people at prayer together cannot be at war with one another. Indeed the purpose of the temple was the end of war according to the vision of Isaiah. All nations shall come to the temple. Out of the temple God shall teach God's ways and swords will be beaten into ploughshares and nations shall not learn war anymore (Isaiah 2:2–4). Our temple is rightly dedicated to the pursuit of peace. However, we lack the radical Acts 2 and 4 community that can be a temple of people committed to the justice and peace of Zion.

8. *Acts for those who read or do not read Restoration scripture.* In the Community of Christ the Book of Mormon is read primarily in the U.S. In the new churches in Asia and Africa for instance, only the Bible is used. This is potentially a divisive situation and problematic for global church identity. However, when we understand that Acts 2 and 4:31–35 find re-expression through IV Nephi, Doctrine and Covenants 36, and Genesis 7 in the Inspired Version, then all church members are on the same grounds when they reread the biblical book of Acts as a central part of our scriptural canon. Restoration scripture can still be influential in new churches and still shape the church's identity when we emphasize Acts, the Sermon on the Mount, the blessing of children by Jesus, or other passages from the Bible that are reworked or quoted in the Book of Mormon and Doctrine and Covenants.

9. *Community of Christ Pentecostalism.* The early Latter Day Saints and also the Reorganization were Pentecostal before the birth of Pentecostalism in the Azusa Street revival of 1906. Pentecostalism in the global South is a major force in the expansion of Christianity.[30] Rereading Acts would enable us to express a

---

[29] World Bank, "Attacking Poverty: Opportunity, Empowerment, and Security," *World Development Report 2000/2001: Attacking Poverty* (New York: Oxford University Press, 2000), 3.

[30] See for example, "Mission and Pentecost," the theme of the whole volume of *Missiology— An International Review* 35, no. 1 (January 2007), and Allan Anderson, "Spreading Fires: The

Community of Christ Pentecostalism that is less about tongues and more about authentic spirituality, inclusion—breaking down ethnic, racial, and national barriers—critiquing violence, and living together lives of economic justice.

10. Integrated not piecemeal—narrative not principles. Acts 2 and 4 present an integrated communal expression of radical justice. It is not piecemeal. Acts is a story told within a greater story of God as a revealing Spirit, the oneness of humankind, economic justice, and temple. Acts is a narrative, not principles or goals. It describes how organic, righteous community comes into being and develops through the work of the central character of the whole book of Acts— the Holy Spirit.

Conclusion

A S A PEOPLE NAMED Community of Christ we can be inspired by the courageous attempt of the early Latter Day Saints to shape community in the light of Acts chapters 2 and 4. We would honor them not by unthinkingly following their conclusions but by following their example of reading Acts rigorously for ourselves today. Then, with the help of the Holy Spirit, we should use it to inspire our vision of community in a wonderfully diverse, yet frequently violent world, with huge gaps between rich and poor. In the rereading of Acts we find our identity, message, and mission as the Community of Christ.

Much of our congregational life is a pale shadow of Acts 2 and 4, and until it is something more, we shall not be used in the hands of God to change the world. However, our reunions and family camps, particularly those with offerings to cover expenses so that people give according to their ability, often meet in the spirit and practice of Acts 2 and 4. Our challenge is to go from one week a year to fifty-two weeks a year living as Zion. I have personally seen this in diverse Christian communities such as Benedictine monasticism, the Bruderhof, and Reba Place Fellowship. There are people who can help us in our journey in these latter days.

Globalization of Pentecostalism in the Twentieth Century," *International Bulletin of Missionary Research* 31, no.1 (January 2007): 8–14.

Appendix: Acts 2 as a Model for the Kirtland Period

Acts 2 *(King James Version)*	Examples in the Kirtland Era 1830–37
	GATHERING And again a commandment I give unto the church, that it expedient in me that they should assemble together at the Ohio (Doctrine and Covenants 37:2a [December 1830]).
1 And when the day of Pentecost was fully come, they were all with one accord in one place.	
	PENTECOST You should go to the Ohio; and there I will give unto you my law; and there you shall be endowed with power from on high and thence, whosoever I will, shall go forth among all nations (Doctrine and Covenants 38:7c [January 1831]; see also Doctrine and Covenants 92:2a–b [June 1, 1833]).
2 And suddenly there came a sound from heaven as of a rushing mighty wind, and it filled all the house where they were sitting.	
3 And there appeared unto them cloven tongues like as of fire, and it sat upon each of them.	
4 And they were all filled with the Holy Ghost, and began to speak with other tongues, as the Spirit gave them utterance.	"The quorums of the Church were organized in the presence of the Church, and commenced confessing their faults and asking forgiveness. The Holy Spirit rested upon us. O may we be prepared for the endowment,—being sanctified and cleansed from all sin" (Leonard J. Arrington, "Oliver Cowdery's Kirtland, Ohio, 'Sketch Book' [January 17, 1836]," *Brigham Young University Studies* 12, no. 4 [Summer 1972]: 416).
5 And there were dwelling at Jerusalem Jews, devout men, out of every nation under heaven.	
6 Now when this was noised abroad, the multitude came together, and were confounded, because that every man heard them speak in his own language.	
In verses 7–15 Peter begins to preach to the crowd from many nations explaining what is happening and leads to the promise of the prophet Joel about the Holy Spirit.	"Near the close of the meeting, 2 o'clock in the morning, almost all present broke out in tongues and songs of Zion" (Arrington, "Cowdery 'Sketch Book'" [February 22, 1836], 420).

Acts 2 *(King James Version)*	Examples in the Kirtland Era 1830–37
	"Let the annointing of thy ministers be sealed upon them with power from on high: let it be fulfilled upon them as upon those on the day of Pentecost: let the gift of tongues be poured out upon thy people, even cloven tongues as of fire, and the interpretation thereof. And let thy house be filled, as with a rushing mighty wind, with thy glory" (Joseph Smith Jr., "Prayer of Dedication," *Latter Day Saints' Messenger and Advocate* 2, no. 6 [March 1836]: 278–79). "There is a Pentecostal time among the saints over a 15 week period from January 21 to May 1, 1836. Included among these experiences was that on Sunday April 3 of a vision of Jesus by Oliver Cowdery and Joseph Smith Jr." (Backman, *Heavens Resound*, 285).
16 But this is that which was spoken by the prophet Joel; 17 And it shall come to pass in the last days, saith God, I will pour out of my Spirit upon all flesh: and your sons and your daughters shall prophesy, and your young men shall see visions, and your old men shall dream dreams: 18 And on my servants and on my handmaidens I will pour out in those days of my Spirit; and they shall prophesy:	PROMISE OF THE LAST DAYS 1834—church renamed Church of the Latter Day Saints; promise of Joel concerning the Holy Spirit applies to this time.

Acts 2 (King James Version)	Examples in the Kirtland Era 1830–37
19 And I will shew wonders in heaven above, and signs in the earth beneath; blood, and fire, and vapour of smoke: 20 The sun shall be turned into darkness, and the moon into blood, before the great and notable day of the Lord come: 21 And it shall come to pass, that whosoever shall call on the name of the Lord shall be saved. *In verses 22–35 Peter continues to preach about the Crucifixion of Jesus and ends with these challenging words to the crowd.*	APOCALYPTICISM "At early Candlelight the heavens began to show forth the signs in fulfillment of the Prophecy of JOEL recorded in the 2nd chap 30th vers of the Book of Joel. the clouds of fire & blood began to arise in the N.E & reached unto the N.W which principly covered the horizon the reflection of the clouds upon the earth which was covered with snow presented a vary red appearance It commenced at 6 oclock & continued until 10 or past" (Dean C. Jessee, "The Kirtland Diary of Wilford Woodruff [January 25, 1837]," *Brigham Young University Studies* 12, no. 4 [Summer 1972]: 384).
36 Therefore let all the house of Israel know assuredly, that God hath made the same Jesus, whom ye have crucified, both Lord and Christ. 37 Now when they heard this, they were pricked in their heart, and said unto Peter and to the rest of the apostles, Men and brethren, what shall we do? 38 Then Peter said unto them, Repent, and be baptized every one of you in the name of Jesus Christ for the remission of sins, and ye shall receive the gift of the Holy Ghost. 39 For the promise is unto you, and to your children, and to all that are afar off, even as many as the LORD our God shall call. 40 And with many other words did he testify and exhort, saying, Save yourselves from this untoward generation.	PREACHING THE GOSPEL a) Latter Day Saint movement from the beginning was very missionary and began work in Canada in 1833. b) Joseph told Heber C. Kimball on June 4, 1837, in the Kirtland Temple: The Spirit of the Lord has whispered to me, "Let my servant Heber go to England and proclaim my gospel and open the door of salvation to that nation." This, the first overseas mission, was very successful and thousands were baptized and gathered to the U.S. (James B. Allen, Ronald K. Esplin, David J. Whittaker, *Men with a Mission 1837–1841: The Quorum of the Twelve Apostles in the British Isles* [Salt Lake City: Deseret Book Co., 1992], 23).

Acts 2 *(King James Version)*	Examples in the Kirtland Era 1830–37
41 Then they that gladly received his word were baptized: and the same day there were added unto them about three thousand souls.	
42 And they continued stedfastly in the apostles' doctrine and fellowship,	LEARNING AND WORSHIP And let the higher part of the inner court, be dedicated unto me for the school of mine apostles (Doctrine and Covenants 92:3f).
and in breaking of bread, and in prayers.	And let the lower part of the inner court be dedicated unto me for your sacrament offering, and for your preaching; and your fasting, and your praying (Doctrine and Covenants 92:3e).
43 And fear came upon every soul: and many wonders and signs were done by the apostles.	
44 And all that believed were together, and had all things common; 45 And sold their possessions and goods, and parted them to all men, as every man had need.	CONSECRATION VERSION 1 And behold, thou shalt consecrate all thy properties, that which thou hast unto me, with a covenant and a deed which cannot be broken (Book of Commandments [Feb. 9, 1831]). CONSECRATION VERSION 2 And, behold, thou wilt remember the poor, and consecrate of thy properties for their support, that which thou has to impart unto them, with a covenant and a deed which cannot be broken; and inasmuch as ye impart of your substance unto the poor, ye will do it unto me (Doctrine and Covenants 42:8b–c, an amendment of above).

Acts 2 *(King James Version)*	Examples in the Kirtland Era 1830–37
46 And they, continuing daily with one accord in the temple,	DIRECTION TO BUILD A TEMPLE Yea, verily I say unto you, I gave unto you a commandment, that you should build an house, in the which house I design to endow those whom I have chosen with power from on high, for this is the promise of the Father unto you; therefore, I commanded you to tarry, even as mine apostles at Jerusalem (Doctrine and Covenants 92:2a–b [June 1, 1833]). The Kirtland Temple was used for worship on Sundays, education of children and priesthood during the week, quorum meetings (high priests on Monday night, seventy on Tuesday night, and elders on Wednesday night), and prayer and testimony on Thursdays.
and breaking bread from house to house, did eat their meat with gladness and singleness of heart, 47 Praising God, and having favour with all the people. And the Lord added to the church daily such as should be saved.	

The Developing Ecumenical Impulses in the Community of Christ since the Presidency of W. Wallace Smith

DALE E. LUFFMAN

Preamble

THIS PAPER WILL endeavor to briefly trace the initiatives taken by various appointee ministers and leaders of the church in encouraging the church toward more intentional involvement in ecumenical endeavor as well as specific World Church initiatives taken to advance ecumenical involvement and participation. Some consideration will be given to resistances and prejudices encountered, as well as ecumenical achievements and engagements that have been significant for the Community of Christ. This paper is but a beginning of a much larger work that needs to be researched and written.

Reflections

HAVING BEEN RECENTLY appointed by the First Presidency to serve on the Faith and Order Commission of the National Council of Churches of Christ [NCCC] in the USA, I arrived in Richmond, Indiana, March 18–20, 2004, with anticipation and apprehension: anticipation because of the nature of the appointment and the potential of serving with denominational representatives of varying Christian communions, and apprehension because I did not know how I or the denomination I represented would be received.

Upon my arrival, I was greeted and welcomed, and soon thereafter joined the Thursday orientation meeting. Two of the first members of the Faith and Order Commission who I would meet would be the chairs of the group to which I would be assigned—the Full Communion Group.

As a representative of the Community of Christ, a movement founded in the midst of the various expressions of Christian Primitivism of the early nineteenth century, I was not sure how I would be received or accepted. Because the Community of Christ shares a common beginning with a much larger and much more well-known group—The Church of Jesus Christ of Latter-day Saints—we have often been judged by who they are and have been. But there I was.

The orientation was designed to orient newcomers, and it did that well. Not only did I garner an understanding and appreciation of the various activities of the Faith and Order Commission, the occasion also provided me an opportunity to orient others to the Community of Christ. It was, for me, an opportunity to talk of a denomination established in over fifty nations that, over the period of the last several decades and arguably over its entire history, has searched for a clearer sense of identity as it has been increasingly drawn out of itself and into the larger ecumenical world. From an identity once framed in terms of who we were not, of authority and absolute truth, the Community of Christ has increasingly embraced an identity that has much in common with many other Christian communions.

During my first hours in the Full Communion Study Group I became aware that many of my denomination's conversations about its own identity and ministry were also conversations that were being had around the table. As O. C. Edwards Jr. reported on the "Meanings of Full Communion: The Essence of Life in the Body," I felt welcomed into a conversation that I had not initially been a part of. What hospitality!

As various approaches and alternatives to full communion in the thought of various Christian beliefs were surveyed, I became aware that the great diversity of thought might be able to include the denomination that I represented in this significant and substantive conversation. As the report was reflected on, I sensed acceptance and respect for me, and also for each and every denomination represented in the ecumenical conversation.

An acknowledgment that not all voices had been heard from and that opportunity for those voices to be heard seemed to be an important part of the agenda for the new quadrennium for the Full Communion study. Accordingly, I was invited to present a paper on "The Community of Christ and Full Communion" at the October 2004 meetings in Pasadena, California.

What was to be an hour or two conversation became a three and one-half hour conversation. Not only was there genuine interest that would lead toward mutual understanding, there were also connections with and clarifications of other Christian Primitivist traditions. Such dialogue that intends to foster understanding and unity seemed to be at the heart of full communion discussions.

As I left Los Angeles for Kansas City, I reflected on what the meetings had come to mean for me and for my being a representative to the Faith and Order Commission of the NCCC from the Community of Christ. I reflected on the distance traveled by those who had been engaged in encouraging the church toward more intentional involvement in ecumenical endeavor and participation. Ecumenical impulses had been developing over the years.

Our Legacy

WILLIAM D. RUSSELL reports that his father, R. Melvin Russell (1898– 1982) had served as an appointee most of his life, mostly as a pastor. Bill states, "I recall that Dad always joined the ministerial alliance or whatever local council of churches existed in the community."[1] Involvement was important because it would make the church known and it would give value to him as pastor of various RLDS congregations. This involvement and his association with other Christian ministers would call for his father's support for what would become the civil rights movement. Melvin's early ecumenical involvement was also represented in several other areas of the church in mid-century. It appears that local initiatives were taken by individual appointees that gave rise to their participation in ministerial alliances during the 40s, 50s, and 60s throughout the North American church. For the most part, however, this was neither orchestrated nor promoted by leadership. There were exceptions. For a number of years there has been local representation in the Independence (Missouri) Ministerial Alliance as well as ecumenical representation in the state of Missouri. The ecumenical and interfaith participation of church leaders in Independence and the surrounding area was more than likely an outgrowth of the church's gathered presence in the Center Place and the strategic opportunities that such participation offered.

It is apparent that by the mid-fifties some individual appointees (whose interest, assignment, and whose administrator permitted them to do so) would venture into representative participation in local ministerial alliances and local councils of churches more aggressively. Representation in statewide councils began to be expressed later. John Blackstock, Garland Tickemyer, and Carl

---

[1] Letter to author from William D. Russell, dated January 21, 2008.

Mesle were known for their early involvement in ecumenical endeavors. Along with Melvin Russell, they were trailblazers.

It was not easy to blaze trails toward ecumenical endeavor. Initially there was often resistance to RLDS representation in local ministerial alliances and councils of churches. Ecumenically oriented appointees would often spend a great deal of time convincing clergy of other faith traditions that we were not who they thought we were. Additionally, the gospel message forged by the Reorganizaton had been an engaging message for pragmatic, conservative members that comprised the church. But the Saints were frequently cautious regarding the involvement of appointees and leaders participating in ministerial alliances and ecumenical endeavors. Often cited were fears that such activity would cause the church to alter or abandon traditional beliefs or practices of the church, or fears that leaders would endorse creeds or theological positions that would be inconsistent with the traditional beliefs and practices of the church.

An increased interest in, and openness to, local and statewide ecumenical involvement began to emerge at the same time that the church began to extend its missionary witness into nonwestern cultures and nations during the presidency of W. Wallace Smith. Gary B. Beebe writes:

> Really, it all started back when I was a very young pastor in the Los Angeles Stake—when the Burbank Congregation joined with a number of other churches, to put on an Easter pageant for the community. Working with other faith groups, discovering the depth of their respective commitments— all helped to begin opening the mind of this young man—that maybe we RLDS were not the only "true church" on the block.[2]
>
> Obviously, a great contribution to opening my faith eyes and heart to God's expansive love at work among all people was the seven years our family spent in Japan under the leadership of Apostle Charles Neff.... Upon our return from Japan in 1969, and with contacts with Dr. Charles Germany [who was serving as a top executive of the National Council of Churches], Seventy Darrell Mink and I traveled to NCCC headquarters in New York City. At this time Darrell was regional administrator of Latin America and I was serving as regional administrator of the Orient. We left the contentious 1970 World Conference on Monday and flew to New York. From there we went to the NCCC offices and met with the leaders of the Orient and Latin American divisions. It was a great time of sharing. The result was that the leaders were so impressed with our presentation regarding the church, its mission and theology, that they invited our leaders to send a representative to the NCCC headquarters to share in the ecumenical conversations taking place at that time. They even offered to provide office space and staffing free

---

[2] Letter to author from Gary B. Beebe, dated January 12, 2008.

of charge if we could send a representative. Charles Neff was excited about the possibility, but could never convince the Presidency to follow through.[3]

The years spent in Portland, Oregon, gave me the greatest hands on experience ecumenically, when the Saints of the Metropole took a very active part in Ecumenical Ministries of Oregon (EMO). Sharing our pulpit with ministers of other denominations, and reciprocating was truly a rich experience. Serving as chair of the bishops of denominational Executives Council was one of the highlights of my years in the Pacific Northwest.

And, finally, my assignment as executive assistant to the Council of Twelve, again under Chuck Neff's leadership, gave me a number of opportunities to work with the Missouri Council of Churches.[4]

Stories of a similar nature could be told by other appointees serving during this era. It was a time of opportunity, and of struggle: to be understood by the larger Christian community, but equally a time of opportunity and struggle to be understood by church leaders and by church members alike. Further, one ought not to underestimate the significant influence of the initiatives of Vatican II on the larger Christian world as well as the RLDS Church with regard to increased ecumenical conversation and dialogue during this era and since.

Reflecting on his involvement in ecumenical endeavors at this time in Columbia, Missouri, and then in the Far West Stake, Lyman Edwards writes:

> It is my conviction that four things are paramount to ecumenical involvement: being there, speaking convictions without pride, bringing skills, and working hard. Our church has trained and equipped us for presiding and similar roles, and with spiritual and theological insights, beyond what many ministers can bring. Being present, responding humbly to questions about us, and then digging in to carry the load, all depend on the individual and to chances that come up.[5]

Lyman served as the president of the Missouri Council of Churches with his tenure beginning the same year that Wallace B. Smith began to serve as president of the church, 1978.

The so-called Presidential Papers were presented to appointees of the church at a January 1979 gathering at the Auditorium in Independence, Missouri. These presentations represented a shift in the manner in which the church would understand itself, and the way in which the message of the church would be communicated. The papers were soon followed by the initiation of the Faith to Grow program. A more favorable climate for ecumenical endeavor

---

[3] The Presiding Bishopric did have a representative on the Stewardship Commission of the NCCC for a number of years.

[4] Letter to author from Gary B. Beebe, dated January 12, 2008.

[5] Letter to author from Lyman Edwards, dated January 11, 2008.

emerged, albeit with resistance in some areas of the church. Aware of the favorable climate and desirous of facilitating support for more intentional ecumenical and interfaith endeavors, R. Alan Smith and I composed a resolution that was ultimately adopted by the 1980 World Conference entitled, "Participation in Interdenominational Christian Ministries."[6] This resolution endorsed participation of the World Church in interdenominational Christian ministries where no traditional beliefs or practices needed to be altered or abandoned. The right of each field jurisdiction to determine the nature of its own participation in interdenominational Christian ministries was affirmed and ecumenical involvement by the jurisdictions of the church was encouraged. This resolution provided support for ecumenical involvement by appointees in the field, support that proved valuable for a number of appointee ministers. Increased activity by various appointees and leaders of the church followed.

During this period of time women from around the church in North America began to increase their participation in local activities of Church Women United, providing one of the most successful venues of interfaith fellowship and worship available to the members of the church.

The 1992 World Conference requested the First Presidency to investigate the benefits, costs, and advisability of membership in interfaith organizations.[7] The resolution encouraged National Churches to investigate carefully membership in their respective national interdenominational organizations. It also urged branches and congregations of the church to investigate participation in local ministerial associations where appropriate.

Action was taken by the 2002 World Conference calling for the First Presidency to appoint a committee on Ecumenical/Interfaith Relations.[8] This resolution was carefully prepared by Scott Sinclair. World Conference Resolution 1275 called for the establishment of a committee to serve as a link between the church and other interdenominational and interfaith groups. This resolution also called for the Community of Christ to consider membership within the National Council of Churches of Christ—USA (NCCC–USA) and the World Council of Churches (WCC). The resolution further called on the church leadership to enter into dialogues with the NCCC and WCC "regarding an appropriate relationship between the Community of Christ and these ecumenical/interfaith organizations." Apostle Gail Mengel was designated as the point person

---

[6] World Conference Resolution (WCR) 1157—Participation in Interdenominational Christian Ministries, adopted April 10, 1980.

[7] World Conference Resolution 1222.

[8] World Conference Resolution 1275.

with the NCCC and Apostle Leonard Young took a similar role with respect to the WCC.

Resistances and Prejudices Encountered

RESISTANCES TO ECUMENICAL involvement by representatives of the church within the larger Christian community have been common. The leadership of the church in Portland, Oregon, in the 1970s became very involved in local and statewide ecumenical initiatives. Becoming a constituent member of Ecumenical Ministries of Oregon (EMO), leaders were represented on various statewide commissions and on the Bishops and Executives Council. But participation in the ecumenical community was resisted by some. A Lutheran Church and a Baptist Church in the Northeast Portland area raised concerns regarding the RLDS Church's orthodoxy and expressed concern that the RLDS Church had been permitted to become a member of EMO. When Rodney Page, executive director of EMO, affirmed that the RLDS Church was truly *Christian* and refused to allow the RLDS Church to be disenfranchised, the Lutheran and Baptist Churches that protested withdrew from EMO. A similar scenario has been played out in Iowa with Ecumenical Ministries of Iowa (EMI).

In Montana, Illinois, Arizona, and other locales the participation of members of the church in interfaith ministries has been questioned. A Billy Graham event in Illinois announced that the participation of our denomination would not be permitted. It required the church to bow out in order for the event to continue. Church representatives in Phoenix were asked to pull out of an interdenominational event that the church was co-sponsoring because the evangelical community had threatened to pull out if representatives of the Community of Christ participated. The church was pulled from the list of sponsors as a matter of expediency to keep the evangelical community from pulling out of the interdenominational event. Pastors and others who endeavor to engage in local ministerial associations often report that their participation is questioned or blocked by conservative evangelicals.

Issues remain—primarily, two questions are raised for us: first, our shared history with the LDS Church, and second, the status of the Book of Mormon as scripture for the Community of Christ.

Successes Worth Celebrating

THERE HAVE BEEN great blessings and lasting contributions that have come from representation in ecumenical and interdenominational ministries by appointees and other leaders of the church. Representative of all the fruits of ecumenical endeavor are the following:

• Creation and involvement in the Institute for Ecumenical Theological Studies (IETS) in Seattle, Washington, the result of participation in the Washington State Association of Churches and coordinated ecumenical effort on the part of David Irby and Francine Wight. Community of Christ members have enrolled in this program of graduate theological education and have been favored with hospitality and acceptance.

• Engagement with ecumenical organizations in Oregon, Iowa, and Missouri to oppose the death penalty has benefited from the leadership of the church in these areas. The death penalty was kept from becoming law in Iowa and Oregon, but, unfortunately, not in Missouri. In Iowa, Des Moines stake president Robert Skoor worked with then Senate president (now US congressman) Leonard Boswell to carefully address the issue of the death penalty when it was before the Iowa Senate in the early 1990s. With help from World Church leaders at headquarters and Ecumenical Ministries of Iowa, Brother Boswell became a significantly important player in helping to defeat a capital punishment bill at that time.

• Leadership to ecumenical communities of all kinds has been provided by appointees and other local church leaders. State level leadership has been provided over the years by John Blackstock, Garland Tickemyer, Lyman Edwards, Roy Schaefer, Joe Serig, and W. Grant McMurray among others in Missouri; Robert Skoor, Dale Luffman, Bill Russell, and Larry McGuire in Iowa; Leonard Young in Michigan; Scott Sinclair and Barbara Carter in California; Gary Beebe, Alex Kahtava, Greg Page, and Brad Shumate in Oregon (this is a representative list, not an exhaustive listing).

In earlier years Lyman Edwards and Gary Beebe served as presidents of their respective statewide councils. More recently Barbara Carter, a mission center president and appointee, served as president of the California Council of Churches.

Gail E. Mengel, Community of Christ denominational ecumenical and interfaith officer, recently completed a term as president of US Church Women United, an auxiliary group of the NCCC. Dale E. Luffman, a member of the Council of Twelve Apostles, is currently serving on the Faith and Order Commission of the NCCC, and Gail E. Mengel is serving on the Justice Commission of the NCCC.

• Ecumenical involvement at the local level contributed to the saving of the church's reputation in Kirtland, Ohio (and around the world), in the late 1980s. When I arrived as the Kirtland Stake president in 1986, I discovered that there was no ministerial association in the area. I visited with several of the clergy in the area and found that they were anxious to form a mutual fellowship and association as well. The United Church of Christ minister, the Unitarian minister, the Roman Catholic priest, and I formed the initial ministerial association. We formed a rich bond. We shared in fellowship, prayer, study, and advocacy. We preached in each other's churches. The Catholic priest, Norm Smith, actually preached in the Kirtland Temple several times. When news of the Avery family killings by Jeffery Don Lundgren hit the airwaves and the newspapers, it was the supportive and affirming witness shared by the Roman Catholic priest and the UCC minister that saved us in that situation. Their comments to the media left no question in the minds of the public regarding our denomination as a Christian body.

The Present Moment

THE ACTION TAKEN by the 2002 World Conference (WCR 1275) called for the church to explore potential membership in the National Council of Churches of Christ—USA and in the World Council of Churches. However, following the world conference, and at the urging of Jim Wallis of Sojourners—who was a close personal friend of W. Grant McMurray—it was decided that it might be better to focus the church's efforts on a new ecumenical group that was forming in the United States called Christian Churches Together (CCT). Arguments in favor of this initiative were that the church would be on the ground floor of a new ecumenical initiative, one that was to focus on issues of economic justice and one that was thought to be far more inclusive than the NCCC. It would also be an opportunity to move toward membership and participation in the NCCC. The World Church Leadership Council took formal action to support the First Presidency in applying for membership in Christian Churches Together in the spirit of WCR 1275.

However, during initial meetings evangelical leaders began to raise questions regarding the church's heritage and its theology. Representatives of our denomination were able to convince those questioning the church that the church is Trinitarian and Christ-centered in belief. But they still objected to our use of additional scripture (Book of Mormon and Doctrine and Covenants). The concerns were significant enough for some that the Community of Christ was denied the opportunity to be a founding denomination of Christian Churches Together.

It was agreed that it would be advantageous to CCT and to the Community of Christ for the church's application to be reconsidered. A representative team was appointed to review the application and to do a site visit, meeting with a selected representative team of Community of Christ leaders. Presidents Stephen M. Veazey and Becky Savage, Apostle Dale E. Luffman, Gail Mengel (the church's first official ecumenical/interfaith officer), and Don Compier (dean of the Community of Christ Seminary) met with the team over two days. It was a stimulating and penetrating conversation. The representative team was impressed by the journey of the Community of Christ from its early nineteenth-century beginnings to the current time when we have taken on a new name and continued to move into the mainstream of Protestant Christianity. They were satisfied and expressed themselves favorably on our being admitted as members of CCT.

Bringing this recommendation to the steering committee of the CCT was another matter. Questions remained with some as to the relationship of the church to the Book of Mormon. Some committee members were concerned by the use of the term "scripture" in relationship to it. Concern was also voiced regarding the Community of Christ's ongoing links to the Mormon tradition. In the end, the steering committee was unable to arrive at consensus (it takes only one objection to block approval) regarding the application of the Community of Christ. The lack of consensus meant that the application would not be forwarded to the rest of the CCT body for approval. Our admission was denied.[9]

President Stephen M. Veazey responded to the communication, expressing great disappointment at their decision and the adopted process of consideration. He expressed hope that the leadership of Christian Churches Together would reconsider their action.[10] Because we were invited to continue to participate in the fellowship of CCT, Gail Mengel continues to attend CCT meetings representing the church in spite of the actions taken.

Participation continues in Church Women United. June 19–22, 2008, a national conference of Church Women United was held at the headquarters complex of the Community of Christ, and women throughout the church continue to be fruitfully engaged in local venues of this ecumenical fellowship. Representation on the Faith and Order and the Justice Commissions of the National Council of Churches in Christ continues to bear good fruit. At meetings of the Faith and Order Commission held in Atlanta, Georgia, April

---

[9] Letter dated October 10, 2007, and signed by Wes Granberg-Michaelson, moderator, Christian Churches Together.

[10] Letter to author dated October 31, 2007, signed by Stephen M. Veazey.

3–5, 2008, overtures were made encouraging the Community of Christ to apply for membership in the NCCC.

But perhaps most importantly, ecumenical and interfaith participation on the part of local leaders and members of the church is increasing in the life of the church. This is good, for it is evidence of the long journey of many who have persistently endeavored to call the church to be increasingly involved in ecumenical dialogue and participation.

Reviewing ever so briefly the initiatives taken by various appointee ministers and leaders of the church in encouraging more intentional involvement in ecumenical endeavor has been a rewarding experience. I thank God for those who have preceded us and the impulse among us, and look forward to the ever-growing fruits of ecumenical engagement by leaders and members of the Community of Christ.

The Prophet and the Papyrus

WILLIAM D. MORAIN

I F ONE ADOPTS a purely secular approach to the study of Joseph Smith Jr., the biographer must necessarily accept the challenge of discovering the real-world origins of the remarkable output of original narrative that Smith produced during his abbreviated lifespan. In the Book of Mormon and other writings are some extraordinary tales and pronouncements that have profoundly engaged a host of followers. Much of their content is so unusual that they deserve the closest critical examination to find those multiple sources from which they have sprung. Although the task will ever be incomplete, the nonrational realm has been the least examined and offers the best opportunities for useful exploration.

For the secular reader the fantasy world created in the violent and moralistic saga of the Book of Mormon finds its homologues in the works of Tolkien and J. K. Rowling—despite lacking the richness of literary elegance and allegory of the latter two. But if the fabled world of Nephites and Jaredites cannot match the grandeur of its parallels among the worlds of orcs and wizards, one must still give credit to the lyrical originality of mind out of which those fantasies once bubbled.

In sleuthing such origins of output, it is noteworthy that Tolkien, as a young toddler living in South Africa, was terrified when bitten one afternoon by a large, hairy tarantula and was saved only by the alertness of his nurse who sucked the toxin out of the gaping wound.[1] It can hardly be coincidental that

---

[1] Humphrey Carpenter, *J.R.R. Tolkien: A Biography* (Boston: Houghton Mifflin Company, 2000), 21.

some of the most terrifying scenes in *The Lord of the Rings* echo this event in their imagery.

But perhaps a more apt example of this sort of literary origin is seen with the horror writer Stephen King, whose early life has been well chronicled by child psychiatrist Lenore Terr.[2] When King was barely four years old, he went out to play by the railroad tracks with his best friend one afternoon. He returned home early, reportedly pale and without speaking. He went directly to his room and remained mute until the following morning. His friend's pieces were brought back in a wicker basket as a result of his encounter with the train wheels. King was never able to recall for his mother what had happened and has today no conscious memory of the event whatsoever, though he does recall that he "peed his pants." But when he turned seven, King began compulsively writing horror stories and has never stopped. Those who have seen the trestle scene in the movie *Stand by Me* based on a King novel can especially appreciate the reference.

In parallel fashion, it was the principal thesis of my book *The Sword of Laban: Joseph Smith Jr., and the Dissociated Mind*, published by American Psychiatric Press in 1998,[3] that much of Smith's adult personality and literary output took their origins in a violent event in his own bedroom at the age of seven. The event was the third and final surgical assault on the boy's left leg bone infection, performed, like the first two, without anesthesia. The procedure was executed by Dartmouth's Dr. Nathan Smith with the bodily assistance of the boy's own father and a group of medical students who aided in immobilizing him. In following the surgical custom of the day, young Smith was almost certainly spread-eagled with restraining cords secured to the four legs of his bed as the large knife, saws, forceps, hooks, and clamps performed their crimson tasks in an episode of unimaginable pain and anxiety. Although ultimately successful from an orthopedic standpoint, the event itself could have been nothing less for the boy than the psychological equivalent of a gang rape with the complicity of his own father.

The aftermath was hardly better. The resulting massive, contaminated, maggot-infested, and draining leg wound would have taken months to heal, and its foul smell was no doubt a contributory reason that the boy was promptly carted away to his uncle's home at the seashore to recuperate. Spending the next three hard winters on crutches as the middle child in an impoverished and dysfunctional family could hardly have contributed to a healthy childhood. And

---

[2] Lenore Terr, *Too Scared to Cry: Psychic Trauma in Childhood* (New York: Harper and Row, 1990), 252–60.

[3] William D. Morain, *The Sword of Laban: Joseph Smith Jr., and the Dissociated Mind* (Washington, DC: American Psychiatric Press, 1998).

it is not surprising that Smith's famous first publication starts with a tale of impending chaos that seeks resolution through a trip to the seashore.

Tolkien, King, and Smith thus share a history of childhood trauma that profoundly affected their later literary output. Recent psychological studies have strongly reinforced the fact that such events in childhood are of far greater impact on personality than those occurring in adolescence or adulthood. The posttraumatic stress disorder of troops in combat, for instance, is the equivalent of the insertion of a virus into the cerebral software, wherein a stimulus such as an exploding firecracker will provoke a frightening flashback. But a severe traumatic experience in *childhood*, in contrast, is the equivalent of rebooting the brain and reinstalling the system software, altering the entire personality around the traumatic event.

A defining feature of the fantasy writings of the majority of these authors is that their voluminous output has been published without illustrations. Instead, the vividness of detail that the writers have skillfully provided has been sufficient for the reader to *see* the story without additional visual aids.

However, in Smith's case there is a single, notable exception and one that strengthens the case for the centrality of the role of his childhood operations. That exception had its origins in the well-described 1835 visit to Kirtland, Ohio, of an Irishman named Michael Chandler with his traveling Egyptian mummy display. In addition to the corpses, one of the mummy cases bore a papyrus roll bearing hieroglyphics and some accompanying pictures. When shown the papyrus by Chandler, Smith claimed to be able to translate some of the writings; in the process so impressing his Kirtland followers that they pooled their funds and purchased the entire exhibit for $2,400.

Smith began to study the papyrus immediately and soon announced the following: "With W.W. Phelps and Oliver Cowdery as scribes, I commenced the translation of some of the characters or hieroglyphics, and much to our joy found that one of the rolls contained the writings of Abraham, another the writings of Joseph of Egypt, etc.—a more full account of which will appear in its place, as I proceed to examine or unfold them."[4]

His examination of the papyrus rolls occupied a substantial amount of his time over the next weeks to months, resulting not only in a purported translation but also in what he described as an alphabet and grammar of the Egyptian language. The final document, apparently incomplete and without reference to Joseph of Egypt, was summarized in his introduction as follows: "A TRANSLATION Of some ancient Records that have fallen into our hands,

---

[4] Joseph Smith Jr., *History of the Church of Jesus Christ of Latter-day Saints*, 7 vols., ed. B. H. Roberts (Salt Lake City, Deseret Book Company, 1927), 2:236.

Figure 1. Original portions of Facsimile 1 (Charles M. Larson, By His Own Hand Upon Papyri: A New Look at the Joseph Smith Papyri *[Grand Rapids: Institute for Religious Research, 1992]). Reproduced by permission.*

from the Catecombs of Egypt, purporting to be the writings of Abraham, while he was in Egypt, called the BOOK OF ABRAHAM, written by his own hand, upon papyrus."[5]

The unique feature of this document is the fact that it is the only one of Smith's that is accompanied by contemporary illustrations. Three pictures accompany the text, all of them copied directly from the papyrus rolls. Significantly, the pictures on the papyrus were fragmented at their edges, almost certainly from the damage sustained when first unrolled.

The most important papyrus illustration to Smith was the so-called Facsimile 1 (Figure 1), which evidently inspired a portion of his narrative of Abraham. As the picture is a principal source for his work, it requires extended examination.

---

[5] *Times and Seasons* III, no. 9 (March 1, 1842): 704.

Figure 2. Line drawing of likely full reconstruction of original Facsimile 1(Larson, By His Own Hand Upon Papyrus*). Reproduced by permission.*

This portion of the papyrus, as with all of the rest, has been repeatedly demonstrated by Egyptian scholars to be a common funerary document based on *The Book of Breathings*, a text in this particular case dating between 50 BC and 50 AD—not in the Abrahamic era 2000 years previous. The papyrus, tucked into the coffin with the mummified corpse in customary fashion, delineated several magic spells that were to be recited by the deceased in order to learn how to breathe again in the afterlife. This particular text identified the actual deceased as Hor, a priest of the god Amon. Based upon examination of many, many similar papyri, the scene almost certainly appeared before being damaged by unrolling as shown in Figure 2.

The illustration shows a supine figure representing Osiris, the god of the underworld. In this case Hor, the particular deceased in the coffin with this papyrus roll, *becomes* Osiris in accordance with Egyptian mythological ritual. To the left the jackal-headed god Anubis is portrayed embalming Osiris as he lies on the traditional lion-headed bier. To the front of the bier is a small table bearing wines, oils, and a papyrus plant. Prostrate Osiris's uplifted right hand

Figure 3. Line drawing of what remained on the papyrus at the time it was first viewed (see Figure 1), (Larson, By His Own Hand Upon Papyrus*). Reproduced by permission.*

is held palm down over his own face in an expression of grief while his soul *ba*, the human-headed bird hovering over his head, waits to enter his body. In the meantime, Osiris's wife, Isis, takes the form of a falcon and hovers above his midsection. With his left hand Osiris holds his phallus in position to impregnate his wife in order that she can bear his son Horus, who will one day kill Osiris's evil brother *Set*, who had murdered Osiris in the first place. In turn, Horus's four sons (Osiris's grandsons) are portrayed as the heads of the four jars beneath the bier. These so-called canopic jars traditionally contain the viscera removed from the body by the embalmer.

But that complete original scene is not what Smith saw as he viewed what remained of that picture, as shown in Figure 3, after those marginal pieces had fallen away upon the first unrolling of the papyrus. To be able to understand why Smith saw what he did in the fragment of what was left, it will be helpful to refer to an important contemporary diagnostic tool used by clinical psychologists in assessing underlying facets of patients' emotions and fears.

The Thematic Apperception Test, or TAT, was developed in 1935 by Dr. Henry Murray at the Harvard Psychological Clinic. Convinced that imagination was more important than perception, Murray created the TAT in an attempt to better discern the dreams, fantasies, projections, conflicts, and creative productivity of his patients. The resulting test consists of a battery of thirty 9 x 12 inch cards, each portraying a black-and-white scene of some ambiguous interpersonal event or situation. In a controlled setting the patient is shown a series of these cards and asked to tell a story about each.

A patient viewing a card typically makes a special identification with a particular character in the picture, thereby creating a protagonist or hero in his/her story. The patient then fills in the details, drawing exclusively on his/her own thoughts and memories since no other sources of information are available, in the process describing the relationship of the protagonist to any other person(s) shown in the picture. A trained psychologist listening to the story can glean many clues about the patient's own fantasies, fears, and conflicts that would have been revealed, including much about the patient's attitude toward whomever the other person represented. In the process, the patient portrays an outcome of the story that unwittingly provides important clues into his/her own core personality. The TAT further assists the psychologist in exposing some inhibitions that the patient is either unwilling to disclose directly or is perhaps unable to disclose through unawareness. This is why clinical psychologists find the TAT to be far more powerful than the Rorschach because of its ability to elicit meaningful projections with vastly greater complexity and detail.

As Dr. Murray himself described the process: "When someone attempts to interpret a complex social situation he is apt to tell as much about himself as he is about the phenomenon on which his attention is focused. At such times, the person is off his guard, since he believes he is merely explaining objective occurrences. [As such] he is exposing certain inner forces and arrangements, wishes, fears, and traces of past experiences."[6]

Returning to the subject at hand, a comparison of Figures 2 and 3 (see next page) discloses some vital differences.

As is obvious, the missing pieces include: (1) Anubis's jackal-head and outstretched hand; (2) Osiris's trunk, left upper extremity, and phallus; and (3) all of the falcon-wife Isis except the tip of one seven-feathered wing.

Now it becomes interesting. In order to preserve all eleven portions of the papyrus roll that were obtained from Chandler, someone had evidently glued them onto some stiff backing paper at a very early date in order to prevent further damage. When the papyrus sheets were rediscovered in 1966, it was apparent that someone had made an attempt at some relatively recent (nonancient) time

---

[6] Christiana D. Morgan and Henry A. Murray, "A Method for Investigating Fantasies: The Thematic Apperception Test," in *Endeavors in Psychology: Selections from the Personology of Henry A. Murray*, ed. Edwin S. Shneidman (New York: Harper and Row, 1981), 390.

Figures 2 (top) and 3 compared

Figure 4. Facsimile 1 with some added sketches of uncertain origin (Larson, By His Own Hand Upon Papyrus). *Reproduced by permission.*

to fill in the missing pieces of the picture by making a crude sketch on the backing paper. Facsimile 1 therefore actually appears as shown in Figure 4.

Substituting for Anubis's jackal-head is now a man's head, and beside it is the upraised right hand bearing a knife in a threatening gesture. And instead of the falcon-wife Isis's left wing, a seven-fingered right hand of the supine victim is seen accompanying a parallel left in a defensive posture that suggests the warding off of a bodily attack. It cannot be determined with any certainty who performed the sketch, but it surely was not a trained artist. Whoever it was, it must have been someone who had extraordinary license to doctor such a sacredly regarded artifact. In an eerily similar parallel to the question of who erased eighteen and one-half minutes of Watergate tapes, the evidence to be presented will strongly suggest that it was the man at the top.

This papyrus picture was, in effect, Smith's very own Thematic Apperception Test, and Dr. Murray would have smiled at the story that Smith spun from it as he fantasized the supine Abraham saying:

Therefore, they ... hearkened not unto my voice but endeavored to take away my life by the hand of the priest of Elkenah.... And it came to pass that the priests laid violence upon me, that they might slay me, also, ... and that you may have a knowledge of this altar, I will refer you to the representation at the commencement of this record [presumably Facsimile 1]. It was made after the form of a bedstead, such as was had among the Chaldeans ... And as they lifted up their hands upon me, that they might offer me up, and take away my life, behold, I lifted up my voice unto the Lord my God; ... and the angel of his presence stood by me, and immediately unloosed my bands, and his voice was unto me: Abram! Abram! behold, my name is JEHOVAH, and I have heard thee, and have come down to deliver thee, and to take thee away from thy father's house, and from all thy kin-folks, into a strange land, which thou knowest not of.[7]

This narrative, of course, closely mirrors the circumstances of Smith's childhood operation in numerous respects, reinforced to him by the position of the upright assailant looming above the legs of the recumbent figure. Smith identifies immediately with the supine figure as his story's Abrahamic protagonist in preference to the other characters in the picture. His narrative begins when the surgeons "hearkened not" to what would certainly have been a seven-year-old's noisy remonstrations when faced with impending assault and continues by describing the altar notably as a bedstead. This is followed by a characteristic rescue fantasy from this threat when the hero's bands were providentially unloosed. And the denouement results in the victim leaving the house of his father and kinsfolk with a trip to a strange land.

In his story, Smith has told us a great deal about himself as well as the childhood event hovering deeply in buried memory. As the supine protagonist, he describes himself in the victim role under existential threat. Helpless on his bedstead, he significantly identifies a collective *they* who were laying hands on him. But with only one assailant shown in the picture, Smith reveals less than consciously an important detail of his own awful childhood experience at the hands of *numerous* surgical assistants and his own father. Further, in his creation of a rescue by Jehovah as a result of his own request, Smith portrays himself to be the God-favored, virtuous hero who is unjustly persecuted by evil men. And in the conclusion of his story, Smith demonstrates his outright rejection of his father and family by being delivered by God to a safe place far from them in a distant land—both a recapitulation of the aftermath of his surgery at the seashore and, in parallel fashion, of the basic narrative theme of the Book of Mormon. Thus in Dr. Murray's words does Smith reveal in his story his "inner forces and arrangements, wishes, fears, and traces of past experiences." And

---

[7] Book of Abraham 2, 4, 5, *Times and Seasons* III, no. 9 (March 1, 1842): 704.

Smith could not have given a better description of his adult personality—his self-perception of a God-favored, virtuous hero who is unjustly persecuted by a conspiracy of evil men, the host of enemies he would one day enumerate in his rough-stone-rolling speech as "priestcraft, lawyer-craft, doctor-craft, lying editors, suborned judges and jurors, and the authority of perjured executives, backed by mobs, blasphemers, licentious and corrupt men and women."[8]

To clarify visually the narrative text of his story in a public forum, Smith later sat with local artist Reuben Hedlock, giving him precise instructions in the fashioning of a quality woodcut that would fill in those missing portions of the papyrus professionally to correspond with his story of a noble prophet under attack. The picture was published in *Times and Seasons* on March 1, 1842, as shown in Figure 5. Smith had Hedlock add numbers to the figure to identify his characters to readers of *Times and Seasons*. Number 1 became the Angel of the Lord poised to rescue number 2 Abraham. Number 3 was designated the idolatrous priest of Elkenah attempting to offer up Abraham as a sacrifice. Numbers 5 through 9 became other named idolatrous gods.

The similarity between Hedlock's skillful representation and those original crude scribbles on the parchment backing are more than enough to suggest that Smith did that original sketch himself. Despite the fact that the dark-standing figure in Hedlock's drawing is obviously Nubian, Smith has inappropriately directed the drawing of a Caucasian head, presumably out of repressed memory. The standing figure is juxtaposed over the legs of the victim with a threateningly positioned and appropriately sized surgical amputation knife, now transposed to the outstretched arm. Although the altar in lionine representation bears little resemblance to a bedstead, and no bands secure the victim's limbs, one is immediately drawn to the body language that Smith has depicted for himself as the victim, with two hands raised, not in grief, but in defensive horror to ward off the imminent attack. This visual expression of abject terror is about as literal a depiction of the emotions Smith surely felt at his childhood operation as could ever be constructed out of what was on that parchment. Smith has not only *told* his story; he has *illustrated* it as well along with its accompanying emotional affect.

In the final analysis Smith's principal contribution to the papyrus picture is the placement of a large knife into the hand of the standing figure. This alone might be overlooked if not for the preeminent role that the very same symbol played in so much of the rest of Smith's body of literary work. Appearing as the sword of Laban, it occupies center stage in the first chapter of the Book of Mormon's first book and becomes the principal talisman of the work when

---

[8] Smith, *History of the Church*, 5: 401.

Figure 5. Hedlock's drawing of Facsimile 1 with missing pieces added under Smith's direction ("A Fac-simile from the Book of Abraham: No. 1," Times and Seasons III, no. 9 [March 1, 1842]: 703).

it is cloned for the armies of the righteous. Smith also claimed to see it in the treasure box with the golden plates on Hill Cumorah and was reported in a comrade's letter to be brandishing it himself against his foes in Missouri.

Of equal importance is the oft-repeated appearance of the angel with the drawn sword that Smith used to justify his introduction of plural marriage. His apparent recurring dream reportedly threatened him with death or loss of important powers on numerous occasions if he did not take more and more women to wife. Since dreams of the recurring variety invariably have a referent in real life, there can be little question about the specificity of this childhood event for Smith or how the important counterphobic defense was working in this sexual construct.[9]

The question might finally be raised concerning any nexus between the picture in question and the rest of the content of the Book of Abraham, particularly those often-cited passages about eschatology, God's domicile on the planet Kolob, and the denial of the priesthood to blacks. In fact, there appears to be no direct connection between such topics and the childhood surgeries. But as in the case of the Book of Mormon, Smith's bestowing the imprimatur of scripture to his narrative by writing under a sacred pseudonym provided a certain cachet of authority to the lofty tales that Smith had been generating since his teen years (what his mother had called his "most amusing recitals" during evening conversations). The superstructure of a new universe of theology would carry greater moment when delivered from Abraham in scripture than from himself in simple revelation. The picture gave him that license and allowed him to tell a gripping story about Abraham, from which the rest flowed.

To conclude, as Yogi Berra once said, sometimes you can observe a lot by just looking. Again, take a long look at Figure 5. What is Smith conveying about his feelings, his fears, and the traces of a horrid experience? Look at the scene. Look at the figure with the knife. And look at the body language of the prostrate victim. Is it Abraham? Or is it a helpless seven-year-old boy? The Book of Abraham contains nearly seven thousand words; this picture can hardly be worth less.

---

[9] Morain, *Sword of Laban*, 193–99.

"Seekers and Disciples": a Sociological Analysis of the Community of Christ

CHRYSTAL VANEL

Introduction: Community of Christ and Sociology

SEVERAL HISTORICAL AND theological studies have been published on the Community of Christ in *Theology* (a Graceland Press yearly publication) and the *John Whitmer Historical Association Journal*. Leaders of the Community of Christ have been either historians (Grant McMurray) or theologians (Apostles Andrew Bolton and Dale Luffman both teach at the Graceland Seminary, where courses on history and theology are offered). There is also a church historian (Mark Scherer) and a church theologian in residence (Tony Chvala-Smith).

Very few studies, however, have been undertaken on the Community of Christ from a sociological perspective. The *John Whitmer Historical Association Journal* offers an interesting article from sociologist Danny Jorgensen on the RLDS Church and postmodernity.[1] Former apostle Maurice Draper is the only known RLDS leader trained as a sociologist.[2] Additionally, there is currently no church sociologist and the seminary offers no courses on sociology.

---

[1] Danny Jorgensen, "Beyond Modernity: The Future of the RLDS Church," *John Whitmer Historical Association Journal* 18 (1998): 6–19.

[2] Maurice Draper, "Sect-Denomination-Church Transition and Leadership Types in the Reorganized Church of Jesus Christ" (master's thesis, University of Kansas, 1964), 161; *Isles and Continents* (Independence, MO: Herald Publishing House, 1982), 296; "The Sociology of Dissent and the Reorganized Church," in *Let Contention Cease: The Dynamics of Dissent in the*

In this article, I propose to study the Community of Christ from a sociological point of view. I argue that the Community of Christ is a modern religiosity, that one may call *modern Mormonism*. It is from a sociological perspective that I analyze the identity(ies) and theology(ies) of the Community of Christ. I have been inspired by the works of two French sociologists—my professor Jean-Paul Willaime and Madame Danièle Hervieu-Léger.

Jean-Paul Willaime is a French sociologist specializing in the sociology of Protestantism. He teaches at the *École Pratique des Hautes Études*, and works for the French National Center for Scientific Research (*Centre National de Recherche Scientifique—CNRS*). He also researched Mormonism, as two of his students did their MA work on this subject.[3]

Danièle Hervieu-Léger is a renowned French sociologist who works at the *École des Hautes Études en Sciences Sociales*. She specializes in sociology of religion, specifically Catholicism and modern religiosity. Modernity according to Hervieu-Léger is defined by three elements: firstly, rationality; secondly, the independence of the individual from institutions; and finally, the independence of institutions from each other (i.e., religious and political institutions are separated). How does religion fit in these elements of modernity? According to Hervieu-Léger, modern religiosity can be illustrated by two figures: the pilgrim (*pèlerin*) and the convert (*converti*).[4]

The Seeker of the Community of Christ and the Pilgrim of Danièle Hervieu-Léger

The Pèlerin (Pilgrim) of Danièle Hervieu-Léger

HERVIEU-LÉGER DESCRIBES "pilgrim religiosity" in her book on religious modernity: "Pilgrim religiosity is individual and is characterized beforehand by the fluidity of the contents of beliefs and in the same time by the uncertainty of community belongings that it can bring."[5] Thus, the modern

---

Reorganized Church of Jesus Christ of Latter Day Saints, ed. Roger D. Launius and W. B. "Pat" Spillman (Independence, MO: Graceland / Park Press, 1991).

[3] Christian Euvrard researched the beginnings of the LDS Church in France (MA thesis) and its current sociological situation today (PhD dissertation); my MA thesis on the Community of Christ.

[4] Danièle Hervieu-Léger, *Le pèlerin et le converti: la religion en mouvement* (Paris: Flammarion, 1999), 289.

[5] "Cette religiosité pèlerine individuelle se caractérise donc avant tout par la fluidité des contenus de croyances qu'elle élabore, en même temps que par l'incertitude des appartenances communautaires auxquelles elle peut donner lieu" (Hervieu-Léger, *Le pèlerin*, 99).

religiosity of the pilgrim, as defined by French sociologist Hervieu-Léger, is: a) individual; b) fluid in its beliefs; and c) not clear in its community identity.

The Seeker of the Community of Christ

THE COMMUNITY OF CHRIST gives a good definition of what it means to be a seeker through its depiction of Joseph Smith:

> The movement's founder, Joseph Smith Jr., was himself a young seeker. His study of scripture and his encounters with other Christians awakened in him a desire to find God's love and guidance for his own life. According to Joseph's earliest recollections, when he was about fourteen years old, sometime around 1820, he took the yearnings of his heart into the woods near his home and began to pray.[6]

The Community of Christ insists on the individual religiosity of Joseph Smith: the young teenager is said to have been looking for God by himself, through *his* study of the Scriptures and *his* encounters with other Christians. Smith's religiosity was to influence his own life. Around 1820, Smith "took the yearnings of his heart" and prayed. We read no mention of Smith's desire to find the only true church, and to belong to an institution. Smith's religiosity is actually described here as outside of institutions: it is an individual religiosity, like the pilgrim's modern religiosity describe by Hervieu-Léger.

Community of Christ or the Communities of Christ?

A Pluralistic Church

COMMUNITY OF CHRIST also presents the "fluidity of beliefs" mentioned by Hervieu-Léger as part of pilgrim religiosity. In the "Our Faith and Beliefs" section of the *Faith and Beliefs* pamphlet, the church affirms: "Recognizing that the perception of truth is always qualified by human nature and experience, there is no official church creed that must be accepted by all members."[7] Thus people are free to believe how they want and what they want. What Hervieu-Léger calls *fluidity* seems to be illustrated by the word *journey* in the Community of Christ as evident in *Seekers and Disciples*:

> Our experience teaches us that following Jesus is a never-ending process that requires us to keep changing and growing. We make mistakes on our journey

---

[6] Andrew Bolton, Anthony Chvala-Smith, and Robert Kyser, *Community of Christ: Seekers and Disciples* (Independence, MO: Herald Publishing House, 2001), 15.

[7] Community of Christ, *Faith and Beliefs* (Independence, MO: Herald Publishing House, n.d.).

with Christ, just as the first disciples did. But God responds to us by offering a fresh, new beginning each day, as we come to God in trust.[8]

Community of Christ members are encouraged to walk on a journey, or in other words, to be fluid. The fluidity and liberty of beliefs produce a pluralism of theologies.

Jean-Paul Willaime defines as *pluralistics* the churches that "present doctrinal pluralism."[9] So it is, in the Community of Christ. Church theologians present diverse theological thoughts: Tony Chvala-Smith is a critic-orthodox, Don Compier has a passion for Jean Calvin, Andrew Bolton prefers peace theology and the Book of Mormon, and Robert Mesle is Graceland's unique process theologian.

Because of the many theologies we find in the Community of Christ, no clear community identity is present. In fact, it seems that we find many communities in the church: the Parkview congregation in Missouri is strongly conservative in its ethics and theology, whereas the Basileia congregation in California is quite liberal.

The institution proclaims its diversity of cultures and theologies in the declaration "We Are One, We Are Many."[10] Many members in the United States study the Book of Mormon during Sunday school class, while in Africa and Haiti, many members have never heard of it.

Political Theology as a Way to Unite the Pluralistic Community of Christ

PEACE THEOLOGY IS what Jean-Paul Willaime calls a "political theology" (*théologie politique*). Political theology "insists on the eschatological dimension of Christianism and on the active participation of Christians to the transformation of the world."[11] The peace theology of the Community of Christ is a political theology as it is highly eschatological. *Faith and Beliefs* affirms this in its statement on "End Time": "The ultimate victory of righteousness and peace over injustice, evil, and sin is assured because of the unfailing love of God and the conviction that Christ is coming again." In part, "The Kingdom" statement reads: "The full coming of the kingdom awaits the final victory

---

[8] Bolton, Chvala-Smith, and Kyser, *Seekers and Disciples*, 18.

[9] "Eglises [qui] reconnaissent un pluralisme doctrinal en leur sein" (Jean-Paul Willaime, *La Précarité Protestante: Sociologie du protestantisme contemporain* [Paris-Genève: Labor & Fidès, 1992], 114).

[10] *Herald* 154, no. 1 (January 2007): 6–7.

[11] "sur la dimension eschatologique du christianisme et sur la participation des chrétiens à la transformation du monde" (Willaime, *Profession: Pasteur* [Paris-Genève: Labor & Fidès, 1992], 148).

over evil when divine rule is established and justice, peace, and righteousness prevail."[12]

In these two theological statements, words like *justice* and *peace* have political connotations. The exhibition against the war in Iraq organized by the American Friends Service Committee, and welcomed by the Community of Christ Temple during the 2007 Peace Colloquy, clearly had political significance.

Because the membership cannot be united on metaphysical issues (some being neoorthodox and Trinitarians, others being liberals and process theologians, etc.) the leadership tries to unite through practical (political) theology. The book *Yearning for Peace: Assemble the Worldwide Orchestra*[13] is a good illustration of peace theology as a way of uniting cultural diversity in the Community of Christ: ministers of many countries present what peace theology means from their own cultural perspective.

Limits of Peace Theology: The Homosexual Issue

BUT PEACE THEOLOGY cannot always unite the diverse membership of the Community of Christ. Since 1982, the official policy of the Community of Christ states that only nonpracticing homosexuals can be ordained to the priesthood. But during the 2002 World Conference, Community of Christ president Grant McMurray admitted that he had witnessed ordination of active homosexuals and he did not oppose it. Thus, McMurray expressed his favor for more openness toward homosexuality in the Community of Christ. Some members in North America and western Europe fully supported the church president, arguing homosexual rights are part of peace theology. But other theologically conservative members, especially in Haiti and Africa, were stunned by the church leader's confession and at least one Haitian congregation left the church.[14] While visiting a Community of Christ congregation in Independence, Missouri, I met an openly gay couple. But during an international leaders meeting taking place at the temple, I also had a discussion with ministers from the Ivory Coast and the Democratic Republic of Congo. They told me that homosexuality was only an American issue, nonexistent in Africa, and that they would never talk about this taboo subject to their parishioners.

Community identity is therefore often not clear within the Community of Christ. It may be more appropriate to speak of Communit*ies* of Christ.

---

[12] Community of Christ, *Faith and Beliefs.*

[13] Darlene Caswell, ed., *Yearning for Peace: Assemble the Worldwide Orchestra* (Independence, MO: Herald Publishing House, 2001), 146.

[14] William D. Russell, ed., *Homosexual Saints: The Community of Christ Experience* (Independence, MO: John Whitmer Books, 2008), 264.

The Convert

The Convert of Danièle Hervieu-Léger

T HE SECOND FIGURE Hervieu-Léger uses to describe modern religiosity is the *convert*:

> The convert manifests and accomplishes the fundamental postulate of modern religiosity that an authentic religious identity can only be chosen ... Conversion is first of all ... the entrance of an individual into a family. This entrance takes place with the incorporation into a catechumenal community whose religious qualifications are measured by the intensity of affective links between its members.[15]

Thus, for Hervieu-Léger, a convert is part of a religious community. The convert enters this religious family by his or her own choice. We can speak of a *family* because of the "affective links" existing between its members.

The Disciple of the Community of Christ

T HE BOOK *Seekers and Disciples* gives a definition of the disciple strikingly similar to the one of Hervieu-Léger's convert:

> It is not possible to be a disciple on your own. You cannot be a solo Christian. You have to enter and become part of a community. The first thing Jesus did was gather a community of disciples around him whose task was to learn, share with each other, and together serve others.... One of the joys of being a Christian is fellowship—simply being together whatever our backgrounds. Community is only possible with others. Together we worship, study, pray, play, and help each other grow as disciples. Together we struggle to make key decisions about our lives as a group or congregation in local meetings or as an international movement at a World Conference.[16]

Like Hervieu-Léger's convert, the disciple of the Community of Christ *enters* into a community. This community is a family: words such as *share, serve, joy, play*, and *help* illustrate the "affective links" existing in the Community of Christ family/fellowship.

---

[15] "Le converti manifeste et accomplit ce postulat fondamental de la modernité religieuse selon lequel une identité religieuse 'authentique' ne peut être qu'une identité choisie ... La conversion se présente avant tout ... comme l'entrée dans une famille. Cette entrée prend corps, concrètement, avec l'incorporation dans une communauté catéchuménale dont la qualification religieuse se mesure à l'intensité affectives des liens entres ses membres" (Hervieu-Léger, *Le pèlerin*, 121–33).

[16] Bolton, Chvala-Smith, and Kyser, *Seekers and Disciples*, 31–32.

The Temple of the Community of Christ:

Where Pilgrims/Seekers and Converts/Disciples Meet

THE COMMUNITY OF CHRIST temple, standing in Independence, Missouri, since 1994, is the perfect illustration of our sociological observations. The temple is a place where one can be alone to seek God. One can walk along the path toward the sanctuary and meditate on the many objects and symbols (such as crosses and flowers) along the way. The *seeker's path* would thus be a more appropriate name.

After walking along the path, the seeker can finally enter the sanctuary and quietly pray or meditate, look at the altar of the temple, often decorated with fabrics of various colors, or gaze at the impressive white ceiling of the nautilus. The seeker, individually searching for God, can also meditate in the chapel of the temple, sit quietly and pray, perhaps thinking deeply about the sacramental moments of his or her own life while looking at the paintings depicting the different sacraments of the church.

The temple is also a place where disciples from the Community of Christ meet together to worship and pray. Although located in the small and somewhat unknown town of Independence, Missouri, the temple is the place where leaders from around the world meet for conferences, theological and administrative meetings, and trainings. During those meetings and worships, often emotionally charged, members of the Community of Christ feel they are part of one spiritual family.

Political/Peace Theology

FROM THE ANNOUNCEMENT of its construction, the temple was to be "dedicated to the pursuit of peace."[17] The sacred building is becoming a symbol of the political/peace theology of the institution to which it belongs. The symbols of the temple represent peace. A prayer for peace is held daily in the temple while a candle is lit. An annual Peace Colloquy takes place in the temple.

Conclusion: Community of Christ as Modern Mormonism

THE COMMUNITY OF CHRIST seeker and disciple perfectly describe Hervieu-Léger's pilgrim and convert. Thus, the Community of Christ appears to offer a modern religiosity. From all the churches dating back to Joseph Smith, the

---

[17] Community of Christ, *Book of Doctrine and Covenants* (Independence, MO: Herald Publishing House, 2000), 156:5a.

Community of Christ seems to be the only modern church. In this way, it is appropriate to describe the Community of Christ as *modern Mormonism*.

But what about the largest restoration movement group, the LDS Church? Is it not a modern church? According to Hervieu-Léger's criteria, it seems that the LDS Church only offers the convert option. Being LDS is to be part of the LDS Church, to strictly follow its rules and believe its dogmas. Using Hervieu-Léger's vocabulary, a member of the LDS Church is part of a family. And this family is eternal because of temple rituals. Furthermore, only LDS members who totally adhere to church orthodoxy can enter the temple and be part of the eternal Mormon family.

In her famous book on Mormonism, Jan Shipps argues that since 1890 and the end of polygamy, the LDS Church entered into the *present*. Shipps's vocabulary is very unclear: what is the *present*? Is it a historical notion representing contemporary history? Or is it a sociological one referring to modernity? Unfortunately, Shipps does not answer those questions and her words remain unclear, thus lacking scientific precision.[18]

Sociologist Armand Mauss describes more precisely and scientifically the dealing of the Utah church with modernity, studying its assimilation with US society: after the religious institution officially gave up polygamy in 1890, Mormons began to assimilate into American culture; but since the 1960s, the LDS Church reacts negatively to this assimilation, perceiving the loss of the Mormon identity it produced.[19]

On the contrary, it seems that since the 1960s the RLDS Church became more assimilated to US society and more integrated into modernity. As remarkably shown by Matthew Bolton, it is in the 1960s that the RLDS Church opened up to the world—as did the US through its military presence—and thus to theological pluralism. Bolton makes a bold comparison—one that surprised my professors at the Sorbonne (*École Pratique*)—comparing the Vatican II of the Roman Catholic Church with the Statement of Objectives of the RLDS Church: both took place in the early 1960s and both opened their respective institutions to modernity.[20]

---

[18] Jan Shipps, *Mormonism: The Story of a New Religious Tradition* (Champaign: University of Illinois Press, 1985), 211.

[19] Armand Mauss, *The Angel and the Beehive: The Mormon Struggle with Assimilation* (Champaign: University of Illinois Press, 1994), 257.

[20] Matthew Bolton, *Apostle of the Poor: The Life and Work of Missionary and Humanitarian Charles D. Neff* (Independence, MO: John Whitmer Books, 2005), 189.

Personal Thoughts about Suffering

JEANNE MURPHEY

Purpose of Writing This Paper

I HAVE FOUND THAT most theories about God are inadequate or unsatisfactory in explaining to me why suffering and evil are a part of our existence. I was born at the end of the Great Depression and was a small child during World War II. This was a time of great suffering for most of the world, and it seems as if parts of the world are never free from suffering. For the greater part of my life I have wondered why this is so. My own suffering seemed trivial compared to horrors such as the Holocaust, extermination wars, starvation, and the poverty in much of our world. I would tell myself how fortunate I was to have been born in the United States, to have a place to live and food to eat, even though I was an unhappy child. I was taught that God loved me, but I didn't really feel that God loved me. I felt insignificant and invisible. Many times I experienced the pain of desertion by my parents, and I felt that God had deserted me too. We were members of a conservative religious denomination (Reorganized Church of Jesus Christ of Latter Day Saints, now named the Community of Christ) so I spent a lot of time in church, and I tried very hard to be a good child. But I felt that I was too unimportant for God to take notice of me.

I survived my childhood, but at a price to myself. As an adult I worked at healing my problems. I grew up believing that I was of no worth and that I was only an obstacle and nuisance to my parents. As a teenager I held a confusing piece of knowledge in my head. I was an only child and would have loved to have a brother or sister. But I *knew* that I did not want another child to be in our home because I did not want that child to suffer what I was suffering. If you had asked me what was so extraordinary about my suffering I could not have given you an answer. It's only as an adult that I have come to understand what that answer is. Now I know that my childhood *knowing* was accurate. I would not have wanted another child to walk the path that I walked.

My Questions

ALWAYS FELT REMOTE from God, and wondered why God should care about me. Adults said that God loved me and did care about me. If God cared about me, why was my childhood so unhappy? I have searched for the answer to that question. Reincarnation theories say that we are born into certain situations so that we can learn from that situation. I couldn't convince myself that my suffering was worth that learning. Another theory says that we choose our birth family. I can't imagine that I would be sick enough to choose to suffer. Another theory says that God suffers with us in our pain. That's sympathetic, but it doesn't offer an alternative to the suffering. Traditional atonement theories say that we are all sinners of such monumental proportions that God had to send his son, Jesus, to die and redeem us. I have so many problems with atonement theories that it would take a while to list them. It will suffice to say that if we are such sinners what is the point of creating us at all?

I grew up with traditional understandings about God. A scripture that was often quoted was John 3:16–17: "For God so loved the world that he gave his only begotten Son, that whosoever believeth on him should not perish; but have everlasting life. For God sent not his Son into the world to condemn the world; but that the world through him might be saved."[1] This scripture was basic to interpretation of the doctrine of atonement. The traditional doctrine of atonement is that God required a sacrifice be made to appease him and also to satisfy the demands of justice. This couldn't be any ordinary sacrifice, such as a sheep or a dove. Only the sacrifice of God's own son was acceptable. So Jesus came to earth and allowed himself to become the sacrifice. As a result of that sacrifice humans could be saved from their sins and become eligible to live eternally.

I have had many questions about this doctrine, and as the years have gone by, I have found myself more and more unable to accept it. How could I honor and respect a God that was so mean-spirited and vengeful? What kind of parent would require the death of his own child in order to meet his need

---

[1] All Bible quotations in this paper are from the Reorganized Church of Jesus Christ of Latter Day Saints/Community of Christ *Holy Scriptures*, "Inspired Version" of the Bible (Independence, MO: Herald Publishing House).

for appeasement? As I became familiar with the writings of some feminist theologians I found that they identified the atonement as divine child abuse. That made sense to me! An article that has become a classic in feminist theology is titled "For God So Loved the World?" The authors ask the question:

> Can the case be made that it is contrary to the gospel to maintain that suffering is redemptive? Our approach is theological, not biblical, and focuses on the issue of the atonement. Classical views of the atonement have, in diverse ways, asserted that Jesus' suffering and death is fundamental to our salvation. Critical traditions have formulated the issue of redemption in different terms but still have not challenged the central problem of the atonement—Jesus' suffering and death, and God's responsibility for that suffering and death. Why we suffer is not a fundamentally different question from why Jesus suffered. It may be that this fundamental tenet of Christianity—Christ's suffering and dying *for us*—upholds actions and attitudes that accept, glorify, and even encourage suffering. Perhaps until we challenge and reject this idea we will never be liberated.[2]

At last I was finding that I was not alone in my concerns about Christian theology.

Another story that has always given me great concern is the Old Testament story of Abraham being willing to sacrifice his son Isaac. This story is the forerunner of the story of Jesus' sacrifice by his Father. How could Abraham possibly be willing to kill his beloved son just because God required it? When I grew up and married and became a mother I had even more qualms about the story. I remember the feelings I had when I held my newborn daughters in my arms after they were born. It was one of the most important moments in my life. If God had required me to sacrifice them, I would have said, "over my dead body."

The Bible is full of stories of evil and suffering. Our world is full of stories of evil and suffering. What is God doing about it? Traditional doctrine maintains that God is all powerful, or omnipotent. So how do believers of traditional doctrine explain God's impotence in regard to suffering?

(1) One answer is what is called the pious-prosperity theory. According to this theory, if you are pious (obedient) you will prosper. If you don't prosper then it must be that you are being punished for disobedience. Many theologians have criticized the concept that suffering is always the result of sin. Wendy Farley stated:

---

[2] Joanne Carlson Brown and Rebecca Parker, "For God So Loved the World?" in *Christianity, Patriarchy, and Abuse*, ed. Joanne Carlson Brown and Carole R. Bohn (New York: Pilgrim Press, 1989), 4.

If the disease that crippled human life were only the guilt of sin, then the atoning death of the Christ would be a revelation of such love, mercy, and redemptive power that it would wipe away the evil of history. We would be like criminals abandoned to the living death of penal servitude who heard the footsteps of someone bringing a key to release us. Inside our gnarled, brutal bodies, our hearts would melt at the love that sacrificed itself for our wicked, undeserving selves.[3]

(2) Another answer comes from the book of Job. That answer is that God allows us to be tested. Job was going along and enjoying his life. Then Satan came to God and challenged him. Satan said that Job would only serve God as long as Job prospered. So God said to Satan, "Behold, all that he hath is in thy power: only upon himself put not forth thine hand."[4] So Satan proceeded to destroy everyone and everything around Job. I find this depiction of God to be deplorable. God is depicted as being weak and foolish because Satan can trick him into letting Job's life be decimated.

(3) Yet another answer is that God punishes people because he loves them. In the book of Revelation (3:19) it says, "As many as I love, I rebuke and chasten; be zealous therefore, and repent." This interpretation has been widely used to impose suffering through the use of physical punishment. One such victim said:

> "Do you really expect me to believe in a loving, omnipotent God? Whatever God is like, I don't want anything to do with someone who let a little girl be battered and bruised and violated by her father and brother." The struggles of childhood victims of abuse to reconcile their experience of violation and victimization sound hauntingly like those of survivors of concentration camps. "Where was God?" "Why did God allow this to happen?" "How can I integrate this experience into the rest of my life and go on living?" "How can I ever trust and be happy again?"[5]

Some contemporary theologians are beginning to address the issue of evil and suffering. They are cognizant of the silence of theology to articulate a response that can help the victims of evil and suffering. In her book *Tragic Vision and Divine Compassion: A Contemporary Theodicy*, Wendy Farley says:

> The phenomenon of undeserved, destructive suffering is not acknowledged by most classical theologians; its recognition poses problems for theodicy that apparently did not exist for Augustine, Thomas Aquinas, or Calvin. In

---

[3] Wendy Farley, *Tragic Vision and Divine Compassion: A Contemporary Theodicy* (Louisville: Westminster/John Knox Press, 1990), 63–64.

[4] Job 1:12.

[5] Carolyn Holderread Heggen, *Sexual Abuse in Christian Homes and Churches* (Scottdale, PA: Herald Press, 1993), 95.

much of the classical theological tradition, the problem of human suffering is obscured by the tradition's focus on sin as the primary expression of evil. Theodicy [defined as a vindication of the justice of God in permitting evil to exist] addressed the question of why *sin* was permitted to introduce evil into an otherwise good creation and what God does to redeem humanity from its guilt.[6]

Farley is concerned with relating redemption to the problem of the existence of evil and suffering. She proposes that a theology of compassion can offer solace to those who suffer. This compassion takes two courses. "The first is to resist the causes of suffering. The second is to resist the power of suffering to dominate."[7] Apostle and theologian Geoffrey Spencer offered the comment that Farley "has proposed that compassion relates a loving God to the world's tragic need, while traditional theology relates a judgmental God to the world's sin. Compassion exposes God's vulnerability—God's power is the power of powerlessness."[8] I am appreciative that Farley made an effort to address the role of God in regard to suffering. But for me her proposal doesn't offer any understanding beyond saying that because God suffers with us we are empowered to survive. Her God, although he suffers with us, is still powerless.

Theologians Joanne Carlson Brown and Rebecca Parker have written about the concept of the Suffering God in their article, "For God So Loved the World?"

> We would not reject the image of God as a Suffering God and would welcome the demise of that distant, impassive patriarch in the clouds who is beyond being affected by the turmoil below. The advent of the Suffering God changes the entire face of theology, but it does not necessarily offer liberation for those who suffer. A closer examination of one form of the Suffering God theology [by Edgar Sheffield Brightman] will reveal that this apparently new image of God still produces the same answers to the question, How shall I interpret and respond to the suffering that occurs in my life? And the answer again is, Patiently endure; suffering will lead to greater life.[9]

Is there an answer that is more satisfactory than to just patiently endure? Realistically I believe that we do have to find a way to endure the suffering that comes our way. In all of the explanations that I grew up with, God was a passive part of the process. One exception to this understanding was a belief in miracles. What are miracles? Why are some people seemingly protected or

---

[6] Farley, *Tragic Vision and Divine Compassion*, 51–52.

[7] Farley, *Tragic Vision and Divine Compassion*, 116.

[8] Geoffrey F. Spencer, *The Promise of Healing* (Independence, MO: Herald Publishing House, 1993), 88.

[9] Brown and Parker, "For God So Loved the World," 14–15.

healed, when so many others are not? It is popular today to talk about angels and miracles. I think that is because they offer solace and comfort in a world that desperately needs a sense of security. Miracles are comforting for those who feel they have been the recipients of one. But what of the countless numbers of people who were not recipients? Do they feel that God is displeased with them and therefore punishing them? Miracles are usually defined as being the result of divine intervention. "Miracles become problems when we think of them as divine interventions violating the laws of nature. The problems are not merely scientific but also theological and moral. Nothing challenges the goodness of God or the justice of the universe more than the stark randomness of such alleged 'miracles.'"[10]

The above quote is from C. Robert Mesle who is a process theologian. He writes about how ancient peoples thought that lightning was a thunder bolt thrown by the gods. To them lightning was a divine intervention in their world. Today we understand that lightning is a phenomenon of certain weather conditions, and not God showing us that he is angry with us. We still have a healthy fear of the consequences of being struck by lightning, but we don't believe that it is supernatural. We know that it is natural. "The gods who threw lightning bolts are gone now. If we tie our God to lightning or anything like it, our God gradually will go away, too."[11]

An Answer

PROCESS THEOLOGY OFFERS a different perspective about our relationship with God, and it is a perspective that speaks to my intellect and my heart.

In spite of my dissatisfaction with traditional theologies I remained active in my church. I think that is because even in the midst of my questions and uncertainty I had been searching for a theology that satisfied me emotionally and intellectually. I had hope that I could find such a theology. It is said that "hope springs eternal," so I continued to seek for a new understanding about my relationship with God.

There are some givens in my theology of life. One given is that every person has the freedom of making choices. I grew up calling this the gift of agency. God will not prevent us from making choices, whether they are good or bad. However, I think that God will entice or try to persuade us to make wise choices, and that this is done without denying or intruding on our agency.

Another given is that God loves us and always wants the best possible results for us. There is a wonderful illustration of this point in the book *Good*

[10] C. Robert Mesle, "On Miracles," *Saints' Herald* 136, no. 5 (May 1989): 19.

[11] Mesle, "On Miracles," 19.

Goats: Healing Our Image of God. A woman came to her pastor to seek guidance and comfort in regard to her son's situation. The son was in trouble with the law because of his involvement in prostitution, drugs, and murder. He was very depressed and suicidal. The mother was concerned about what was going to happen to her son. The pastor privately thought that nothing good was going to happen to the son. But being a wise pastor he didn't say that. Instead he asked her to imagine that she and her son were sitting next to God. He asked her to imagine what God would do. Then he asked her to describe what was happening as she imagined the scene. She said that her son felt so lonely and empty. She wanted to throw her arms around him, so she did. Then God put his arms around both the mother and the son, and they cried together. The pastor said, "I was stunned. What Hilda taught me in those few minutes is the bottom line of healthy Christian spirituality: God loves us at least as much as the person who loves us the most."[12] That is the kind of love that I want to believe in and experience.

What I find meaningful in the process theology schema is that as humans we interact with God. We are not passive beings who are acted upon. In the New Testament it is recorded that Jesus said that henceforth he no longer calls us servants, but now calls us friends.[13] Being a friend implies a mutual sharing and relationship. As I understand process theology, it is about the relationship of all elements of our universe, whether physical or spiritual. Marjorie Suchocki, a well-known process theologian, says that our relationships to others are integral to our identity and existence.

Who we are depends on our own individual creative responses to physical and psychical relationship. Our bodies are formed in and through incorporation of carbon molecules originating in distant stars; the air we breathe is itself a gift from the breaths of all who have lived before us; our health depends on our integral and synergistic relationship with a host of microbes and cells living within us. Our spiritual lives and our whole world of meaning are formed through our creative response to a vast number of relationships, the most important of which are those closest to ourselves in terms of partnership, kinship, friendship, and colleagueship.

We are creatures of relationship, not puppets, not driven by relationship, but existing in and through our own creative response to relationships in various circles of importance to us. We receive from others, integrate what we receive into ourselves, and give back of ourselves to those others and indeed, to the

---

[12] Dennis Linn, Sheila Fabricant Linn, and Matthew Linn, *Good Goats: Healing Our Image of God* (Mahwah, NJ: Paulist Press, 1994), 11.

[13] John 15:15

whole universe. This is a rhythm that happens again and again, ad infinitum, to every existing thing whatsoever.... It is a dynamic describing all existence. It is the way of the universe.[14]

> And God also exists in creative response to relationships. The joys of creatures become the joys of God, and the sorrows of creatures the sorrows of God. Further, in process modes of thought, God is not just the passive participant in the life of the cosmos, but the creative lure of the whole process of existence. God offers to each element in the world a way that it might most creatively respond to the influences it receives, and the world takes that influence into itself, becoming as it will, offering the result to the universe, and also back to God. God takes the results of the world's becoming into the divine nature, there values it, integrates it judgmentally into the divine self, and on the basis of what the world is becoming and God's own character, offers a possibility back to the world for the good once again.[15]

As I tried to comprehend this interpretation of our relationship with God, I needed to put it in my own words. Suchocki had given us her synopsis of the process, which was based on her study of the work of Alfred North Whitehead. Her statement was very profound and I wanted to try to understand it and then apply it to my own experience. I apologize if I have done too much simplification of her concepts.

In my college science courses I learned about cause and effect, and that for every action there is a reaction. So, for this explanation I view myself as the initiator of action; that is, I perform some task or behavior. There are results and consequences of my behavior. These results and consequences (input) go to God, where they are taken in and assimilated, maybe into something like an extremely intricate computer system, which is incomprehensible to me. And while God is inputting my results, the same is being done for all peoples. After mulling over what options will be possible, given my previous choices, a set of possible choices comes back to me.

I believe that God always wants my life to be better, so if there are any positive possibilities, they will be included in what returns to me. But sometimes life is so terrible that all of the options are negative ones; however, there may be one or more suggestions that are not quite as terrible as the others. It is not God who is determining the options. God only digests the input that we send out. We determine what becomes input through our choices and actions. Since we are not solitary beings, our options are also determined by the input coming from many others. If there are any positive options available, those positive

---

[14] Marjorie Suchocki, "A Theology of Creation," *Theology: Process Theology and Religious Pluralism* 9 (2002): 28–39.

[15] Suchocki, "A Theology of Creation," 31.

options will be part of the output from God. And then the cycle starts again, and repeats over and over and over.

This explanation was meaningful to me. When I first heard it I had an "ah ha" feeling. Here was an explanation that recognized that I was a partner with God. I had to try and think it through to understand why I felt that this was so significant. I concluded that it was significant because it dealt with the issue of power. People who are the victims of evil, or who are in the extremities of suffering, feel powerless. This is intolerable to their psyches because they have an urgent need to believe that they have some control or power over what is happening to them. In Maslow's hierarchy of needs "the first need of humans is for survival, and the second need is for safety."[16]

Consider the victims of physical or sexual abuse. Blume says:

> In incest one person is active and one passive, one dominates and one acquiesces. The battered woman feels that she must be doing something wrong and that, if she could only correct it, her husband would stop beating her. She maintains this self-blame as a way of preserving the illusion that she can somehow control her husband's or lover's behavior—that she is in control of her environment. The child victim of incest also maintains this view. For both, the alternative would be even more difficult to face: *powerlessness.* It is less threatening to see oneself as somehow responsible and, therefore, guilty than to admit that one has been basically powerless and, therefore, the victim of a situation out of control.[17]

The idea that we are partners with God is exciting! The suffering God is powerless except to offer comfort. So both the victim and God are powerless in the face of evil and suffering. The God of process theology takes action. Suchocki states that God is not just a "passive participant." When we as individuals believe that we have any options, we can have a sense of hope for the future. As long as action is possible there is opportunity for change. We hope that that change will bring us healing and relief from our suffering.

In my understanding of process theology, God is active in the process of healing. Feminist theologian Rita Nakashima Brock has written about the healing relationship: "In healing, the function of the healer is not to gain power but to share it. In the sharing process, woundedness reveals the sacred. Between healer and sufferer, an inequality of power exists that denies the afflicted the capacity to become whole. Hence, the flow of power between healer and afflicted

---

[16] Charles Whitfield, *Healing the Child Within* (Deerfield Beach, FL: Health Communications, Inc., 1987), 18.

[17] E. Sue Blume, *Secret Survivors* (New York: John Wiley and Sons, 1990), 111.

represents the balancing of power inequities and the emergence of wholeness."[18] I think Brock's description of power flowing between the sufferer and God is a wonderful example of process theology.

In process theology interpretations, I find understanding and hope. As I apply it to my own situation it goes this way: first of all, I'm born, and that's a significant statement because I was not wanted. Next, all of the circumstances of my life were relayed to God. God took in my circumstances and saw that there were several possible choices for what would be the next event in my life. These possible choices returned to me. I made a choice from the possible options, and the people around me also made choices. Once these choices had been made, then they again flowed back to God. If the choice made was the best choice from the options available, then the next round of options from God would have the potential of improving my situation, because God wanted my situation to improve. If the choice made was one of the worst options available, then my situation would probably deteriorate. Our agency (ability to choose for ourselves) is always a factor in making our choice. God does not prevent us from choosing for ourselves.

In this theological interpretation God and I are interacting. God cannot wave a magic wand and put me in a different home and place. But God continually sends me options that have the possibility of improving my condition. My situation improves, stagnates, or deteriorates according to the choices made. Whatever the choice is, it returns to God, and another set of options returns. This is a continuous unending process. I believe that there were peripheral people in my young life who extended love and kindness to me. These people were channels for positive growth options. I was able to internalize some of their concern for my welfare. And because of their concern I was able to think that maybe I wasn't always an inadequate person.

Elie Wiesel, a survivor of the Holocaust, said, "Make no assertions about God which you could not make while standing over a pit of burning babies."[19] I have heard Bob Mesle say that when he reads stories from the scriptures he always asks, "What happened to the women and the children?" If what happened to them was that they were raped or killed, or some other heinous thing, then Bob cannot honor that story. The statements from both of these men resonate strongly within me. Another friend of mine has said that "when it comes to God we flush our brains down the toilet," meaning that people who are usually rational often become irrational when the issue is God. I think that

[18] Rita Nakashima Brock, "And a Little Child Will Lead Us," in Brown and Bohn, *Christianity, Patriarchy, and Abuse*, 55.

[19] Anna Richardson, *Double Vision: A Travelogue of Recovery from Ritual Abuse* (Pasadena, CA: Trilogy Books, 1997), 7.

it is irrational for us to be asked to worship a deity who is jealous, legalistic, and powerless to help us. That is the God that I was taught about as a child. I much prefer being in relationship with a God who offers hope to those who have "walked through the valley of the shadow of death." This God is our Friend, Companion, and Healer. This is the God I see in process theology.

Signal Communities in Witness of Peace[1]

BY DONALD E. PITZER

Introduction

I AM HONORED TO address this distinguished international gathering on the vitally important subject of peace. It is of great significance when religious bodies, such as the Community of Christ, give top priority to bringing their spiritual, intellectual, and communal resources to bear witness of peace. For far too long religious division, religious diversity, and religious exclusiveness have made religions contributors to conflict rather than promoters of peace.

Today, in this time of war, we are assembled to consider *signal communities'* witness of peace. Peace is an increasingly more urgent matter. We have split the atom, stood on the moon, and discovered DNA as the building block for life. Yet the world seems as ignorant and impotent as ever about the top item on the human agenda—how to live together peacefully, productively, and happily based on mutually deserved trust. In the supposedly civilized twentieth century our wars killed 120 million people, about half civilians. That number equals almost one thousand Independence Missouris. How can we make harmony from our diversity, resolve our conflicts with words rather than arms, and empower leaders without reaping authoritarian control, abuse, and aggression? How can we implement the simple but difficult solution of Jesus: "Love your enemies and pray for those who persecute you" (Matt. 5:44). He said, "Blessed are the peacemakers," not blessed are the war makers (Matt. 5:9).

---

[1] Delivered as a plenary address at the 2008 Peace Colloquy of the Community of Christ, Independence, Missouri, October 4, 2008.

We might hope the world is now ready to consider what small, voluntary communal laboratories teach us in their witness of peace and justice. After all, communities *are* the witness of peace, the stage for seeking, testing, and acting out peace. Thousands of historic and current communal groups provide that stage for our instruction.

My purpose in this keynote is twofold: first, to place the Latter Day Saints' communal efforts, especially the signal communities of the Community of Christ, in the context of this instructive communal legacy, and second, to point out specific witnesses and lessons from communal societies. Pursuit of these lessons has kept me researching communal groups for forty years, thirty of them as director of the Center for Communal Studies at the University of Southern Indiana. I have approached communal societies as social microcosms that test social and political theories, economic systems, and religious doctrines and practices. I have found the lessons they teach to have individual, community, and worldwide implications.

Latter Day Saints in Communal History

BEFORE EXPLORING THESE lessons let us turn to our first objective—to place zionic Latter Day Saints' communalism in communal history. The Saints' communities are part of a social phenomenon with both ancient and modern expressions. Historically, communal societies were organized as communes with common property. We easily recognize many of these: the first-century Christians in Jerusalem; monastic orders; Protestant sects such as Moravians, Mennonites, Shakers, Harmonists, Oneidans, Hutterites, and Bruderhof; and Jews still living in kibbutzim in Israel.[2] During the last century, communal groups increasingly organized with less economic sharing as cooperatives, collectives, joint-stock companies, land trusts, and nonprofit corporations. Members enjoyed more individual freedom and became more engaged in governance. Groups now prefer being called "intentional communities" or "planned communities" instead of "communes" or "communal societies." We recognize these today as ecovillages, retirement centers, and cohousing projects. Included is Harvest Hills as a signal community of the Community of Christ, right here in Independence

---

[2] For historical and present information, see the websites of historic and current communities referred to in this address. This address draws from the essays, bibliography, and list of fourteen hundred communal groups founded in the United States up to 1965 in Donald E. Pitzer, *America's Communal Utopias* (Chapel Hill: University of North Carolina Press, 1997). Also used is Timothy Miller, *The 60s Communes* (Syracuse, NY: Syracuse University Press, 1999), which has the best historical survey, vignettes, and list of communal groups in the United States that began in the 1960s and beyond. Articles and book reviews in *Communal Societies, Journal of the Communal Studies Association* are also a vital resource.

since 1970.[3] Variety, nonviolence, and humanitarian witness mark thousands of contemporary communities.[4]

The expanded forms and uses of communal living have made it difficult for a general definition to keep pace. For decades I required my students to learn a definition that I tried to stretch over all past and present communal groups no matter what they did or called themselves or however they organized their finances. It went like this: "Communal societies are small, voluntary social units, partly insolated and isolated from the general society in which their members practice an ideology, an economic union, and a lifestyle and experiment with their ideal systems—social, economic, political, religious, and philosophical—in the hope that their utopian vision will be realized worldwide by divine aid or human effort." A few students, or maybe I should say many, found this a little long and a lot complicated. And it proved inadequate to describe the kaleidoscopic changes within the founding movements and over centuries of time.

Thus, the definition is in flux. It is adjusting to include the realities of what I began calling in the 1980s "developmental communalism."[5] Developmental communalism is a theory that sees each movement that adopts any form of communal living as passing through a developmental process—before, during, and often after its communal stage. This approach views communal living as a *means* to an end, not an end in itself. Developmental communalism also frees us from judging the success of communal groups by the length of time they remain communal. Rather, it focuses on the *movements* that establish communal sanctuaries during an early stage—often for security, solidarity, and survival—

[3] James A. Christenson, *Zion In Our Neighborhood: The Story of Harvest Hills, 1970–1995* (Leawood, KS: Leathers Publishing, 1997). Bryan Monte, "Harvest Hills: Graying Not Growing," *John Whitmer Historical Association Journal* 28 (2008): 188–210; paper also presented at the joint conference of the John Whitmer Historical Association and the Communal Studies Association, Kirtland, Ohio, September 29, 2007.

[4] For a detailed list, information, and articles on contemporary communities internationally, see *Communities Directory: A Comprehensive Guide to Intentional Communities* and *Cooperative Living* and *Communities*, a quarterly magazine, both published by the Fellowship for Intentional Community (Rutledge, Missouri), <http://www.ic.org >. Geoph Kozeny's ninety-minute documentary, "Visions of Utopia: Experiments in Sustainable Culture," is an inside look at seven current communities, available at <http://store.ic.org/catalog/product_info. php?cPath=30&products_id=29>. See also, Miller, *60s Communes*.

[5] Donald E. Pitzer, "Developmental Communalism: An Alternative Approach to Communal Studies," *Utopian Thought and Communal Experience*, ed. Dennis Hardy and Lorna Davidson (Queensway, England: Middlesex Polytechnic, 1989); reprinted in *Community Service Newsletter* 39 (January/February, March/April 1991) and in *The Guide To Communal Living: Diggers and Dreamers 94/95* (Redfield Community, Winslow, Buckinghamshire, England: Commune Network, 1993). Developmental communalism is also the theoretical base for Donald E. Pitzer, *America's Communal Utopias*.

and then shows their vitality by developing into new organizational forms and employing new methods. The communal method necessitates creating and managing a whole social structure on a small scale. This alone can pose an unbearable burden to founding movements.

First-century Christians in Jerusalem chose the communal developmental process. According to Acts 2:44, 45, "All that believed were together, and had all things common; And sold their possessions and goods, and parted them to all men, as every man had need." Sometime after Ananias and Sapphira were stricken dead because they lied about sharing all the sale of their land (Acts 5:1–10), the church relaxed the communal requirement to permit believers to live anywhere and to own private property. This developmental move, combined with forsaking the Hebrew customs of animal blood sacrifice and circumcision, liberated the faith to grow into the Greek and Roman worlds.

Early Christianity's adaptability proved essential to its expansion but raises the specter of what I call a communal double jeopardy threat. Movements lively enough to develop into new organizational structures, ideas, and methods tend to save their movements but lose communal living. Witness the Moravians, Owenites, Inspirationists of Amana, Iowa, and, as we shall see, even the Latter Day Saints. On its other side, the double jeopardy threat dictates that movements that make communal living a required commitment or tenet of faith usually discover they have injured or eventually killed their movement as with the Shakers and Harmonists. Demise is certain for groups like these and monastic orders that demand celibacy unless they gain new members from the outside.

As many of you could detail better than I,[6] the Latter Day Saints' movement provides a unique example of developmental communalism. Soon after the publication of the Book of Mormon and the establishment of the church in 1830, both the leaders and working-class poor who largely composed the membership felt a magnetic tug toward the communal living promises of security, solidarity, and survival. Prophet Joseph Smith Jr. and others knew the communal example of the first Christians and likely the economic success of the Shakers and Harmonists. Early leader Sidney Rigdon had even heard Robert Owen speak about his New Moral World utopia and socialistic model at New Harmony, Indiana.[7] But the plan revealed to Smith in 1830 and 1831 contained novel elements and justifications. It not only brought justice to the poor, it ingeniously combined private enterprise with community of goods.

---

[6] See, for example, Andrew Bolton, "Pentecost and All Things Common—Acts Chapter 2 and 4:31–33 as Template for Community in Kirtland, Ohio, 1830–1837," *Restoration Studies* X (2009): 57–77, and Ronald E. Romig and Anne L. Romig, *Stewardship Concepts and Practices: Studies in Restoration History* (Independence, MO: Herald Publishing House, 1992).

[7] Bolton, "Pentecost and All Things Common," 63.

As practiced at Kirtland, Ohio, and Independence, Missouri, in the 1830s, the system of consecration and stewardship provided that members consecrate all their possessions and annually all their surplus earnings to the bishop. In return they received a stewardship in property and funds to use as they chose (Doctrine and Covenants 42:8a–9b).[8]

This arrangement was to restore the perfect social order of peace, justice, and equality that existed for God's people of Zion in the ancient United Order of Enoch. As stated in the Doctrine and Covenants, "And the Lord called his people Zion, because they were of one heart and one mind, and dwelt in righteousness; and there was no poor among them" (36:2h, i). Reviving the United Order also tied the zionic Saints to the millennial purpose of the holy city of Zion—a city built by Enoch and taken up into heaven to become the center of God's kingdom in Jackson County, Missouri, after Christ's return (Doctrine and Covenants 36:3a–d). Restoring the United Order also placed the Saints of the 1830s in the tradition of the Nephites who, according to the Book of Mormon, enjoyed the blessings of the United Order when they practiced it in America in the first two centuries of the Christian era (IV Nephi 1).

The United Order gave the early Mormon adoption of communal living a divine sanction and infused it with a zeal for the millennial cause of Zion. But it did not prevent the public hostility and perpetual migrations that upset the stability of the church's financial base. These realities induced the Saints to suspend their United Order communalism. In its place at Nauvoo, Illinois, tithing became the movement's developmental change that proved to be financially sufficient, less difficult to administer, and more conducive to nationwide and worldwide expansion.

In its post-communal phase, the Latter Day Saints can be compared to the Amish who for three hundred years have lived in tight-knit communities but without demanding community of goods. They and the Latter Day Saints both have practiced the communal ideal of close association, fellowship, and assistance without losing their movement to the communal double jeopardy threat. Regrettably, however, unlike the Amish and Mennonites, the Latter Day Saints lost their peace witness. When the Saints' movement began, the young Smith advocated the nonviolent stand of Jesus and the primitive Christians, and Sidney Rigdon held to his previous Campbellite pacifism. But mob persecution and militia murders in the 1830s severed this peace commitment and both men ever after justified the Saints responding with "redemptive violence."[9]

---

[8] Doctrine and Covenants (Independence, MO: Herald Publishing House, 2007), 55–56.

[9] Andrew Bolton, "Anabaptism, the Book of Mormon, and the Peace Church Option," *Dialogue* 37, no. 1 (Spring 2004): 92–94.

This makes all the more remarkable the developmental process through which the Reorganized Church of Jesus Christ of Latter Day Saints has come in the last several decades. The very change of the name to Community of Christ in 2001 announced the renewed emphasis on the zionic mission as a witness for peace and justice in community and reflects the early nonmilitant leadership of Joseph Smith III.[10] In March 2007, guidance of President Stephen M. Veazey confirmed the priority of establishing signal communities (Doctrine and Covenants 163:2b; 3a, b; 5a). The Council of Twelve was admonished to "lead the church's mission of restoration through ... the establishment of signal communities of justice and peace that reflect the vision of Christ" (163:5a). In one of the most dynamic paradigm shifts and revivals of communal usage within a movement in communal history this guidance further asserts: "The hope of Zion is realized when the vision of Christ is embodied in communities of generosity, justice, and peacefulness" (163: 3a; see also 2b, and 3b, c). Thus zionic *signal communities* are being created anywhere, everywhere, and including anybody while not negating the prophesied *single community* of Zion as the future center of the millennial kingdom. According to the Community of Christ statement of faith and beliefs, signal communities are, in fact, using communalism for a new mission—to infuse the realities of God's kingdom into *every* human dimension—"families, congregations, neighborhoods, cities, and throughout the world."[11] Martin Luther King Jr. envisioned the world becoming what he called the "Beloved Community"—"a community of love and justice" where "brotherhood is a reality."[12] Signal communities can move us in this direction.

Peace Lessons from Communal Millennialism

ON THIS HOPEFUL note we go to our second objective—examining lessons from four dimensions of communities' witness for peace—from millennialism, humanitarianism, pacifism, and authoritarianism. Beginning on the global level with millennialism, we will work our way toward the community and individual levels. Communitarians often have found global peace and justice through future divine intervention more easily embraced than

---

[10] Bolton, "Anabaptism," 93–94.

[11] See "Zion" (Community of Christ, "Faith and Beliefs," <http://www. cofchrist.org/ourfaith/faith-beliefs.asp> [accessed August 26, 2008]).

[12] King's description of the purpose of the newly formed Southern Christian Leadership Conference as stated in its 1957 newsletter, quoted in an article in *Christian Century*, April 3, 1974, 361–62, based on Kenneth L. Smith and Ira G. Zepp Jr., *Search for the Beloved Community: The Thinking of Martin Luther King Jr.* (Valley Forge, PA: Judson Press, 1974).

peace and justice here and now at the personal level, possibly because peace with one's self and one's neighbor is such a daunting *everyday* challenge.

Millennialism promises peace through the appearance of a Savior, a Godly kingdom for at least a millennium, a thousand years. This is one of the most potent ideas in history, and its most powerful expressions have come in the Western World. In Hebrew and Jewish faith it has meant that the Messiah will *yet* appear. Christians believe that Jesus was the Messiah and will appear again as the Prince of Peace. Many Muslims look for the Twelfth Imam, who disappeared in the tenth century, to return and rule over a perfect world order.

Christian millennialism became the motivating belief for many religious movements, but a vulnerable communal witness for peace. Millennialist communal groups teach us that excessive reliance on divine intervention to bring peace on earth usually results over time in frustration and sometimes contributes to the decline or demise of the founding movement. Forty celibate male millennialists emigrated from Europe to Pennsylvania in 1694, the year they thought Christ would return. Their commune was called the Woman in the Wilderness after the prophecy in Revelation 12 about the woman who would flee the dragon after begetting the millennial Christ. When their leader, Johannes Kelpius, died in 1708 after claiming to be immortal, the men scattered, some of them so distressed they took wives.

Shakers, officially The United Society of Believers in Christ's Second Appearing, were *optimistic* millennialists.[13] The eight who emigrated from England to New York in 1774 believed Christ's spirit had already returned to earth in the female form of their leader, Mother Ann Lee. Despite the violence of the American Revolution and Civil War, Shakers thought peace would increase as the divine spirit gradually permeated all humanity. Some twenty thousand Believers lived in one or another of the Shakers' nineteen settlements, but now only seven reside in their last community at Sabbathday Lake, Maine. These remaining few are still optimistic. As the now deceased Sister Gertrude Soule told me in 1983, raising one hand: "Mother said when the movement gets down to the number of fingers on one hand there will be a great revival."

The Harmonists, who followed their German prophet George Rapp to the United States after 1803, were *pessimistic* millennialists.[14] Their reading of prophecy indicated that world conditions would become steadily worse until

---

[13] See Priscilla J. Brewer, *Shaker Communities, Shaker Lives* (Hanover, NH: University Press of New England, 1986) and "The Shakers of Mother Ann Lee," Pitzer, *America's Communal Utopias.*

[14] See Karl J. R. Arndt, *George Rapp's Harmony Society: 1785–1847* (Rutherford, NJ: Fairleigh Dickinson University Press, 1965) and "George Rapp's Harmony Society," Pitzer, *America's Communal Utopias.*

Christ's return. For a century these celibate Harmonists watched the war-weary world deteriorate. Rapp died at age eighty-nine in 1847, still expecting Christ's return during his lifetime. His Harmony society ended in 1916.

Millennialism's lesson about peace is clear. No matter how much a redeemer is anticipated, the solution to today's problems is not to sit idly by awaiting this event. The witness for peace demands that we actively engage in the nonviolent peace process in the present, addressing the suffering and injustice of our own times.

Ultimately, the peace witness of the shrinking Shakers and defunct Harmonists is judged by their humanitarian deeds rather than by their millennial beliefs. The Kentucky Shakers are celebrated for ruinously overextending their own resources to feed and care for both Union and Confederate soldiers during the Civil War.[15] The Harmonists are applauded for generously aiding the Zoarites, Hutterites, and other sectarian immigrants.

Peace Lessons from Communal Humanitarianism

THIS LEADS US to our second lesson—the relationship between humanitarianism and peace—that by dispensing justice and mercy to the poor, diseased, and distressed we relieve the suffering that often causes violence, revolution, and war itself.

You might be surprised that secular, rather than religious, communitarians provided the major thrust for the communal humanitarian witness of the nineteenth century. The violence of the French Revolution and the poverty of the Industrial Revolution brought Charles Fourier and Etienne Cabet of France and Robert Owen of Scotland to found utopian movements that began more than sixty socialistic communal experiments in America and Europe. The Owenites, in and beyond their communal phase, urged emancipation of the slaves and helped usher in modern women's and workers' rights, public schools and libraries, and consumer/producer cooperatives.

For centuries monastic orders have understood the immediacy of human need and responded with hospitality, hospitals, and schools. Mother Teresa won the Nobel Peace Prize in 1979 for the service of her missionaries of charity among the poor and diseased beginning in Calcutta. Her Order's witness now reaches to six hundred missions in 120 countries.[16]

---

[15] Thomas Clark, *Pleasant Hill in the Civil War* (Lexington, KY: Keystone Printery, 1974): 32–33, 38, 60.

[16] Louise Chipley Slavicek, *Mother Teresa: Modern Peacemakers* (New York: Infobase Publishing, 2007), 90–91.

Habitat for Humanity International, launched by Millard and Linda Fuller at Koinonia Partners, is undoubtedly the best-known humanitarian project to emerge from an American intentional community. Koinonia Partners was rightly honored last evening with the 2008 Community of Christ International Peace Award for its courageous initiatives for peace and justice. Its Habitat outreach alone has built more than 250,000 homes for over a million industrious poor people in every state of the United States and ninety foreign countries.[17] How many here, like former president and first lady Jimmy and Rosalynn Carter, have assisted Habitat? If you want to help just call 1-800-Habitat.

By 2005, Habitat ranked tenth in income among charities in the United States with nearly one and a half billion dollars ($1,500,000,000).[18] That's a wonderful one and five with eight zeroes. But contrast that with the projected bill for the Iraq war alone—three trillion dollars ($3,000,000,000,000). That's a three with *twelve* zeroes, three thousand billions. If all the Iraqi people were divided into families of four, with three trillion dollars, Habitat could build a $422,000 home for each family in Iraq—or a $200,000 home for every such family of four in both Iraq *and* Afghanistan! What will it take for humanity to come to its senses, beat its swords into plowshares, and use its resources for *con*struction rather than *de*struction?

The communal humanitarian lesson in witness of peace is that we must first actively address poverty, disease, and despair if we hope to make an assault on abuse, violence, and war.

Peace Lessons from Communal Pacifism

OUR THIRD LESSON relates to pacifism, the persuasion that nonviolent resolution of disputes is the route to true and lasting peace. Just as Jesus did not resist his assailants and explained to Pilate that "if my kingdom were of this world, then would my servants fight" (John 18:36), many communal pacifists have died rather than fight—Amish, Mennonites, and Hutterites among them. Many others have witnessed for peace in community—Shakers, Harmonists, Quakers, Brethren, Community of Christ, Catholic Worker's, Jehovah's Witnesses, and monastic orders.

But most Christians, despite the example and teaching of Jesus and the witness of the early church, accepted the arguments for participating in a *just war* once the Roman state accepted Christianity. St. Augustine in the fourth

---

[17] "Habitat for Humanity Fact Sheet," <http://www.habitat.org/how/factsheet.aspx> (accessed August 20, 2008).

[18] "The 50 Largest US Charities Ranked by Total Income," *Christian Science Monitor*, November 20, 2006, 17.

century, St. Aquinas in the thirteenth, and others opened the door for Christians to enter the military. Warfare was justified if the bloodshed was defensive, for a moral cause, and declared by a legitimate governing leader to restore the peace after diplomatic means were exhausted. Much Christian support for war during the last century rested on the assumption that God blessed nationalism, empire building, and defending or spreading democracy.

The witness and actions of pacifistic communalists have modified this trend. They have sometimes helped convince governments to enact laws that respect the beliefs of conscientious objectors and noncombatants and to seek peaceful, diplomatic solutions to international conflicts. Harmonist delegates successfully got a provision for payment in lieu of armed service written into Indiana's first constitution in 1816. The Zoarites in Ohio declared in their principles of separation: "We cannot serve the state as … soldiers, since a Christian cannot murder his enemy, much less his friend."[19] But they later compromised their pacifistic principles during the Civil War to accommodate a few members who chose to fight to free the slaves. The Shakers sent resolutions to President Theodore Roosevelt from their peace conference during the Russo-Japanese War in 1905. They uncompromisingly asserted that "all wars are equally barbarous and equally unnecessary, their desolating cruelty effecting nothing for the cause of justice or human liberty, and to be regarded only as a return to primitive savagery." They called for peace conferences to precede military action, international arbitration, armaments reduction, and disarmament. Roosevelt went on to arbitrate an end to the war and win the Nobel Peace Prize. Should we give the Shakers any credit? Maybe.

In 1989, the Nobel Peace Prize honored perhaps the most famous communal pacifistic witness ever, that of the fourteenth Dalai Lama. This Buddhist and Tibetan leader has nonviolently led the effort to save the culture, if not the independence of his native land since the Chinese takeover in 1959. Even the recent Tibetan violence cannot diminish his consistent pacifistic witness.[20]

At a conference with the Hutterites at Bon Homme in South Dakota, we were shown a graphic example of communal pacifists' witness: graves of two of their young men who were inducted against their conscientious objection stand in World War I. Both were murdered in military incarceration, then sent home in the uniforms they refused to wear. You remember how the pacifistic Amish of Lancaster, Pennsylvania, demonstrated the depth of their nonviolence and forgiveness when a deranged man killed and wounded children in their school

---

[19] Quoted in Philip Webber, *Zoar in the Civil War* (Kent, OH: Kent State University Press, 2007), 3.

[20] Pico Iyer, "A Monk's Struggle," *TIME*, March 31, 2008, 44–53; Jonathan Mirsky, "How He Sees It Now," *The New York Review of Books*, July 17, 2008, 4–6.

in 2006. In their great grief the Amish not only forgave him, they sent provisions to his family, which responded with appreciation to this healing gesture.

I brought my *peace pole* today. It reminds me of the first one I saw in the Atarashiki-mura (New Village) north of Tokyo. This six-foot-tall pole proclaims in eight different languages "May Peace Prevail on Earth." With my peace pole came a message that expresses the communal New Village's faith in the role of the individual as a peacemaker. It states: "We are facing an age where the politics of the world *must* be carried out by each individual. Every individual who repeats the words 'May Peace Prevail on Earth' thus becomes a great force for realizing peace in the world." As Dr. Dean Ornish observed: "When you embody peace, people around you feel it …. When you meet hatred with love, fear with hope, that transforms you and those around you."[21]

We know that pacifism is a radical position. It raises the troublesome question of if, when, how, and how much force should be used. But its communal witness clearly teaches us to address conflicts on the lowest personal and community scales as soon as possible. Christian pacifistic groups often follow the lowest-level directive for conflict resolution in Matthew 18:15–17, 21–22. Members are to first go alone to kindly discuss a dispute, then to take one or two witnesses, and finally to bring the matter to the community. Eberhard Arnold, founder of the Bruderhof communities, insisted on this process and reminded the members: "Only when two people do not come to an agreement quickly is it necessary to draw in a third person."[22] Resolving problems quickly makes me think of something I wrote a good while ago.

> In the beginning the wound can be healed by a kiss
> In the beginning the flood can be damned by a toothpick
> In the beginning the fire can be snuffed by a breath
> In the beginning the war can be avoided by a smile
> In the beginning[23]

---

[21] "How to Stress Less," *Newsweek*, August 14, 2006, 60.

[22] In "The First Law in Sannerz," Arnold stated this more fully as: "Direct address is the only way possible; it is the spontaneous brotherly or sisterly service we owe anyone whose weaknesses cause a negative reaction in us. An open word spoken directly to another person deepens friendship and will not be resented. Only when two people do not come to an agreement quickly is it necessary to draw in a third person whom both of them trust. In this way they can be led to a solution that unites them on the highest levels."

[23] March 19 calendar entry in Donald E. Pitzer and Connie L. Pitzer, *Pi Tze For You Volume II: More Musings to Amuse and Bemuse* (Evansville, IN: self published, 2007).

Peace Lessons from Communal Authoritarianism

S O LET US look at our fourth and final lesson. This one derives from communities' attempts to control diversity, deviant behavior, and authoritarianism. Communal experience teaches that the more homogeneous the group, the greater the conformity, unity of purpose, and longevity. Homogeneous ethnic and religious communities with deep common roots and commitments usually find it easier to achieve that balance between unity and diversity that produces harmony. Heterogeneous groups with fewer common ties and united mostly by secular ideals usually find harmony and longevity significantly more elusive.

All intentional communities—just like society at large—must deal with deviant behavior. Their members are *Homo sapiens*—people not only with proclivities for cooperation, benevolence, and altruism, but also for aggression, territoriality, and hierarchical dominance. At the end of a tour of the Deer Spring Bruderhof in Connecticut, I thanked the community as "a wonderful people." When their patriarchal leader, Hans Meyer, stood to respond, he said, "We are *not* a wonderful people. We struggle every day to keep ourselves under control and to obey the will of God."

Communal groups, like other voluntary associations like churches, do have important advantages over the general society. Members make commitments, sometimes vows, to be in accord with the beliefs, purposes, and practices of the organization and to obey its rules. This lays a foundation for order, conformity, and peace. If members do not conform, there are consequences: denial of privileges, shunning as in Amish circles, and ultimately excommunication.

The sobering lesson from communal control of diversity and deviant behavior is that, even with all their advantages, intentional communities still find this a daunting task. And perhaps the greatest challenge is to find ways of transferring communal successes to larger and larger human venues, including nations. In this, we must be realistic in considering the peacekeeping *disadvantages* that nations face in managing their diversity and deviant behavior. Except in theocracies, governments have no spiritual authority. They can only follow the communal example to a point: making laws and punishing violators. Perhaps shockingly, the United States imprisons a greater percentage of its population than any other country, and almost 50 percent of all prisoners worldwide.[24] All nations must accept newborns, legal immigrants, and naturalized citizens. The United States tests the limits and potential of diversity while holding to its motto *E Pluribus Unum*, "of many one." China is an amalgam of fifty-six ethnic

---

[24] Roy Walmsley, "World Prison Population List," 7th ed., National Institute of Corrections, Bureau of Prisons, United States Department of Justice, February 27, 2007, <http://www.nicic. org/Library/022140> (accessed 26 August 2008).

groups. Iraq is torn by Kurdish, Shiite, and Sunni differences. The diversified and disharmonious Soviet Union lasted less than a century.

Results from communal laboratories suggest that nations should cultivate a genuine harmony in diversity, a genuine unity of hearts, minds, and spirits. India has taken the first bold initiative at a state-sponsored communal experiment to unite *international* diversity. With the blessing of the United Nations through UNESCO, India founded Auroville in 1968 as "the first and only intentionally endorsed ongoing experiment in human unity." Seventeen hundred people from thirty-five nations now live in communal Auroville attempting "to realise human unity—in diversity."[25]

While we recognize the difficulties communities and governments have in controlling their domains, we can never excuse their descent into the abyss of authoritarianism. Charismatic, ego- and power-driven leaders make unreasonable demands that rob their disciples of their possessions, privacy, independent judgment, civil rights, and sometimes their very lives. We know the celibacy of Ann Lee, George Rapp, and monastic orders; the complex marriage and eugenic experiment of John Humphrey Noyes at Oneida, New York; the polygamy of Joseph Smith Jr. and Warren Jeffs; and the suicides of Jim Jones.

If leaders are restrained by consensus decision making, such abuses might not occur. Born out of the freedom-loving youth movement in 1972, Alpha Farm in Oregon pioneered this method—a process of open discussion with full participation by all members until decisions are arrived at unanimously, if possible. As you can imagine, consensus decision making can be lengthy, but it can keep the authoritarian demon from the door while emphasizing the importance of the individual in governing, conflict resolution, and peace.

Communal history shouts this lesson loudly: "Beware Authoritarianism!" Authoritarian abuse must be questioned, resisted, and rejected. This is true whether it raises its ugly head in the name of God, of peace, or of security; be it in an intentional community, a Nazi Germany, a Communist Soviet Union, or a democratic United States of America.

Conclusion

In conclusion, the communal witnesses and lessons for peace we have examined today lead us to conclude that even in community, peace depends on each individual. All members are part of the matrix of peace and any person out of order disturbs the peace of all. Each individual must resolve his or her own conflicts within the communal setting and arrive at internal control with the resources of his or her own spiritual, moral, and rational grounding.

---

[25] "Auroville in Brief," <http://www.auroville.org/av_brief.htm> (accessed July 24, 2008).

Albert Bates of The Farm community in Tennessee calls it "Reform by the square inch."

Yet, we also must conclude that, while peace is rooted in the individual, it can only be displayed in community, in association with others. Therefore, communities *are* the witness for peace. Communities are the stage for acting out and demonstrating peace, cooperation, and harmony. Only in relation to others can we know ourselves fully and test our moral fiber.

How then can we individually and in community uphold peace, even fight for peace, as contradictory as that might sound? We fight for rights. We fight for principles. We fight for territory. We fight for oil. At this time and this place let us find the resources and resolve to fight for peace. This must mean doing battle armed with love—love for ourselves, our Maker, our neighbors, and our world. Again, Jesus reminds us: "Love your enemies" (Matt. 5:43). As revolutionary as this sounds, if we cannot embrace the truthful negotiation and reasonable compromise that are the basis for mutually deserved trust, we will repeat the misunderstanding, hatred, and warfare that have characterized our traditional fight for peace. In his March 2007 guidance on signal communities, President Veazey urged "redemptive relationships in sacred community. The restoring of persons to healthy or righteous relationships with God, others, themselves, and the earth … (Doctrine and Covenants 163:2b). This will never be easy, but it *is the way* of all true religion, good government, and proper reason. It is the *only way* beyond the killing of more in the future than in the past.

Gandhi advised: "Be the change you want to see in the world." St. Francis prayed: "Lord make me an instrument of your peace." Therefore, let us sing out with all our hearts, "Let there be peace on earth and let it begin with me." Let peace begin with me and *you*. Let peace begin with me, you, and *us*. Let peace begin with me, you, us, and *them*. Let us begin!

Standing on Strong Shoulders: Church Identity and Historical Consciousness[1]

MARK A. SCHERER

D EAN COMPIER, faculty colleagues, graduates, students, and friends of the seminary: I am honored to be installed as associate professor of history and faculty member of Graceland University and the Community of Christ Seminary. It is a humbling experience to find myself standing before you in this educational setting sharing my thoughts. I consider this truly a great honor.

The Complexity of the Task

S O... HERE I AM—a historian professionally prepared in a *secular* university and now commissioned to profess religious history in a *sacred* seminary setting, festooned in the sartorial splendor of my academic garb, still wondering if this position is really right for me. Perhaps my wondering will always be with me. My planet orbits in a fascinating intellectual solar system that causes me to navigate the fine line between historical objectivity and the church's Christian mission. I yearn for objectivity to which all good historians aspire, but of course, know the impossibility of this goal. But mine is also a unique

---

[1] This paper was presented by the author as his faculty installation address in the position of associate professor of history in the Community of Christ Seminary, Graceland University, Independence, Missouri, May 21, 2008.

ministry of memory. All this means I must confront the dilemma of how to deal honestly with issues and events that are historically significant to understanding the church story even though that same information would never be placed in a missionary tract.

I am the church historian of a denomination steeped in historical tradition, only some of which is actually sustained by fact; a church where historically, like all the rest, decision makers are, in equal portions, guided by the powerful indwelling of the Holy Spirit and the powerful urges of their own humanity. I cannot explain one without explaining the other, without being attacked as either a faith promoter or faith destroyer. So, to fill this perplexing job description, what is one to do? I see three options: to just look the other way and plead no knowledge to anything controversial that comes across my desk; to deny what is verified by the best scholarship and simply run out the clock on my career; or to take a moderate course that claims ownership of both dimensions of the church story, learn from its lessons, counsel the quorums and orders of the church of my findings, then let my honesty and integrity be my testimony. I think you know my preference.

The Elusive Search for Truth

MINE, AND HOPEFULLY yours, is a search for elusive truth. Early in the previous century, Albert Einstein proved that truth's nature is relative. Although truth is a moving target through space and time, it nevertheless always seems to emerge; in its own time truth always finds a way. Such is also the case with our church story. As much as it is possible to know it (and there are always surprises around the corner), at least for now our vision of what happened in the early life of the church has become relatively clear. Hmmm, I wonder if historian Inez Smith Davis ever said that! If what I say about our vision is accurate then *our willingness to tell historical truth is just as important as knowing it.*

Still, we must continue to ask questions. Historically, scripturally, or theologically, we have nothing to fear from honest answers discovered in our questioning. For, in my opinion, if truth creates obstacles in our journey to build "signal communities" and "to share the peace of Jesus Christ," then we are traveling the wrong road.

The Importance of Sound Historical Methodology

S ound historical methodology provides the bedrock for seminary education. As one who professes history to the student of scripture I would say that it is impossible to understand the *holy text* without first understanding the *historical context*. And to the student of theology, I would say that it is impossible to understand the *holy thought* without first understanding the *historical thinker*.

If the discipline of history is the solid bedrock of seminary education then what is to be the role of the competent historian in the seminary setting? Appearances and expectations can be deceiving. A whale is not a fish even though it looks like a fish and swims under water. And historians of religion are not theologians even though in the seminary they appear to be the same. Religious history is a discipline that studies the beliefs, words, and deeds of those within a faith group across space and time. It is a study that demonstrates the blessings received, the pains and frustrations experienced, and the challenges encountered by each generation of a sect or denomination's believers.

Sound religious history is not and cannot become a mere tool of parochial denominational promotion. When the expectation for the historian is reduced to apologetic faith promoter then the historian is relegated to denominational spin meister. This, of course, does not remove the possibility for the historian to receive and to share their own testimony of the presence and guidance of Jesus Christ in their life. Believe me, I acknowledge that as my personal testimony every day. Rather, it means that there must be developed an intellectual and spiritual maturity that provides for the inexorable separation between divinity and humanity.

So much of our church story as we understand it today is personal testimony, and ranges far beyond the historian's task. Yet it is to this task that I am called. For example, I cannot say for certain that in a dedication service on Sunday, April 3, 1836, after the Kirtland House of the Lord pulpit veils were lowered, that Jesus Christ himself appeared to Joseph Smith Jr. and Oliver Cowdery. Or whether Moses actually appeared and conferred on the two men the keys of the gathering of Israel and the leading of the ten tribes from the land of the north, only to be followed by Elias who conferred on the two church leaders the gospel of Abraham, and then finally, Elijah who gave them the keys to priesthood authority and the charge to prepare for the Second Coming. I cannot say *for certain* what happened in the Sacred Grove in Palmyra, New York, when the young Smith put his knee to the ground and poured out his heart's desires. And parenthetically, I don't think Joseph could either since he gave so many different versions of the event. But, at least for me, his confusion is very strong evidence of his spiritual encounter because that is what happens when the Divine mind touches the human mind. Finally, I am not certain that there were actual metallic plates so important to the Book of Mormon story. As a historian, however, I can only tell you that all of this is to what Smith testified.

In none of these key events in the church story does my hesitance suggest my doubt that the events actually happened. But for some this will appear to be faith destroying. Indeed, even analyzing the Kirtland Temple epiphanies, or the experience of the First Vision, or the historical veracity of the Book of Mormon, will be considered heresy, since for many these stories are part of their personal testimony. Here is where I happily bequeath to the theologian the task of explaining the testimonial components of a believer's faith.

But *asking questions* is by definition the historian's profession.[2] And providing direct answers will not be heresy *unless we have canonized our church story.* The presence of this condition means that a portion of our people worship a prophet from Palmyra, rather than a carpenter from Nazareth. These people are sharing the prominence of Joseph Smith rather than the peace of Jesus Christ. Our history should not accommodate such a view. My purpose here is not to assign blame, but if this is a problem within our faith, then why is it so? Does the blame fall on the membership for not delving more deeply to achieve a clearer understanding of the church story? Or does the blame encompass also the leadership (me included here) for not encouraging the exploration of the three pillars of responsible membership—study of scripture, history, and theology? Perhaps there is plenty of blame to go around. Here is where the seminary administration, faculty, and students can move the church forward with such great strides.

The Need for Historical Consciousness

I ARGUE THAT A mature, twenty-first-century denominational identity is built on a healthy *historical consciousness.* Without such a consciousness church members fall prey to anyone willing to tell a good story to accomplish their own personal agenda; fiction replaces fact. In 1834, Joseph Smith Jr.'s personal army of two hundred men, women, and children, armed to the hilt with all manner of weaponry, marching some eight hundred miles from northern Ohio to western Missouri to forcibly liberate Zion, becomes the Latter Day Saints' blessed army of the Lord. At Far West, between 1837 and 1838, Smith's Danite henchmen created to enforce, by violence if necessary, the *right thinking* of the membership, all of a sudden becomes a Far West Latter Day Saint community service organization, and the call-up of his five-thousand-man personal army, at Nauvoo, Illinois, by 1844, the nation's single largest state militia unit, becomes

---

[2] The original Greek understanding of the term "history" means "to inquire."

a mere ceremonial militia company to protect western Illinois from Indian attacks.

When we study our history we study ourselves. Without a mature historical consciousness, the coexistence of conflicting narratives causes a believer's sense of self to become confused.[3] Then, when the truth emerges, as it always does, unknowing members become the victims of abuse, and set themselves up for an identity crisis that is sure to follow. Ultimately, church members wonder how this conflict was allowed to happen and become disillusioned.

Excuse-making and Institutional Identity

THOSE OF US who are members of the seminary's sponsoring denomination should not have to make excuses for our identity. Instead, we should be proud of who we are. We are the Community of Christ! We have so much to offer a wanting world. Our rich heritage empowers us to make a significant contribution to key segments of the world community. Let me provide but one of many examples. A vital characteristic of our church story centers on the theme of persecution and marginalization. As a people we were brutalized by American frontier society and were victimized by state-sponsored terrorism that called for our physical extermination. So we fled, we prospered, and then fled again, and again. This persecution is ingrained in our identity—it's part of who we are—and came with a very heavy price in both lives and property.

Rightfully, we can approach large segments of today's society—in Africa, in the Caribbean, in Europe, in Asia, and here in the Americas—who have been and still are being marginalized, and say to these victims of abuse: Come! Come and see who we are. Come and learn of our ways. We understand your tribulations. We know what it means to have powerful social and governmental forces arrayed against you because of your beliefs and your life's circumstances. Join us and you will be loved and accepted in our diverse community as a sacred child of the most-high God, and find peace. These are our sacrificially earned credentials.

Ignoring, twisting, and/or repressing through our silence a clear and accurate understanding of who we are means we cannot even know what credentials we have earned to even share with a wanting world. The sacrifices of those who have gone before us are all for naught. We cannot stand on the shoulders of their achievements because of the deafening roar of our silence or simply look away, in some cases, with disdain. Nor can we despise the enterprise and lessons of history.

---

[3] I would like to thank Matthew Naylor for his assistance with this phraseology.

In May 1865, just weeks after the conclusion of the American Civil War, freed slaves evidently heard the gospel message and were baptized into the Reorganized Church of Jesus Christ of Latter Day Saints. Some were gifted with calls to sacramental ministry. These priesthood calls must have been forwarded to the Joint Council of the First Presidency and Quorum of Twelve Apostles for processing because there were no specific provisions to ordain men of color.

No doubt there were struggles in our highest church leadership council as they addressed this difficult issue, certainly with high emotions expressed on both sides. Prophetically and courageously Joseph Smith III brought forth Doctrine and Covenants Section 116 that granted priesthood authority to men of color at a volatile time that had the potential for so many to leave the church. And I would speculate that some did. But we recovered as a stronger church because the undeniable call was for the church membership to be prophetic and, more importantly, because it was the right thing to do, no matter the cost.

But we do not have to go back 143 years to find acts of institutional courage. During the April 1972 World Conference, I sat in the choir loft behind the rostrum in a packed auditorium conference chamber to hear the reading of Section 150 brought by President W. Wallace Smith. Polygamist tribesmen had been baptized into the Reorganization in the East Orissa Province of India. The church was called to "bear the burdens of their sin, nurturing them in faith, accepting that degree of repentance which it is possible for them to achieve, looking forward to the day when through patience and love they can become free as a people from the *sins of the years of their ignorance*."[4]

I remember in the conference chamber that a vigorous floor debate ensued. I also remember discussions in the hallways about people threatening to leave the church if the revelation was canonized. I know this because I engaged with some in that conversation. I speculate that some did leave the church. But we survived our losses and emerged even stronger. Contained in Section 150 was the undeniable call to be prophetic and our people responded because it was the right thing to do, no matter the cost.

Theologians would have to address the issue of where God's grace for us would have been, had the decision in 1865 been to remain in our ignorance by rejecting priesthood ministry for men of color. Theologians would have to address the implications of receiving God's grace, were we to have denied baptism to the Sora tribesmen. But what are the implications of receiving God's grace if we today allow our own membership to live in ignorance historically, scripturally, or theologically? What is to be lost with ignorance? What is to be gained with knowledge?

---

[4] Doctrine and Covenants 150:10b (italics added for emphasis).

Challenging issues have always confronted the church. Every generation has confronted movement-changing issues of identity, mission, message, and beliefs. Historically, how previous generations dealt with their struggles reveals much about their willingness to be the body of Christ. Today we stand on the strong shoulders of those giants. And future generations will take note of our courage so they can stand on our strong shoulders. Historians of the coming generations will be watching.

The Illumination of Enlightened Education

I HAVE ALWAYS BELIEVED in the healing effects of education, and I continue to believe that it is education that brings the balm of Gilead to the sin-sick soul. It is the illumination of education that casts the light of knowledge into the darkened room of ignorance. It is the sweet fragrance of learning that removes the stench of prejudice and injustice.

The need for education has always been in the minds of church leaders as an important characteristic and closely held value of who we are as a people. In all three eras of our church story—the era of restoration, the era of reorganization, and the era of world-wide community—we have lifted up the importance of an educated membership.

Educational Emphasis in the Era of Restoration

THE MOST DIRECT restoration era expression of the importance of education occurred on the morning of July 4, 1838. In his public oration on that day of patriotic celebration, Sidney Rigdon discussed the need for an intelligent membership. From the stand in Far West, Missouri, and with an oratorical skill that only Rigdon commanded, the great speaker loudly proclaimed:

> Next to the worship of our God, we esteem the education of our children and of the rising generation. For what is wealth without society, or society without intelligence. And how is intelligence to be obtained?—by education. It is that which forms the youthful mind: it is that alone, which renders society agreeable, and adds interest and importance, to the worship of God. What is religion without intelligence!—an empty sound.[5]

On February 3, 1841, in his mayoral inaugural address to the citizens of Nauvoo, Illinois, John C. Bennett took the occasion to criticize prevailing educational methodology when he identified a gap between what was learned

---

[5] Sidney Rigdon, *Oration Delivered by Mr. S. Rigdon on the 4th of July, 1838* (Far West, MO: n.p., 1838), 8, Community of Christ Library-Archives.

and what was really understood and retained. He lamented to his community audience:

> Every boarding school Miss is a Plato in petticoats, without an ounce of that genuine knowledge… to escape perils with which she must necessarily be encompassed. young people are taught to use a variety of hard terms, which they understand but imperfectly;—to repeat lessons which they are unable to apply;—to astonish their grand-mothers with a display of their parrot-like acquisitions;—but their mental energies are clogged and torpified with a variety of learned lumber, most of which is discarded from the brain long before its possessor knows how to use it. This is the quackery of education.[6]

Educational Emphasis in the Era of Reorganization

A HALF CENTURY LATER, during the reorganization era, came this observation: "Etiquette is not taught in the camp, nor the art of war in the nursery, neither are priests educated at Oxford, nor Rabbis with the Jesuits; nor can we reasonably expect a plentiful supply of genuine Latter Day Saint elders to be furnished by the schools of the Gentiles."[7] Thus, Graceland College was set on a hill of glacial till soil in southern Iowa. This physical setting was chosen because "no stagnant water would form pools and the morning winds would sweep across it in such force to blow away malarial exhalations." Colonel George Barrett called the twenty-acre tract, donated by Marietta Walker, a "graceful land." And on September 17, 1895, Graceland College launched its mission as a place of learning.[8]

Educational Emphasis in the Era of World-wide Community

A ND NOW, in this era of world-wide community, our church seminary's principal task is "to serve the Gospel of Jesus Christ and the mission of the church, Christ's body." It is the mission of this seminary to create an ethos where students can be equipped "to proclaim with power the matchless Christ and to promote authentic Christian discipleship and community."[9] We have always been about educating our membership!

---

[6] John C. Bennett, "Inaugural Address," *Times and Seasons* 2, no.8 (February 15, 1841): 317.

[7] *Journal of History*, quoted in Paul M. Edwards, *The Hilltop Where: An Informal History of Graceland College* (Lamoni, IA: self published, 1972), 13.

[8] Edwards, *Hilltop*, 18.

[9] "Reflection on the Ethos of the Community of Christ Seminary," *Seminary Faculty Handbook, 2008–2009* (Independence, MO: Graceland University Seminary, 2008), 3.

Shortly after the launching of the new American nation, an observer asked Thomas Jefferson about the importance of an educated citizenry in the new national community. The Virginian profoundly stated that a citizen of the United States could not be both ignorant and free. Jefferson's reply is as appropriate for us today as it was more than two hundred years ago. A citizen in our new church community—the Community of Christ—cannot be both ignorant and free. In light of the issues facing our church today, our seminary may well be our most valuable tool to explore and to teach the church membership how best to share the peace of Jesus Christ, but with honesty and integrity. You, the students of the seminary, and especially the seminary graduates here today, become the brightest stars in the church's firmament—not from a position of intellectual arrogance, or esteemed academic achievement, but as you are endowed with the heavy responsibility that comes with having learned the lessons of history, the spiritual understandings of theology, and life-aligning insights of scripture study.

Conclusion

I AGREE WITH WILLIAM FAULKNER when he stated that "the past is not dead. In fact, it's not even past." There is an inseparable relationship between the past, present, and the future. Our understanding of the present is anchored in understanding our past. And our future course is shaped by our thoughts and actions in the present. Our minds require the nourishment of legitimate historical inquiry in order to bear the intellectual fruit that brings enlightenment to the soul. I am grateful for our seminary experience and I am so optimistic about what lies ahead for us in our journey as a people because of the significant contribution that we are able to make as *leaders in learning* during these pivotal times.

Thank you for entrusting me with this position on the seminary faculty.

Utopian Vision and Prophetic Imagination: Reading the Book of Mormon in a Nineteenth-century Context

ANDREW BOLTON

Introduction

A MAJOR CURRENT CONTROVERSY about the Book of Mormon is this: is it really ancient history that can be verified by archeology, or is it a product of Joseph Smith Jr.'s inspired imagination in a nineteenth-century historical context? This debate is taking place within a larger debate about modernity and post-modernity in the wider Latter Day Saint scholarly community.[1] Instead of conservative and liberal preoccupations with origins of the Book of Mormon I want to advocate for a third way—that of taking seriously the Book of Mormon in terms of its evangelistic proclamation of Christ, and its teachings on faithful discipleship and radical social justice. I want to suggest that the Book of Mormon describes glimpses of the kingdom of God on earth, or to put it another way, gives accounts of religiously inspired utopia.

Utopianism is social dreaming of a better world. A positive utopia is an imagined place, described in some detail, that is a *eutopia*, a good place. *Dystopia*

---

[1] John-Charles Duffy makes a thorough survey of the struggles, within the Mormon scholarly communities, of positivism and antipositivism, modernity and postmodernity in terms of Mormon truth claims. See John-Charles Duffy, "Can Deconstruction Save the Day? 'Faithful Scholarship' and the Uses of Postmodernism," *Dialogue: A Journal of Mormon Thought* 41, no. 1 (Spring 2008): 1–33.

or negative utopia is a bad place, a warning of what could happen.[2] In this paper I seek specifically to look at the positive and negative utopian stories in the Book of Mormon as one expression of prophetic imagination on behalf of a fallen world. First, though, I want to deal with a modern problem—the belief that only truth proven by science or mathematics is really true.

The problem around the origins of the Book of Mormon is one of modernity, specifically how truth is verified. The philosophy of logical positivism, which grew out of the Vienna Circle after World War I and was popularized by British philosopher A. J. Ayer among others, defined truth in only empirical and mathematical ways. Put simply, something is true if you can prove it by mathematical logic or by scientific experimentation, and these are the only *meaningful* statements. All other statements are meaningless. Ethical statements are just emotionalism.[3] Logical positivism is a very clear expression of the Enlightenment, the British empirical philosophical tradition, and the success of science.[4] Logical positivism has been persuasive in Western culture and has influenced also how modern history is written in the discipline's drive for facts that can be supported by evidence. Karen Armstrong calls this use of reason and empirical way of thinking *logos*, "the rational, pragmatic, and scientific thought that enabled men and women to function well in the world."[5]

If the only *meaningful* statements are those that are scientifically or mathematically verifiable, and if ethical statements are only *emotionalism*, then one cannot say if the Holocaust or slavery or torture or any human rights abuse is wrong, or right. Any ethical statement is thus of no consequence in terms of truth or human meaning. Many, including myself, would thus argue that logical

---

[2] For definitions of terms here I am helped by the following: *Utopianism*—social dreaming; *Utopia*—a nonexistent society described in considerable detail and normally located in time and space. In standard usage utopia is used both as defined here and as an equivalent for eutopia; *Eutopia* or *positive utopia*—a nonexistent society described in considerable detail and normally located in time and space that the author intended a contemporaneous reader to view as considerably better than the society in which the reader lived; *Dystopia* or *negative utopia*—a nonexistent society described in considerable detail and normally located in time and space that the author intended a contemporaneous reader to view as considerably worse than the society in which the reader lived. Taken from Lyman Tower Sargent, "In Defense of Utopia," *Diogenes* 53, no. 1 (February 2006): 15.

[3] A. J. Ayer (1910–89) popularized logical positivism in the English-speaking world by his book *Language, Truth and Logic* (1936) that he wrote when only twenty-four years old (Edward N. Zalta, ed., *Stanford Encyclopedia of Philosophy*, "Alfred Jules Ayer," [Stanford: Stanford University, 2008], <http://plato.stanford.edu/entries/ayer/#7> [accessed November 25, 2008]).

[4] A good summary of logical positivism is found in the entry for logical positivism in Anthony Flew, ed., *A Dictionary of Philosophy* (London: Pan Books, 1979), 214–15.

[5] Karen Armstrong, *The Battle for God—A History of Fundamentalism* (Ballantine Books, New York, 2001), xvi.

positivism on its own is an inadequate philosophy. As Karen Armstrong puts it, *logos* cannot answer what is the ultimate value of human life, or explain the meaning of life.[6]

If logical positivism or *logos* is not enough, what else do we need for the sake of our fuller humanity? I want to suggest that we need to know ethical truths that make for the flourishing of humanity and the earth. We need to understand the meaning of life in order to deal with life. These truths are not verifiable by science or logical reasoning. Nor can they be expressed in algebraic formulas. Only story or *mythos*, told orally first and then written down and tested by generations of human experience, can create and explore wise answers to our ultimate human questions.

Armstrong argues that in the premodern world both *mythos* and *logos* were regarded as essential, but in the modern world we have written off *mythos* as superstition.[7] In fact we do not understand *mythos* in the modern world with any insight or respect for its role. It is dismissed along with fairy tales. The great temptation for some modern religious believers, devoid of any understanding of *mythos*, and possessing an inadequate understanding of science, is to attempt to turn scripture into facts, or scientifically provable statements. This is the project of fundamentalists who betray both faith and science in pursuing their mistaken ends. In confusing *mythos* with *logos*, religious fundamentalists think they are able to repel the assault of science on faith by the use of science. The result includes, for example, attempts to teach creationism. When absolutized, this can also lead to launching jihadism or crusade—violence against others—and betrayal of the finest insights of the faith itself. Fundamentalism in the Latter Day Saint traditions includes a major preoccupation with Book of Mormon archeology, and that, I suggest, can only get us in trouble. Thus I want to argue that there should be two wheels on our religious bicycle, one called *logos* and the other *mythos*. The wheel missing at present is *mythos*.

So I argue for rediscovering the importance of *mythos* in our lives, to read stories that help us perceive mystery beyond our senses, intimations of Spirit, to be grasped by prophetic imagination, and be caught by what is truly meaningful. Understanding *mythos* rightly is how we should read not only the Bible but also the Book of Mormon. Indeed, I want in the rest of this paper to connect the prophetic imagination of Joseph Smith Jr. with the *mythos* of eutopian and dystopian visions in the pages of this controversial Latter Day Saint scripture.

---

[6] Armstrong, *The Battle for God*, xvii.

[7] Armstrong, *The Battle for God*, xvi–xvii.

Like Thomas More's *Utopia*,[8] the Book of Mormon is set in the New World. For More, the good society he was describing was contemporary in time to his, just separate geographically. When More was writing, the Americas had been discovered by Europeans less than twenty-five years and a great deal was unknown for Europeans in that continent. For Smith, writing in the late 1820s, the Americas had been explored and inhabited by Europeans for over three centuries, but the past was still a big mystery. So Smith creates a utopian saga set far back in the past, but with meaning for his day, about hope for a better future. The Book of Mormon, whilst set in the past like a historical novel, is not about ancient history; rather it is about criticizing the present by dreaming of a better world in the future.

More's *Utopia* is written in a clever way that enables him, through literary devices, to be merely the "reporter" of conversations that describe the island of Utopia whilst protecting More from being identified as author of forceful criticisms of English and European societies—particularly dangerous when Henry VIII was monarch. Smith's literary device is the use of Mormon, the general, scholar, and prophetic leader, who is the abridger of the plates and commentator at points throughout the story. Mormon, the narrator, is Smith, very cleverly hidden. The reader has to confront directly Smith's story with its impressive narrator, not the semiliterate, treasure-seeking farm boy Smith who is much less impressive than the fictional Mormon and would thus be more easily dismissed.

In fact, Thomas More is more like Mormon than Joseph Smith is. Smith is writing on the margins of his society as a semiliterate farm laborer. More is upper class, knighted *Sir* Thomas, a brilliant scholar who collaborated with Erasmus, and was later to rise to great prominence in 1529–32 as Lord Chancellor under King Henry VIII. Both Smith and More were deeply religious men, and both are influenced by Acts chapter 2 with its descriptions of the first Christian community in Jerusalem living in the Holy Spirit with all things in common. Smith reads it directly in the Bible; More also finds it embodied in the monastic tradition which he admired. Both seek a more Christian society, More in Europe, Smith in America. Both meet violent deaths. More is beheaded because out of conscience he resists King Henry's divorce and remarriage. Smith is assassinated because of the vision he seeks to realize in distorted ways in militant and polygamous Nauvoo, Illinois, 1839–44.

The Book of Mormon tells the stories of different peoples who came, like Smith's ancestors, to the promised land of the Americas. The Book of Mormon peoples, like the Pilgrim Fathers, were people of faith too. The Book of Mormon

---

[8] Thomas More, *Utopia*, trans. Paul Turner (London, Penguin Books, 1961).

story centers, for the most part, around Israelites who migrated about 600 BCE and whose descendents became the people of Nephi and also the Lamanites. Smith's story allows the descendents of the Lamanites to be recognized by his contemporaries as the Native peoples of the Americas, who according to the Book of Mormon are part of God's covenanted people and should be respected not despised. Like Smith's gentile neighbors these people of Israelite stock need to find their way back to the God of their ancestors to be included in the fold of God. The purpose of the text is set out in the preface: "to the convincing of the Jew and Gentile that Jesus is the Christ, the Eternal God, manifesting himself unto all nations." An important theme in the utopian vision of the Book of Mormon is thus the inclusion of both Jews and Native Americans with Europeans in the fold of God and the promise of Zion, the kingdom of God on earth. This contrasts starkly with the genocidal practices of most European descendents as the frontier moved west. Professor Seth D. Kunin, anthropologist and trained as a rabbi, has argued that in the mythemes of the Book of Mormon there are no permanent outsiders.[9]

The path to utopia consistently described in the Book of Mormon is that of faith in Christ: "And we talk of Christ, we rejoice in Christ, we preach of Christ, we prophesy of Christ, and write according to our prophecies, that our children may look for a remission of their sins (II Nephi 11:48). "Feast upon the words of Christ; for, behold the words of Christ will tell you all things that you should do" (II Nephi 14:4).

Like More's Utopia, the story of the Book of Mormon also criticizes Smith's contemporary society. Consider what historian Nathan Hatch incisively says in his book *The Democratization of American Christianity*: "The Book of Mormon is a document of profound social protest, an impassioned manifesto by a hostile outsider against the smug complacency of those in power and the reality of social distinctions based on wealth, class, and education."[10]

Karl Sandberg takes this theme further when he writes:

> In fact, if we attend carefully to the Book of Mormon ... what we have is a letter to the dispossessed and the sore beset. The dispossessed are the remnant of the house of Israel, as we read on the title page, the scattered and uprooted descendants of those what had once been the family of God and who were

---

[9] Seth D. Kunin, personal communication with the author. See also Seth D. Kunin, "The Death/Rebirth Mytheme in the Book of Mormon," *Mormon Identities in Transition*, ed. Douglas J. Davies (London, Cassell, 1996), 192–203. Kunin was at the University of Nottingham in the UK when I was in contact with him 1995–97, but is now at the University of Durham as executive dean of the Faculty of Arts and Humanities.

[10] Nathan O. Hatch, *The Democratization of American Christianity* (New Haven: Yale University Press, 1989), 115–16.

now to be gathered back into the family of God through the Gospel of Christ. The sore beset are those alienated from society, the outcasts and the down-and-outers, the humble seekers after Christ who are threatened by unbelief and unbelievers and false teachings, all of which threatened the collapse of the world. The Book of Mormon is about those who feel the foundations of the world are shaking and who are looking for bedrock. It is a book responding to the rupture and dislocation of modern times.[11]

So faith in Christ is inseparably connected with just treatment of the poor. For instance King Benjamin's great sermon on conversion includes these words: "I would that you should impart of your substance to the poor, every man according to that which he has, such as feeding the hungry" (Mosiah 2:43). The covenant of baptism includes being willing "to bear one another's burdens that they may be light" (Mosiah 9:39). The spiritual practice of continual prayer cannot be separated from practical acts of mercy to those in need (Alma 16:219–24).[12]

There are battles and rumors of war among the Nephites and Lamanites and one can easily become ambushed by all the violence in Alma and Helaman where wars seem to continue endlessly.[13] There is a path to Utopia clearly described in the first three quarters of the book but Utopia is far from realized and the path is not convincing. Then the reader is brought to the coming of Christ, announced by a new star and light all night at his birth, and earthquakes, destruction, and darkness at his crucifixion.

The description of the appearance of the resurrected Christ in light and slow descent from heaven can so capture the reader that they also want to join the Nephites in adoration and address him as the "Most High God!" in worship (III Nephi 5:17). Jesus begins by teaching about peace in the church and baptism (III Nephi 5:23–47) and then he teaches a slightly reworked version of the Sermon on the Mount that retains all its radical implications for discipleship (III Nephi 5:48–6:37). There is healing (III Nephi 8:6–11) and a wonderful reworked account of the blessing of children, followed by communion, prayer, church discipline, and ordination of the twelve disciples (III Nephi 5:12–27, 28–46, 47–52, 53–68, 69–75). In the remaining chapters of III Nephi there are baptisms, passages from Isaiah quoted, and further counsel by Jesus.

---

[11] Karl C. Sandberg, "Masonry and the Making of Mormonism" (presentation, Mormon History Association 1995 Conference, Queens University, Kingston, Canada, May 1995).

[12] For more on the theme of justice for the poor in the Bible, Book of Mormon, and Doctrine and Covenants, see my unpublished paper "Economic and Social Justice in the Early Restoration—the Epistemological Privilege of the Poor" (obtainable from the author).

[13] For a survey of violence and nonviolence in the Book of Mormon see Andrew Bolton, "The Book of Mormon—An Asset or Liability for Becoming a Peace Church?" *John Whitmer Historical Association Journal* 19 (1999): 29–42.

It is in IV Nephi 1:1–26 that utopia is fully come and lasts approximately two hundred years. The story here is of conversion, all things common, human equality, blessed marriages, and peace in the land because of the love of God that dwelt in the hearts of the people. This account of utopia (which could also be called realized eschatology, Zion, or the kingdom of God on earth) is an imaginative reworking of Acts 2 and 4:31–35. Finally, utopia is realized, as eutopia, a good place.

The fall of utopia comes quickly and is described in the remainder of IV Nephi 1:27–59. The dystopia (bad place) that results, as people abandon Jesus and become divided into classes and resume the violence of war, is vividly described in tragic detail in the words of Mormon (Mormon chapters 1–3). Mormon perishes with all his people and his son Moroni, in lonely anguish, concludes the story (Mormon chapter 4). This is immediately followed by the description of another dystopia in the Book of Ether where two rival peoples with common ancestry destroy each other. Two longer accounts of dystopia after a brief account of eutopia reinforce a clear message: follow the teaching of Jesus fully or end up destroying yourselves.

The first subversive act in any society is imagining a better one. Old Testament scholar Walter Brueggemann speaks of prophetic imagination.[14] I want to suggest that imagination of a just world is the first prophetic action. The exodus of slaves from Egypt to a land of milk and honey had first to be a burning imaginative vision before it could be a reality (Exodus 3:1–10). We have to first of all imagine swords being beaten into plowshares before nations in reality disarm (Isaiah 2:2–4). We have to imagine Eden and then the restoration of Eden, when wolf will lie down with lamb, and a little child leading them, before a world is created safe for all children (Isaiah 11). The monastic movement, Anabaptist Hutterians, the early Latter Day Saints' United Order, and many other communal Christian movements have all been born by reading and reimagining Luke's account of the coming of the Holy Spirit at the first Pentecost and living all things in common in Acts chapter 2. In another paper I have described the powerful formative influence of Acts 2 and Acts 4:31–35 in early Latter Day Saintism in the Kirtland era 1830–37 and its new scriptures.[15] Utopian writing is that leap of prophetic imagination that criticizes the present order by imagining a new order. Zion in other words has to first be imagined before it can be.

---

[14] Walter Brueggemann, *The Prophetic Imagination*, 2nd ed. (Minneapolis: Fortress Press, 2001).

[15] Andrew Bolton, "Pentecost and All things Common—Acts 2 and 4:31–33 as Template for Community in Kirtland, Ohio, 1830–1837," *Restoration Studies* X (2009): 57–77.

Science can help us predict some elements of a possible future by extrapolating trends from what is happening now. The consequences of global warming and climate change are a good example here. Past performance, though, does not necessarily predict future performance and, as statisticians say, "Thou shalt not extrapolate!" Indeed, only utopian imagination can help us envision new, more just, less violent, and sustainable ways of living. In telling, creating, and recreating utopian myths we are helped to imagine a more humane and green future. Without imagination, we cannot avoid the potential hells or embrace the possible heavens in our future.

What is not yet cannot be expressed scientifically or factually because it is still unknown. That is perhaps why Jesus used parables and made up stories, to help us imagine the kingdom of God that is still future, still yet to be. That is perhaps why at the height of the US civil rights movement, Martin Luther King Jr. preaches, "I have a dream" to rally people to the cause of making racial equality a reality. Equality has first of all to be dreamed before it can become a reality. *Mythos* enables us to share dreams, parables, and stories of what is not yet, so it can yet be. In this way the Book of Mormon is parable, a dream, an inspired prophetic imagination, to help us hope, faith, and work for a better day. The utopian vision in the Book of Mormon is like an icon that points beyond itself to something more—the possibility of the kingdom of God on earth. The model of Zion described briefly in IV Nephi refers to a future event, as an architect's plans precede a new building. The utopian vision in the Book of Mormon hangs as a new picture of possibility in the gallery of our minds.[16]

The path to utopia and utopia itself in the Book of Mormon is described clearly and in vivid detail in terms of Christian discipleship. Nothing is said of practical mechanisms and systems for realizing utopia. However, this is the essence of *mythos*, to cast a vision of possibilities. It also means that the utopian vision is not quickly dated by time or technology, because it is not tied to the *logos* thinking of a particular age. The actual implementation of Zion requires *logos*, practical reasoning and testing of what works and does not work with frail and never fully converted humans. Both *logos* and *mythos* are necessary for realizing utopia—we need both as wheels on our bicycle of hope. Using only *mythos* or converting *mythos* into *logos* only gets us into trouble. To go to Native Americans and tell them that the Book of Mormon is their ancient history is a form of mental colonization. This changes the message of the Book of Mormon dramatically. When read as *mythos*, the book is declaring the dignity and humanity of Native Americans, Jews, and all people. All are equal, declares Jacob, for "one being is as precious in [God's] sight as the other" (Jacob 2:27). When

---

[16] Thanks to Dale Luffman for this image of "hanging pictures in the gallery of our minds."

read as ancient history by white people unconsciously or consciously racist, it becomes oppressive and dystopian when foisted on marginalized ethnicities as their real history.[17]

Evaluation of a particular utopian *mythos,* incarnated through *logos* in human experience, is always in terms of its fruits, to quote Jesus (Matthew 7:15–20).[18] "Is there real potential here for the flourishing for all humans in a greening earth?" is a key question of evaluation of any utopian vision. It is also important to be critical of utopian visions and amend them. For example in the Book of Mormon the voice of women is very limited. Nearly two centuries after the publication of the Book of Mormon many of us think a better utopia is the full inclusion of women with equal voice and ministry.

Our situation at present in the Community of Christ is that both liberals and conservatives misunderstand the nature of myth and the use of science/ archeology in their treatment of the Book of Mormon. Both often neglect to pay serious attention to the story in the text. We need a third way in order to take seriously the prophetic, utopian imagination of Smith expressed through the Book of Mormon story. In the Community of Christ we might then be able to find a deeper connection, both with the founding experiences of our movement and our contemporary mission of fostering "signal communities of justice and peace that reflect the vision of Christ."[19]

Nowhere does the Book of Mormon say to dig in archeological sites to find the truth of its message—for truth is not there. The only promise of establishing the spiritual truth of the Book of Mormon is to be found by reading Moroni 10: 4–5; that is to pray, having faith in Christ. The answer to openness and prayer is the testimony of the Holy Spirit that following Christ fully is the key to a better world—for that is the message of this book of scripture.

In conclusion, it is interesting to note that Dr. Timothy Miller, an academic authority on communal societies, working at the University of Kansas, argues that the "Latter Day Saint movement has created one of the most widely distributed

---

[17] Many thanks for conversations with John Glaser, Don Compier, and Joy Persall. Joy Persall's account growing up as a Native American church member is deeply disturbing, as she describes dealing with the messages given to her as a child; that her skin and the skin of her family would turn white as they became more righteous. The result of this was feeling that she and her family were left out of the hope of Zion since her skin pigmentation did not change.

[18] For one approach to evaluate the success of a utopian community, see also Don Pitzer, "Developmental Communalism—An Alternative Approach to Communal Studies," *Utopian Thought and Communal Experience,* ed. Dennis Hardy and Lorna Davidson (Enfield, England: Middlesex Polytechnic, 1989).

[19] Doctrine and Covenants 163:5a.

and long-lived tapestries of intentional communities in world history."[20] I want to suggest that it is at least in part due to the utopian imagination fostered by the Book of Mormon.

---

[20] Timothy Miller, "Social roots of the Mormon United Order" (presentation, Centers for Studies on New Religions [CESNUR] 2005 International Conference, Palermo, Sicily, June 4, 2005, <http://www.cesnur.org/2005/pa_miller.htm> [accessed November 26, 2008]).

Sacred Spaces, Imagined Geographies, Invisible Cities

G. ST. JOHN STOTT

Rarely does the eye light upon a thing, and then only when it has recognized that thing as a sign of another thing: a print in the sand indicates the tiger's passage; a marsh announces a vein of water; the hibiscus flower, the end of winter. All the rest is silent and interchangeable; trees and stones are only what they are.[1]

—Italo Calvino

Sacred Spaces

REPORTS OF RELIGIOUS experience—accounts of how people believe that divine or supernatural power broke through into their world—are usually given a location in time and space. Even if some details are lost in transmission to later generations, those fresh from the experience usually do not hesitate to give at least some account of when and where their lives were changed. Saul, for example (to begin with the most famous and defining vision in the Christian tradition), told Ananias that the vision that had left him blind and helpless had occurred at a certain time (three days before they met) and at a certain place (on the road from Jerusalem). We might, of course, question whether this conversation took place,[2] but if we do—if we take the story seriously

---

[1] Italo Calvino, *Invisible Cities* (1972), trans. William Weaver (London: Vintage, 1997), x.

[2] From one perspective, because it goes against the implications of Acts 9:17; from another because, given the contradiction between what Luke reports and Paul's own accounts in Galatians

enough to question its details—it is because we know that in the first century CE there was a road between Jerusalem and Damascus, and that it is not *prima facie* impossible that a zealot for the law would travel it in order to suppress outbreaks of heresy. And even if we think that last claim is too strong, and we question whether Saul's authority as a Pharisee would really have extended as far as Damascus,[3] we can legitimately raise the question because Luke's account can be set against a specific sociocultural background, and therefore read (or disputed) as history.[4]

This interest in a particular stopping point on a particular road might be thought theologically unsound, in that all space is sacred.[5] Nevertheless, in our personal and cultural memories "some parts of space are qualitatively different from others"[6] (in some cases because of personal experience, in others because the stories associated with them define and legitimate the religious experience of the culture to which we belong), and our comfort in reading or hearing those stories increases if their physical geography can be identified. Although, as David Henige has observed, the ability to assign a location to a place does not *ipso facto* increase the probability that what we read of its history is true[7]—just because we think we know where Bethany was does not necessarily mean that we can or should believe the story of the raising of Lazarus[8]—but the *inability* to specify where a place was can be problematic. If the place names used by Luke had not referred to known real-world locations our reading and our response would be different. We might still take him at his word, falling back on an appeal to the

---

1 and I Corinthians 9, we might wonder whether there even was an Ananias. Indeed, even within Acts the importance of Ananias seems to be questioned, in that the more Luke expands Paul's call as apostle to the Gentiles the less scope he allows for Ananias's ministry (Ronald D. Witherup, *Conversion in the New Testament* [Collegeville, MN: Liturgical Press, 1995], 67). That said, if we assume that Saul would have told someone of his experience, "Ananias" can represent that addressee for the purposes of my argument.

[3] Ernst Haenchen, *The Acts of the Apostles: A Commentary*, trans. Bernard Noble and Gerald Shinn (Oxford: Oxford University Press, 1971), 320n2.

[4] The rhetorical dimensions of Luke's account might be thought to invalidate its claims to be taken seriously as a history (see Richard I. Pervo, *Profit with Delight: The Literary Genre of the Acts of the Apostles* [Philadelphia: Fortress Press, 1987]), but Daniel Marguerat's response seems just: Acts is "historiography with an apologetic aim" (*The First Christian Historian: Acts of the Apostles*, Society for New Testament Studies Monograph Series 121, trans. Ken McKinney, Gregory J. Laughery, and Richard Baukham [Cambridge: Cambridge University Press, 2002], 34).

[5] Psalms 104; cf. Deuteronomy 10:14; I Chronicles 29:11; Psalms 24:1, 89:11.

[6] Belden Lane, *Landscapes of the Sacred: Geography and Narrative and American Spirituality* (New York: Paulist Press, 1988), 16.

[7] "'This Is the Place': Putting the Past on the Map," *Journal of Historical Geography* 33, no. 2 (April 2007): 239.

[8] John 11:43–44.

authority of the biblical text (in the words of the children's hymn, "this I know / Because the Bible tells me so"), but our reading of the story would be less certain if we did not know where the apostle was going when his life was changed.

In exploring this connection between stories of religious experience and real-world geography, I am not, however, concerned to consider further what we might make of an unknown road in first-century Palestine (part of a counterfactual history of the apostle Paul). My interest is in Bountiful, the city in the Americas where according to the Book of Mormon the resurrected Christ descends from heaven and ministers to the Nephites (by the book's report, the ancestors of the Native Americans).[9] Surely, by any standard, the place where the resurrected Lord taught crowds of some twenty-five hundred people would count as sacred space, and if its location were known, Bountiful could not help but be a place of reflection and pilgrimage. Unfortunately, however, we cannot walk where Jesus walked in his New World ministry, for we do not know where Bountiful was—even Joseph Smith Jr, who claimed that he had translated the Book of Mormon from a "reformed Egyptian" source, had no idea where it was located—and necessarily this not only frustrates the hopes of would-be pilgrims, it also affects the way we read Smith's work.

Initially, as we might expect, Smith believed that the Nephite homeland was in New York State.[10] Some have thought that his inspiration for the Book of Mormon was triggered by the discovery of an Indian artifact while hiring out as a well-digger and treasure scryer,[11] and if that was the case it would have been natural for him to presume that the site of his *trouvaille* could be associated with the geography of the work. But it would also have been natural to make this association if, as Smith would report, the Book of Mormon was the translation of gold plates whose existence had been revealed to him by an angel. The discovery of the plates near his home would have naturally suggested

---

[9] To be precise, the ancestors of the Indians were the Lamanites, the other party to the civil war that destroyed the Nephites in the fifth century CE. Prior to Christ's coming both Lamanites and Nephites had defined themselves by lineage, tracing their descent from the Lehi who had led his family from Jerusalem at the beginning of Zedekiah's reign. However, after Christ's coming the name indicates political allegiance not lineage, and many (if not all) of these Lamanites would have been descendants of the Nephites ministered to by Christ. For the Book of Mormon account of Christ's New World ministry, see III Nephi 5–13 [11–28]. References to the Book of Mormon are to the 1908 *Authorized Edition* of the Reorganized Church of Jesus Christ of Latter Day Saints (now Community of Christ), followed in square brackets by the equivalent chapter and verse in editions published by The Church of Jesus Christ of Latter-day Saints.

[10] Oliver Cowdery, "Letter VII," *Latter Day Saints' Messenger and Advocate* I, no. 10 (July 1835): 158.

[11] Fawn M. Brodie, *No Man Knows My History: The Life of Joseph Smith, the Mormon Prophet* (New York: Alfred A. Knopf, 1945), 40.

that the Nephites had fought their final battles in upstate New York. Later, however, he would tell his followers that Book of Mormon history unfolded in the Midwest,[12] speculate that the first Nephite settlements had been on the coast of Chile,[13] and then in 1843 announce that the ruins of Yucatan explored by John Stephens were Nephite in origin. "Mr. Stephens' great developments [sic] of antiquities are made bare to the eyes of all the people by reading the history of the Nephites in the Book of Mormon," Smith would explain. "They lived about the narrow neck of land, which now embraces Central America."[14] (Excited by what he had read, he now believed that the Nephites' landing had been in the Isthmus of Darien.) Smith, we can conclude, uncritically took evidence of past Amerindian cultures, wherever found, as evidence for the truth of his translation—and understandably so. If, as he believed, the Book of Mormon really was the history of the ancestors of the American Indian, then the mounds he explored in Illinois had to have been the remains "of that once beloved people of the Lord,"[15] and so for that matter did the ruins he read about in Stephens' 1841 work, *Incidents of Travel in Central America.*

Smith's followers, no doubt alert to the apologetic potential of setting Book of Mormon narratives against the background of the Mayan structures of Yucatan, generally ignored other locations in favor of Mesoamerica. "Now, since that invaluable book made its appearance in print," Apostle Orson Pratt boasted as early as 1848, referring to the Book of Mormon, "it is a remarkable fact the mouldering ruins of many splendid edifices and towers, and magnificent cities of great extent, have been discovered by Catherwood and Stephens in the interior wilds of Central America, in the very region where the ancient cities described in the Book of Mormon were said to exist."[16] However, despite such optimism, and the allied conviction that a Book of Mormon geography can be

---

[12] As when the area south of modern Valley City, Illinois, was identified with the Book of Mormon city of Desolation (Kenneth W. Godfrey, "What Is the Significance of Zelph in the Study of Book of Mormon Geography?" *Journal of Book of Mormon Studies* 8, no. 2 [1999]: 70–79).

[13] James A. Little and Franklin D. Richards, *A Compendium of the Doctrines of the Gospel* (Salt Lake City: Deseret News, 1882), 289.

[14] "Extract: From Stephens' 'Incidents of Travel in Central America,'" *Times and Seasons* III, no. 22 (September 15, 1842): 915.

[15] Dean Jessee, *The Personal Writings of Joseph Smith* (Salt Lake City: Deseret Book, 1984), 324; Scott Kenney, ed., Wilford Woodruff Journals, 9 vols. (Salt Lake City: Signature Books, 1983–84), 1:10.

[16] Orson Pratt, *Divine Authority, or the Question, Was Joseph Smith Sent of God?* (Liverpool: R. James, 1848), 13. The Yucatan thesis had received greater publicity than the others as Smith's praise of Catherwood and Stephens had been published in a church newspaper, whereas earlier theses had just been *ad hoc* suggestions on the prophet's part.

constructed ("A careful reader of that interesting book," Pratt wrote, "can trace the relative bearings and distances of many of these cities from each other; and ... determine, very nearly, the precise spot of ground they once occupied"), generations of Mormon archaeologists have failed to find Bountiful, or indeed any other location named in Smith's work.

This failure is perhaps little other than we might expect. As Dee F. Green has noted, "no Book of Mormon location is known with reference to modern topography,"[17] and the consequences of this should be obvious. I will point to two. First, we cannot read the Book of Mormon as a work of geography. (A text can only be read geographically when it can be mapped onto known locations or geographical features.) Second, we cannot read it as a work of history. A text can only be read historically when it can be read against other texts (broadly construed to include all artifactual evidence)[18]—and largely because of the problem of geography, we cannot do that in the present case. We cannot even begin to talk meaningfully of Nephite history because we do not know where the Nephites lived.

Some might disagree, arguing that we can trust the work's historicity because of the witness of the Spirit, but that is to confuse testimony and historiography. If we would read a text as a historical document then, as Jon D. Levenson observes, the interpretative arguments offered "must be historically valid, able, that is, to compel the assent of *historians* whatever their religion or lack thereof, whatever their backgrounds, spiritual experiences, or personal beliefs, and without privileging any claim of revelation"[19]—and in the case of the Book of Mormon the task is beyond us. To argue thus is not to dismiss the importance

---

[17] "Book of Mormon Archaeology: the Myths and the Alternatives," *Dialogue: A Journal of Mormon Thought* 4, no. 2 (Winter 1969): 77–78; Hugh Nibley, *An Approach to the Book of Mormon* (Salt Lake City: Deseret Book, 1964), 370. Several authors have claimed Book of Mormon cities can be mapped onto real-world locations (John L. Sorenson gives a summary of the principal theories in *The Geography of Book of Mormon Events: A Source Book* [Provo, UT: FARMS, 1990]), but their accounts differ widely and none have led to the discovery of archeological evidence for the existence of Book of Mormon peoples.

[18] We can provisionally work without artifactual and textual evidence when we have geographical coordinates for a narrative (stories of the biblical David provide a case in point—see P. Deryn Guest, "The Historical Approach in Crisis? Fact, Fiction and Current Debate in Old Testament Study," *Scripture Bulletin* 27, no. 2 [July 1997]: 42–54), but this is impossible for the Book of Mormon. For the difficulty of reading without these coordinates, consider the disorienting beginning of Italo Calvino's account of the journey to Diomira—"Leaving there, and proceeding three days towards the east"—where "there" is undefined: *Invisible Cities*, 7.

[19] *The Hebrew Bible, the Old Testament, and Historical Criticism: Jews and Christians in Biblical Studies* (Louisville, KY: Westminster / John Knox Press, 1993), 109 (italics in original). Levenson rightly notes that that the value-neutrality of the historical approach makes it difficult to defend the value of the enterprise itself, but my concern here is not to determine whether there is value in the study of the Book of Mormon, but what is entailed in reading it as history.

of testimony, or to seek to subject everything to scientific proof. William Alston puts it well: one "can form beliefs that make claims about objective reality, and thus possess a truth value, without having any idea of how they could be tested by sense perception."[20] However, the warrant provided by the witness of the Spirit does not play a part in the discourse of history, not even in the case of the Nephite record.

We have, of course, traditionally read Moroni 10 as an invitation to us to pray over the nature of the work (its truthfulness, and therefore its historicity),[21] but we have misread it in doing so. Smith no doubt knew that he would be expected to provide evidence for his inspiration. If a man claims to have received revelation, Richard Watson explained in 1825, "his belief has no authority to command *ours*. He may actually have received it but we have not the means of knowing it without *proof*." He needed, Watson continued, "some external authentication of his mission."[22] We can expect Smith to have been familiar with this line of thought and perhaps even to have known Watson's text, which was the standard work of Methodist theology in early nineteenth-century America,[23] but we should not therefore presume that he would have thought that Moroni's words promised the validation his calling needed. Although the Spirit confirms what is true, the truth of the Book of Mormon message lies in its witness to Christ and advocacy of a life of discipleship—a truth discovered experientially as people prayerfully respond to its message "and walk uprightly before God"[24]—not in its being an ancient American history.[25]

---

[20] *Perceiving God: The Epistemology of Religious Experience* (Ithaca, NY: Cornell University Press, 1991), 224.

[21] Moroni 10:4–5 [10:4–5].

[22] J. M. Clintock, ed., *Theological Institutes; or, A View of the Evidences, Doctrines, Morals and Institutions of Christianity* (1825–1829), 2 vols. (New York: Carlton & Porter, 1850), 1:71.

[23] For Smith's interest in Methodism, see Orasmus Turner, *Pioneer History of the Holland Purchase of Western New York, including Some Account of the Ancient Remains* (Buffalo, NY: Jewett, Thomas & Co., 1851), 214; Linda K. Newell and Valeen T. Avery, *Mormon Enigma: Emma Hale Smith* (Urbana: University of Illinois Press, 1994), 25.

[24] Moroni 7:14–15, 10:6 [7:16, 10:6]; Ether 1:106 [4:11–12]); I Nephi 5:3 [16:3]; G. St. John Stott, "A Conjectural Reading of the *Book of Mormon*," *Forum for Modern Language Studies* 42, no. 4 (October 2006): 453.

[25] This would have been obvious to those of the book's first readers who were interested in ministry to Native Americans, for missionaries would teach "that the Spirit of [the] 'Great Father' would enable those who currently asked him, to know and feel that [their] preaching was true" (R. D. Smith to the [Methodist] *Christian Advocate and Journal and Zion's Herald* 12 [June 1829]: 41). The need to evaluate separately the theological content of the Book of Mormon and Smith's claims to have translated a pre-Columbian text was established by Joseph Smith III as early as 20 January 1883 (Joseph Smith III to R. Patterson, 20 January 1883, *Saints' Herald*, [17 March 1883]: 30, no.11 [17 March 1883]: 162).

The witness of the Spirit does not excuse us from the historian's task, and that being so, in reflecting on this task, we might remember the observation of R. G. Collingwood that "a given statement made by a given author, must never be accepted for historical truth until the credibility of the author in general and of this statement in particular had been systematically inquired into"; until the author has been "placed ... in the witness-box for cross examination." (This is particularly the case, Collingwood argued, when "our witness alleges a fact wholly without analogy in our own experience"—which is surely true of the Book of Mormon.)[26] Without evidence that links the work to specific locations in Mesoamerica or elsewhere,[27] we cannot apply Collingwood's standards to a discussion of Smith's translation. As noted above, we cannot read the Book of Mormon as history. We can only read it as we would read a fiction—without presuming reference.

Imagined Geographies

To read a work "as we would read a fiction" is not, I hasten to add, to read it having identified it *as* a fiction. That might be thought surprising, for our way of reading follows from the way we have identified our text.[28] Consider something as simple as a reference to a place: to London, say, or New York—or Bountiful. The context in which we read of a city or town changes the way we think of it, as the French literary critic Jean Roudaut notes: we take a reference to a city in a work of geography to be a reference to a place which has architectural form, and political and economic organization, even if its name is unknown to us; but we take a "real" city referred to in a work of fiction to be imaginary within that fiction.[29] However, to read a work as a work of fiction is not necessarily

---

[26] *The Principles of History and Other Writings in Philosophy of History*, ed. W. H. Dray and W. J. van der Dussen (Oxford: Oxford University Press, 1999), 14; *The Idea of History* (Oxford: Oxford University Press, 1946), 137.

[27] In theory the Ancient Near East background to the Book of Mormon *is* definable, as we know the time and place where its narrative begins. However, although there have been some interesting studies of the setting of the first chapters of I Nephi (the most ambitious being the essays in John W. Welch, David Rolph Seely, and Jo Ann H. Seely, eds., *Glimpses of Lehi's Jerusalem* [Provo, UT: Neal A. Maxwell Institute, 2004]), there are too many outstanding problems for us to say that Lehi's Jerusalem is recognizable.

[28] Hans Robert Jauss, *Toward an Aesthetic of Reception*, trans. Timothy Bahti (Minneapolis: University of Minnesota Press, 1982), 39; cf. Siegfried J. Schmidt, "Towards a Pragmatic Interpretation of 'Fictionality,'" *Pragmatics of Language and Literature*, ed. Teun A. van Dijk (Amsterdam: North Holland Publishing Company, 1976), 163.

[29] *Les Villes imaginaires dans la littérature française: les douze portes* (Paris: Hatier, 1990), 39. Consider Phillip Pullman's *His Dark Materials* trilogy (published 1995–2000). Obviously enough, Lyra's Oxford cannot be visited (after all, it is in a different world to ours); but neither

to make a judgment about its reference in the way that Roudaut suggests we do. As Kendall L. Walton has noted, we can choose "to accept the insight and stimulation [texts] offer without bothering to evaluate their veridicality.... We may want to understand a story as fiction, as prescribing imaginings. We still need not decide if it is true or even ask."[30] Given the problems noted above, I suggest that that is the stance we should adopt toward the Book of Mormon.

My reasons for arguing thus should not be misunderstood. For nearly two hundred years polemicists have happily seized upon the failure of Book of Mormon scholarship to provide evidence that the work is the history that it claims to be, and then used this as a bridgehead from which to challenge the work's status as latter-day scripture. However, this is a battle I am not interested in joining. My present interest is in *how* we read the Book of Mormon, not what it is that we are reading.[31] However, that said, it is impossible to remain completely above the fray. Although I do not want to pursue here the question of the work's historicity, I cannot ignore all the questions that are raised by Smith's testimony. Given the variations in his references to Book of Mormon geography noted above, it would be easy to question the seriousness with which

---

can Will's Oxford. It too is imaginary, even though its geography is in many ways similar to that of the real-world university city.

[30] *Mimesis as Make-Believe: On the Foundations of the Representational Arts* (Cambridge, MA: Harvard University Press, 1990), 98—see also his "Fearing Fictions," *Journal of Philosophy* 75, no. 1 (1978): 5–27; cf. Gregory Currie, *The Nature of Fiction* (Cambridge: Cambridge University Press, 1990), 24. Note also the observation of R. Pack, *Wallace Stevens: An Approach to His Poetry and Thought* (New Brunswick, NJ: Rutgers University Press, 1958), 122—"the opposite of 'fiction' is not 'truth' but 'fact.'"

[31] Remembering the contention that the "surest thing we know about Jesus" in the synoptic gospels "is that he positively would not let people *define* him, would not let them say *who* or *what* he was, before they had grasped the values represented in his words and deeds" (Juan Luis Segundo, *Jesus of Nazareth Yesterday and Today*, 5 vols., trans. John Drury [Maryknoll, NY: Orbis Books, 1984–88], 2:16 [italics in original]), I believe that we would do better seeking to grasp the values of the Book of Mormon before worrying about what it is. However, if we have to call it *something* in the meantime, I would suggest "para-biblical literature." I take the term from H. L. Ginsberg, "Review of Joseph A. Fitzmyer's *The Genesis Apocryphon of Qumran Cave 1: A Commentary*," *Theological Studies* 28 (1967): 574, though given Ginsberg's distinguishing such literature from midrash I accept that the fit might be questioned. For an approach to the Book of Mormon as midrash, see Anthony Chvala-Smith, "The Spirit, the Book, and the City: Retrieving the Distinctive Voice of the Restoration," *John Whitmer Historical Association Journal* 19 (1999): 25; for *midrash* as "the rabbis' reconstruction of God's word to the Jewish people and not the rabbis' reconstruction of what happened in the biblical past," see Chaim Milikowsky, "Midrash as Fiction and Midrash as History: What did the Rabbis Mean?," *Ancient Fictions: The Matrix of Early Christian and Jewish Narrative*, ed. Jo-Ann A. Brant, Charles W. Hedrickand, and Chris Shea (Atlanta, GA: Society for Biblical Literature, 2005), 125; Jacob Neusner, *Midrash as Literature: The Primacy of Documentary Discourse*, Studies in Judaism (Lanham, MD: University Press of America, 1987), 14.

he made them; and if that *is* questioned (if, for example, it is thought that Smith was making things up as he went along) then the very idea of taking time to discuss the geography of his work might seem strange. I cannot fully address this question here, but I do need to make three points. First, as Marvin S. Hill pointed out many years ago, what ever else we might want to add to the mix of Smith's character, we misjudge the prophet if we deny him religious seriousness.[32] There is no reason to presume that he did not take his gifts and calling to heart.

Second, although forensically desirable, consistency is not to be expected of testimony unless there are external constraints requiring it, and Smith was not likely to have been aware of any such. As Walter J. Ong noted, "the abstractly sequential, classificatory, explanatory examination of phenomena or of stated truths" is unlikely without an ongoing engagement with written texts[33]—and though Smith certainly was literate he was more comfortable in an oral world than one of books: dictating his oracles rather than writing them, arguing doctrine with visitors rather than debating in print, basing his theology on what he had just read or heard rather than seeking to integrate his thinking into a systematic whole. When he wanted his thoughts reduced to systematic form, he relied on others.[34] If we remember Peter Laslett's definition of literacy—the ability to "read and write, and record, and refer again, and criticize, and tell others what was the truth of the matter and what should be done about it"[35]—we should recognize that Smith does not use all of the skills Laslett lists. He moves directly from reading to the desire to tell others "the truth of the matter" without bothering to record, reference, and critique.[36] As a result, his teachings were an

---

[32] "Joseph Smith and the 1826 Trial: New Evidence and New Difficulties," *BYU Studies* 12, no. 2 (Winter 1972): 223–34.

[33] *Orality and Literacy: The Technologizing of the Word*, ed. Terence Hawkes (New York: Methuen, 1982), 8–9, 104.

[34] See, for example, John Taylor's reminiscence in his sermon of 31 December 1876, *Journal of Discourses*, 26 vols. (London: Latter-day Saints' Book Depot, 1854–86), 18:330.

[35] *The World We Have Lost Further Explored* (New York: Scribner's, 1984), 233.

[36] Even within the Book of Mormon, it might be remembered, the written text is relatively unimportant. Although it "enlarge[s] the memory" (Alma 17:37 [37:8]), it only rarely serves as a point of engagement. The report that the people of Ammonihah searched "the scriptures" after hearing Alma and Amulek preach (Alma 10:32 [14:1]) provides a rare exception to this generalization, only to raise fresh questions of its own: what is meant here by "scriptures," and what technology of reproduction meant that they *could* be searched? George Reynolds found it enough to reference "the records that contained the holy scriptures" (*The Story of the Book of Mormon* [Chicago: Henry C. Ettin, 1888], 128) but such an approach only begs the question of *which* records, and still leaves "the scriptures" undefined.

exercise in what Claude Lévi-Strauss called *bricolage*[37]—the use of whatever was at hand, the exploitation of ideas gathered by chance from what he had read or heard—and he would have been unlikely to look for consistency in his words. To adopt the formula of Werner Kelber, each testimony would have been an "autonomous speech act"; Smith would not have thought or needed to check one against another.[38]

Of course, there are few statements that can be made about Smith that are uncontroversial, and this is no exception. His use of secretaries to note his actions and words might be seen less as a sign of orality than as evidence for a conscious process of "heroization" (as Foucault noted, "The chronicle of a man, the account of his life, his historiography, written as he lived out his life, [can form] part of the rituals of his power").[39] The possibility merits exploration, but I suspect that we are on a better track with the idea of orality: after all, Smith's reliance on scribes began with the translation of the Book of Mormon, when his use of a seer stone precluded his writing for himself,[40] and it seems to have continued because of his evaluation of the relative effectiveness of speech and writing—in which the latter had lower status. "When a man speaketh by the power of the Holy Ghost," we read in the Book of Mormon, "the power of the Holy Ghost carrieth it unto the hearts of the children of men";[41] there was, however, no such guarantee for the written word and indeed, to make a bad situation worse, prophets could be poor writers.[42]

---

[37] *The Savage Mind* (1962), trans. John Weightman and Doreen Weightman (New York: Oxford University Press, 1996), 19. The term is not being used in a disparaging sense, and would potentially put Smith in good company. Jeffrey Stout has talked of Aquinas as a *bricoleur*— arguing that he made use of the moral resources at his disposal without concern for system-building (*Ethics after Babel* [Princeton: Princeton University Press, 2001])—and though his argument is controversial it can serve to show that talk of *bricolage* should not be taken as a put-down.

[38] Werner H. Kelber, "The Case of the Gospels: Memory's Desire and the Limits of Historical Criticism," *Oral Tradition* 17, no. 1 (2002): 64.

[39] *Discipline and Punish: The Birth of the Prison* (1977), trans. A. Sheridan, *The Foucault Reader*, ed. P. Rabinov (New York: Pantheon Books), 203.

[40] See G. St. John Stott, "The Seer Stone Controversy: Writing the *Book of Mormon*," *Mosaic: A Journal for the Interdisciplinary Study of Literature* 19, no. 3 (1986): 36–53.

[41] II Nephi 15:1 [33:1]; cf. Romans 10:17 ("faith comes by hearing").

[42] Like Mormon (Ether 5:23, 40 [12:23, 40]), Smith recognized his weakness as a writer: Jessee, *Personal Writings of Joseph Smith*, 287; Revelation to Joseph Smith Jr., dated November 1831, *Book of Doctrine and Covenants* (Independence, MO: Community of Christ, 2000), 67:2a [67:5– 7 in LDS editions; also published as Document 74, H. Michael Marquardt, *The Joseph Smith Revelations: Text and Commentary* (Salt Lake City: Signature Books, 1999)]. Arguably such failings did not matter: the calling of a prophet was to declare the word; if others could record, systematize, and "prove" it, so much the better, but that was not the prophet's task. See, for

Needless to say, Smith's orality deserves fuller consideration than is possible in this paper;[43] but I trust it can be seen from this limited treatment that there is no compelling reason to doubt that he serially believed in his geographies, and, trusting his inspiration, was unconcerned to ensure that his ideas cohered. This brings me to my third point: Smith believed that he had the gift of translation.[44] The idea of this gift was no doubt suggested by the reference to that of interpretation of tongues—*hermeneia glossa*—in I Corinthians 12:10. For conservative biblical commentators like Matthew Henry, this was a charisma that gave the gifted the ability "to render foreign languages readily and properly into their own,"[45] and this construction of Paul's words, going back to the second-century assertion in Irenaeus' *Against Heresies* that those "who through the Spirit speak all kinds of languages, and bring to light for the general benefit the hidden things of men, and declare the mysteries of God,"[46] would have hardly needed elaboration for Smith to believe that the words that came to him were not simply inspired but the substance of what had been written in Ancient America. Here too more work is called for, but even in its present form my point should be thought relatively uncontroversial: rightly or wrongly Smith believed that the words that came to him in offering a translation or delivering an oracle were of God. His boast would have been that of Micaiah son of Imlah: "As the LORD liveth, what the LORD saith unto me, that will I speak."[47]

---

example, F. Mark McKiernan and Roger D. Launius, eds., *An Early Latter Day Saint History: The Book of John Whitmer* (Independence, MO: Herald Publishing House, 1980), 31–32.

[43] Thus I do not have space here to discuss the fallibility (and malleability) of memory, though it will have to be considered in a fuller study; for an introduction to the issues in memory research, see Elizabeth Loftus, "Our Changeable Memories: Legal and Practical Implications," *Nature Reviews: Neuroscience* 4, no. 3 (March 2003): 231–34; and neither can I discuss the way Smith's followers' desire to reconcile evidence of Amerindian civilization with the Book of Mormon story could have influenced his testimony, though it too would have an important place in a fuller treatment; for an introduction to the dynamics involved, see Walter Kelber, *The Oral and the Written Gospel*, 2nd ed. (Bloomington: Indiana University Press, 1997), 14–15; G. St. John Stott, "Prophetic Testimony and the Negotiation of Power," *Southern Review: Communication, Politics & Culture* 40, no. 3 (2008): 57–67.

[44] Why he thought there was something to translate lies outside the scope of this paper: for a beginning of an answer, see G. St. John Stott, "Joseph Smith's 1823 Vision: Uncovering the Angel Message," *Religion* 18 (1988): 347–62.

[45] *Matthew Henry's Commentary on the Whole Bible: Complete and Unabridged*, 2nd. ed. (Peabody, MA: Hendrickson, 1991), *ad loc*; Howard A. Snyder, *The Radical Wesley and Patterns for Church Renewal* (Downers Grove, IL: Inter-Varsity Press, 1980), 96. For the Book of Mormon association of this gift with a seer stone, as in Smith's own practice, see Mosiah 5:72, 75 [8:13–14].

[46] Alexander Roberts and James Donaldson, eds., *The Ante-Nicene Fathers: Translations of the Writings of the Fathers down to AD 325*, 10 vols. (1885–97; Peabody, MA: Hendrickson Publishers, 1994), 1:531.

[47] I Kings 22:14.

There is, in short, no reason to presume that the Book of Mormon was *written* as fiction. But that was not what I set out to show. My point was just that without the possibility for real-world reference (or until we can make real-world reference) it should be *read* as such. Here too misunderstanding is possible, so again let me try to make myself clear. I do not propose that we read the Book of Mormon as a novel (that would, as it happens, be a disappointing exercise; as Neal Chandler has pointed out, it lacks the "whole recalcitrant, embarrassing variety of life" that we expect to find in such works[48]—but even if that was not the case such a reading is not what I have in mind). As noted above, in reading a work as fiction, we are simply reading it *without* presuming real-world reference for its place and personal names.

Consider, for a less-charged example of reading without reference, how we might approach Sir Arthur Conan Doyle's "The Problem of Thor Bridge" if we did not already know it to be a short story. The first sentence of Conan Doyle's text is: "Somewhere in the vaults of the bank of Cox and Co., at Charing Cross, there is a travel-worn and battered tin dispatch box with my name, John H. Watson, M.D., Late Indian Army, painted upon the lid." The box contains accounts of cases referred to Sherlock Holmes and written up by Watson, though presumably not that of the death at Thor Bridge (if it is in the hands of its publisher it is not in the vaults of Cox and Company). What are we to make of this? Read in the context of their first publication, as the first sentence of a story published in *The Strand Magazine* for February 1922, we would not hesitate before identifying these words as the beginning of a piece of fiction: but published elsewhere (in a magazine specializing in stories of true detection or popularized forensics, let us suppose), without any attribution to Conan Doyle and without there being other Holmes stories to suggest that Dr. Watson was a nonhistorical character, we might not be so certain. The sentence might strike us as overliterary (for the dispatch box to be just "somewhere" in the vault is arguably too imprecise to be convincing),[49] but Cox and Company of 16 Charing Cross

---

[48] Neil Chandler, "Book of Mormon Stories That My Teachers Kept From Me," *Dialogue: A Journal of Mormon Thought* 24, no. 4 (Winter 1991): 30. Works approaching the Book of Mormon as literature, such as Richard Dilworth Rust's *Feasting on the Word: The Literary Testimony of the Book of Mormon* (Salt Lake City: Deseret Book, 1997), can illuminate the text but do not make a strong case for reading the Book if one does already accept it as scripture.

[49] If the number of such *literary* features reaches a critical mass, then, even in the absence of extratextual signals of literary intention, we might decide that we *are* reading a work of fiction. Whether we might legitimately do so in the case of the Book of Mormon, and whether even if we did we should conclude that Smith consciously authored the text, are questions that lie beyond the scope of this paper; here I am simply concerned to note how even those who take the historicity of the Book of Mormon for granted should still read it as a fiction—while those who presume that it is a fiction, should see their doing so as an invitation to read in a certain matter,

did act as bankers for British regiments, and although John H. Watson does not appear in the Army list it could be that the author really was an ex-Indian Army doctor, albeit writing with an assumed name. In short, without the evidence for Conan Doyle's authorship (or knowledge of the Holmes canon) we might well hesitate before dismissing the idea that there was such a box or that there had been a suicide at Thor Place (the crux of Watson's report). Yet to hesitate in this way would not be to presume that either Watson or Thor Place really existed. Though both might well have done (remember, in this thought experiment Watson is not known to be a fictional character), with no evidence other than a single case report we would have no reason to affirm that they did. If we wanted to engage with Watson's narrative we could only do so meaningfully by reading it *as* fiction—that is without presuming reference—while suspending judgment as to whether it *was* fiction, pending further research.

This brings us back to the question of geography. If we did read in this way, although the Thor Bridge narrative would possess spatiality (as Marcel de Certeau observed, "Every story is a travel story—a spatial practice"),[50] its spatiality would be a construct, a product of our imagination. This is not because there might not have been a real-world Thor Place but because, not knowing whether there was (and if so, where we should locate it—other than somewhere near Winchester) we can only make sense of its action by constructing a mental map: a schematic representation "of the spatial configuration of the textual world."[51]

It is the same, I would suggest, with the Book of Mormon, where Mormon reports toward the end of his history: "I Mormon ... made this record out of the plates of Nephi, and hid up in the hill Cumorah all the records which had been entrusted to me by the hand of the Lord, save it were these few plates which I gave unto my son Moroni,"[52] and here too we a have a claim that there is a repository of records unknown to historians or archivists (this time the plates

---

not as a judgment that excuses them from further discussion and legitimates disengagement from its text.

[50] *The Practice of Everyday Life*, trans. Steven Rendall (Berkeley: University of California Press, 1980), 115.

[51] Marie-Laure Ryan, "Cognitive Maps and the Construction of Narrative Space" *Narrative Theory and the Cognitive Sciences*, ed. D. Herman (Stanford, CA: CSLI Publications, 2003), 236; cf. Edward W. Soja, *Thirdspace: Journeys to Los Angeles and Other Real-and-Imagined Places* (Cambridge, MA: Blackwell, 1996), 78–79; Henri LeFebvre, *The Production of Space* (1974), trans. Donald Nicholson Smith (Oxford: Blackwell, 1991), 38–39. We construct mental maps of real-world geography too, but these can be validated: those of non-referring narratives cannot, and this makes them of particular importance to our understanding of such works.

[52] Mormon 3:7–8 [6:6–7], punctuation modified. The manuscript used for the printing of the Book of Mormon was unpunctuated (Dan Vogel, *Joseph Smith, The Making of a Prophet* [Salt

hidden up "in the Hill Cumorah," not the papers stored in Cox and Company's vault),[53] and a separate text ("this record" rather than Thor Bridge case) that would be published. And as in our example, I suggest (given that there is no evidence of fictional or fraudulent intent on Smith's part)[54] we can choose to suspend judgment as to the historicity (or fictionality) of the claim. As in the (counterfactual) case of a text of a Sherlock Holmes story that could not be attributed to Conan Doyle, we can choose to read the Book of Mormon as a nonhistorical text without deciding that it *is* a work of fiction—and in doing so, leave the debate over historicity to one side.

Invisible Cities

THIS HOPE FOR a less controversial, less historical reading of the Book of Mormon might seem irrelevant in the present context, for to insist that Bountiful is only to be found in (our) imagined geography might be thought fatal to any hope of finding sacred space through the pages of the work. However, such doubts are premature. In the Latin pilgrimage tradition, Glenn Bowman observes, "It is from the significance, not the places, that one draws inspiration, and the places serve primarily as loci where the pilgrims are better able to body forth the subjects of their meditations in their imaginations." And he goes on: "The experience of interiorization can take place away from the sites; it is the image, not the place, which is important."[55] Even if we knew where Bountiful was, that is to say, the image of what happened there could be thought more important than the physical location where it supposedly occurred.

We might note in this connection the way in which the people of Bountiful come to understand the significance of Christ's descent. The "great multitude" gathered around the temple at the time had been "talking of Jesus," but neither institutional religion (the temple) nor received knowledge (the discourse) equips them to understand God's interpellation. Although they hear "a voice, as if it

---

Lake City: Signature Books, 2004], 471), and the punctuation of contemporary editions is too heavy.

[53] These other plates found their way into the visions of early Mormonism: see Brigham Young, discourse of 17 June 1877, *Journal of Discourses*, 19:38.

[54] As John Searle noted, "One cannot truly be said to have pretended to do something unless one intended to pretend to do it" (*Expression and Meaning*, 65); cf. Roger Pouivet, "The Ontology of Forgery," trans. Marcel Lieberman, *Interdisciplines: Art and Cognition Workshops*, <http://www.interdisciplines.org/artcognition/ papers/2/version/en>, (accessed 11 January 2008), and there is no evidence of that intention.

[55] "Christian Ideology and the Image of a Holy Land: The Place of Jerusalem Pilgrimage in the Various Christianities," *Contesting the Sacred: The Anthropology of Pilgrimage*, ed. John Eade and Michael J. Sallnow (Urbana: University of Illinois Press, 2000), 114, 115.

came out of heaven," it has no meaning for them; they can only "cast their eyes round about, ... [understanding] not the voice which they heard."[56] Even when they are overwhelmed by the Spirit—pierced to the center, overcome with God's power, their hearts aflame—still they do not understand, for spiritual manifestations offer no certainty, and religious experience is not, in itself, a source of understanding.[57] It is only when the Nephites actively seek insight that they can grasp what is happening. It is only when they "open their ears" and "look steadfastly towards heaven"—we should note the change from the earlier looking "round about"—that the message is clear: "Behold my beloved Son."[58]

Needless to say, an imaginative response to this invitation to faith in Christ (and an understanding of what it entails) does not require that we walk the streets of Bountiful or even know that such streets exist. Indeed, paradoxically, what such a response requires (if we are to recognize the complexity of the image presented in this passage from III Nephi 5 [ch. 11 in LDS editions]), is not a familiarity with Nephite urban geography but a cognitive map of Smith's text—a map in which the relative locations of its cities are more important than their latitude and longitude. Bountiful, after all, was named after the wilderness area in which it was built. The name had previously been used for a strip of land on the Red Sea coast ("called Bountiful, because of its much fruit"), and amazement at nature's abundance in the New World had led to its use to describe a wilderness area there (this time one "filled with all manner of wild animals of every kind").[59] However, Bountiful's claim to fame did not just rest on the natural resources of its region. It would also become a center for Nephite worship (a temple would be built there—something only previously reported of the Nephites for Nephi, their first settlement in the New World, and

---

[56] III Nephi 5:3–4 [11:2–3].

[57] III Nephi 5:5, 6 [11:3, 4]. As John Dominic Crossan notes, writing of Christ's appearance to the disciples on the Emmaus road (*The Birth of Christianity: Discovering What Happened in the Years Immediately After the Execution of Jesus* [New York: Harper San Francisco, 1988], xi), without "scripture and eucharist, tradition and table, community and justice ... divine presence remains unrecognized and human eyes remain unopened"—and no less necessary, I would add, is reflection and thought.

[58] III Nephi 5:6–7 [11:5], punctuation modified. Even Christ's descent calls for active understanding. When the people see "a man descending out of heaven ... clothed in a white robe" (9–10 [8]) they "wist not what it meant, for they thought it was an angel" (10 [8]); it is only when *his* testimony confirms that of the voice from heaven that they fully understand who it is (8, 12 [7, 11]). For the links between intellection and revelation in Smith's thinking, see Stott, "Seer Stone Controversy," 41–42.

[59] I Nephi 5:62–63 [17:5]; Alma 13:75 [22:31]; and cf. Alma 25:52 [55:26] ("the city Bountiful") and I Nephi 5:67 [17:6] ("we called the place [we settled] Bountiful").

their capital Zarahemla),[60] and as we have seen it was the place where Christ ministered to his people. The city's name was therefore clearly iconic, expressive of God's providence and love.[61]

No less iconic, however (and what moves us from the metaphoric to the spatial), is its location. Book of Mormon geography is defined with reference to an isthmus (a "narrow neck of land") separating the land to its north from that to its south. The Nephites had settled the land to the south, and Bountiful was in "the northern parts" of their territory, with the land Bountiful stretching into the isthmus itself. Beyond its borders was the "land northward," or more precisely the "land Desolation." This too was a familiar name—used before for the ruins of Ammonihah (whose people had claimed that their city could not be destroyed, but were proven wrong when "in one day it was left desolate; and [their] carcasses were mangled by dogs and wild beasts of the wilderness. . ."),[62] and it is not surprising that the same equation of desolation with destruction should be used in the naming of what lay to Bountiful's north. It too was a land "which had been peopled, and [whose people had] been destroyed," leaving their bones to be discovered by those who came after.[63] Two lands, two definitions of wilderness; on the one hand a morally desolate home of savagery, on the other a source of blessings and plenty—images well-known to early nineteenth-century Americans.[64]

Again, I must make it clear that these reflections are not intended as a contribution to a debate on Book of Mormon origins. To point to American parallels in this way is not to insist on a nineteenth-century origin for the work. It is merely to read it with an eye to the "beliefs, knowledge, and familiarity with conventions" presumed by its author(s)—as Peter J. Rabinowitz suggested some

---

[60] II Nephi 4:22 [5:16], Jacob 1:17 [1:17]; Mosiah 7:13 [11:10] (the temple at Nephi); Mosiah 1:27 [1:18] (Zarahemla); III Nephi 5:1 [11:1] (Bountiful).

[61] Some have noted that Bountiful could be seen as a translation of the biblical *tob* (good)—as in "the land of Tob" (Judges 11:3; cf. Exodus 3:8; II Kings 3:19)—but, whether or not Smith would have known that, it is significant that the meaning of Bountiful is transparent, whereas that of Zarahemla is not. (Zarahemla is another favorite for those who would discover Old World roots for Book of Mormon naming patterns: see Stephen D. Ricks and John A. Tvedtnes, "The Hebrew Origin of Some Book of Mormon Place Names," *Journal of Book of Mormon Studies* 6, no. 2 [1997]: 258–59, for the suggestion that it means "seed of compassion.") In John Bunyan's *Pilgrim's Progress* (1678), Smith's first audience might have remembered, Bountiful is the sister of Mercy, and both graces are defined in relationship to their treatment of the poor (World's Classics edition, ed. W. R. Owens [London: Oxford University Press, 2003], 215).

[62] Alma 11:14–19 [16:9–11] (the language is influenced by Jeremiah 15:3), 13:76–77 [22:32].

[63] Mosiah 5:62–63 [8:8]. We should add to the evidence of bloodshed that for deforestation: Helaman 2:5–6 [3:5–6].

[64] The classic account is that of Roderick Nash, *Wilderness and the American Mind* (New Haven, CT: Yale University Press, 1967).

thirty years ago, if we do not approach narrative works in this way "our reading experience will be more or less seriously flawed"[65]—and to recognize that when it comes to the Book of Mormon the authorial audience was that of 1830. (After all, by its own account it was edited to meet the needs of a latter-day audience,[66] and translated "by the gift and power of God" to fulfill its purpose.[67]) As we read, we should be listening to the voices of the New Nation, not those of millennia before.

For even a casual reader in 1830, I suggest, the contrast between the land Desolation and the land Bountiful would have been clear: on the one hand there was the abundance of God's blessings; on the other, their absence. It is particularly significant, therefore, that following the spiritual decline of the Nephites, we cease to read of the city of Bountiful and instead only read of the "city of Desolation."[68] Possibly no new city is described here, and Desolation *was* Bountiful. After all, the city Desolation was "in the borders [of the land Desolation], by the narrow pass," and Bountiful was strategically situated near that very same pass[69]—and while that might mean that we have two cities (Desolation, to the north of the narrow pass and guarding the way south; Bountiful, to the south and guarding the way north) it could also mean that there was a single city (Bountiful / Desolation) overlooking the pass and able to prevent movement in either direction. However, whatever the case, what concerns me here is that we never read of both cities existing at the same time, even though both are of Nephite construction.[70] When we read of Bountiful,

---

[65] "Truth in Fiction: A Reexamination of Audiences," *Critical Inquiry* 4, no. 1 (Autumn 1977): 126 (a revised version of the article was published in *Before Reading: Narrative Conventions and the Politics of Interpretation* [Columbus: Ohio State University Press, 1988], 15–46); "Where We Are When We Read," *Authorizing Readers: Resistance and Respect in the Teaching of Literature*, ed. Peter J. Rabinowitz and Michael W. Smith (New York: Teachers College Press, 1998), 5. For a similar argument explicitly addressing the reading of scripture, see J. Louis Martyn, "Listening to John and Paul on the Subject of Gospel and Scripture," *Word & World* 12, no. 1 (1992): 70. Martyn is drawing on the ideas of Walter Bauer.

[66] Mormon 1:82 [3:17]; Ether 1:34 [2:11].

[67] Book of Mormon, title page.

[68] Mormon 1:71, 2:3 [3:7, 4:2].

[69] Mormon 1:69 [3:5]; Alma 24:10 [52:9].

[70] As the land northward was "the place of [the] first landing" of the people of Zarahemla (Alma 13:74 [22:30]), those maintaining that there were two cities could argue that Desolation was built by the Mulekites—perhaps on a Jaredite site (Omni 1:39 [1:22]; the Mulekites were descendants of a group led to the New World by of the sons of Zedekiah: thus Helaman 2:129 [6:10], contradicting II Kings 25:7; the Jaredites were led to the New World from Babel, but like the Nephites destroy themselves in a civil war). However, by the time that Desolation is first mentioned, Jaredite civilization has imploded and the Mulekites are counted as Nephites. We have two Nephite cities; two Nephite icons.

there is no mention of Desolation; when we read of Desolation, there is no mention of Bountiful—and whatever a cartographer might decide, at any one time our mental map has only one city in the narrow neck of land. In the covenantal theology of the Book of Mormon blessing and cursing follows from the way people respond to the moral demands of the gospel.[71] To adopt the words of Edward Schillebeeckx, again and again, "in acceptance or refusal, [they make] a response to the anonymous grace of God, his call to salvation,"[72] and it is this dynamic, not Mesoamerican topography, that defines our mental map.

With that in mind we might remember our epigraph. "Rarely does the eye light upon a thing," Calvino's Marco Polo reflects, as he tells Kublai Khan of the route he followed to reach Tamara (one of his "invisible cities"), "and then only when it has recognized that thing as a sign of another thing."[73] These words might, of course, be applied to the Book of Mormon itself, and it is certainly worth noting that if people "light upon" it and recognize its inherent authority, it is because they see it "as a sign of another thing"; not because they can use it as a Baedeker. In this context it is enough for Bountiful to be what C. D. Martin calls a "constructed" referent.[74] We need not see the Book of Mormon thus, of course, any more than we need see anything in this way. The hibiscus that can be seen as a sign of spring can also be seen as just a flower; and the Book of Mormon that can be seen as a sign of God's self-revelation can also be seen as just a book—indeed as an unreadable book, as "chloroform in print."[75] But even if that is the case, and the work is not seen as a sign in its own right, the details of its nonreferring geography *should* be recognized as "images of things

---

[71] See G. St. John Stott, "Amerindian Identity, the Book of Mormon, and the American Dream," *Journal of American Studies of Turkey* 19 (2004): 22, 24–26; for this theme in the Old Testament, see Ernest W. Nicholson, *God and His People: Covenant and Theology in the Old Testament* (Oxford: Clarendon, 1986). The summary in J. Gordon McConville, *Grace in the End: A Study in Deuteronomic Theology* (Grand Rapids, MI: Zondervan, 1993), 132–33, could be applied to the Book of Mormon: "The gift of the land is not a thing in itself, but initiates a scenario in which a people lives before their God in covenant faithfulness."

[72] *Revelation and Theology*, 2 vols., trans. N. D. Smith (New York: Sheed and Ward, 1967–68), 1:4; the choice is defined in Deuteronomy 30:15.

[73] *Invisible Cities*, 13. Calvino is not suggesting that everything has such significance, or the significance is inherent in what is seen; his point is simply that some phenomena assume an unanticipated symbolic importance as we encounter them.

[74] *Language, Truth and Poetry* (Edinburgh: Edinburgh University Press, 1975), 89n88. I use Martin's term without any presumption of deception on Smith's part.

[75] Mark Twain, *Roughing It* (1872), *The Innocents Abroad; Roughing It* (New York: Library of America, 1984), 617. There is some irony in the way that apologists who have seen the Book of Mormon as a sign that God is a God of revelation have tended to ignore the work's contents: see A. Bruce Lindgren, "Sign or Scripture: Approaches to the Book of Mormon," *Dialogue: A Journal of Mormon Thought* 19, no. 1 (Spring 1986): 69–75.

that mean other things."[76] As icons they are pointing beyond themselves. Just as Calvino's invisible cities are images of Venice ("Every time I describe a city I am saying something about Venice," Polo explains), so Bountiful is an image of the Kingdom of God.[77]

But this is not all. Bountiful is not (or need not be) just an image—just a focus for meditation and reflection. It can also be an agent of change, pointing *through* its failure of reference to the need to locate and live the city's story in real space and time.[78] A narrative can offer a model of what might happen as well as a record of what took place, and as Richard Jenkins has pointed out "a model always refers to a future event." Although this event need not occur (always, faced with God's grace, there are decisions to be made), "the model creates the possibility that it can do so,"[79] and in such a context the historicity of the model is by the way. Indeed, it has been argued, it is precisely the lack of real-world reference that makes nonhistorical geographies powerful invitations to act. When places described don't exist, the French writer Georges Perec observed, "space becomes a question, ceases to be self-evident, ceases to be incorporated, ceases to be appropriated"[80]—and *as* a question it precipitates activity. So it can be with the Book of Mormon, I suggest: the work's stories of sacred space can precipitate (or potentially can precipitate) the readers' sacralization of their present life.[81]

That one might respond to scripture—that one might put down a work determined to live life differently—is, of course, unsurprising. The late Wolfgang Iser suggested that a work's significance "does not lie in the meaning sealed

---

[76] Calvino, *Invisible Cities*, 13.

[77] Ibid. Complicating the analogy is that while Polo is talking about Venice, Calvino is thinking of San Remo. It is beyond the scope of this paper to speculate on what lay behind Bountiful.

[78] For the need for religion to be defined with "sensual concretion," see Theodor Adorno, *The Jargon of Authenticity*, trans. Knut Tarnowski and Frederic Will (London: Routledge, 1973), 56.

[79] "Thinking and Doing: Towards a Model of Cognitive Practice," *The Structure of Folk Models*, ed. Ladislav Holy and Milan Stuchlik (London: Academic Press, 1981), 94

[80] *Species of Spaces and Other Pieces* (1974), trans. and ed. John Sturrock (London: Penguin Books, 1997), 90–91; cf. Diane Davis, "Addressing Alterity: Rhetoric, Hermeneutics, and the Non-Appropriative Relation," *Philosophy and Rhetoric* 38, no. 3 (2005): 208.

[81] In talking of a *model* I am not assuming that the Book of Mormon provides us with a *blueprint* for kingdom-building. I am mindful of Calvino's Fedora and its museum of crystal balls, each of them a vision of the perfect Fedora of the future (*Invisible Cities*, 32–33). Because the city is continually changing, each one becomes obsolete as it is being constructed. Although we can find in the Book of Mormon an illuminating commentary on what is entailed in the call of Zion, we cannot find a manual of instructions. As Claude Bremond has reflected (*Logique du récit* [Paris: Seuil, 1973]), the way in which we actualize a schema is not made explicit in its definition.

within the text, but in the fact that the meaning brings out what had previously sealed within us." Indeed, he noted, "Through gestalt-forming, we actually participate in the text, and this means that we are caught up in the very thing we are producing": reading in the light of our own history, we transform ourselves and our world with what we read.[82] There is, perhaps, little that is remarkable in the idea that it could be so with the Book of Mormon. And yet I feel that the possibility that it could, needs affirming, for so much emphasis has been placed on the historicity of the work that we can forget what is important about it is the response that we have to its words. Even if the places that define the kingdom are unknown, indeed even if they are unknowable, the narratives that describe them both give us "a horizon of possible experience, a world in which it would be possible to live," and challenge us to make the possible—the sacred—real.[83] Faced with this gift and challenge, we can create Bountiful.

This is not, I hasten to add as I conclude, an argument for seeing the Book of Mormon as a utopian work: as I have argued elsewhere, Smith's account of the collapse of Nephite and Jaredite society points to the inevitability of the failure of any attempt to build the kingdom this side of the eschaton.[84] However, the realism I see in the work does not nullify our responsibility to (try to) actualize our vision of discipleship.[85] However we read it, the Book of Mormon invites us to assume the responsibility of building Zion. That is why I would agree with one of Jeanette Winterson's characters when she reflects that

---

[82] *The Act of Reading: A Theory of Aesthetic Response* (Baltimore: Johns Hopkins University Press, 1978), 157, 132; cf. Marie-Laure Ryan, *Narrative as Virtual Reality: Immersion and Interactivity in Literature and Electronic Media* (Baltimore: Johns Hopkins University Press, 2001), 193: "Meaning [in a literary text] is not a preformed representation encoded in words and in need of decipherment but something that emerges out of the text in unpredictable patterns as the reader follows trails of associative connotations or attends to the resonance of words and images with the private contents of memory."

[83] Paul Ricoeur, "Life in Quest of Narrative," *On Paul Ricoeur: Narrative and Interpretation*, ed. David Wood (London: Routledge, 1991), 26; cf. Stuart Brock, "Fictions, Feelings, and Emotions," *Philosophical Studies* 132, no. 2 (January 2007): 236–37; Karen J. Wenell, "Contested Temple Space and Visionary Kingdom Space in Mark 11–12," *Biblical Interpretation: A Journal of Contemporary Approaches* 15, no. 3 (2007): 324.

[84] Stott, "Conjectural Reading," 453–54. The task is perhaps Sisyphean, but unlike Albert Camus (*The Myth of Sisyphus*, trans. Justin O'Brien [London: Penguin, 1975]) I ground my realism in human weakness, not life's meaninglessness.

[85] Neither, for that matter, would a reading that uncritically saw Smith's work as a utopian text. "The conventional utopia," Herbert Muschamp has written, "—the imaginary ideal city or world—seems to me a transitional state between belief in an almighty dignity, a supreme being capable of bending the laws of nature, and the acceptance of personal responsibility in whatever sphere life happens to place us" ("Service Not Included," *Visions of Utopia*, ed. Edward Rothstein, Herbert Muschamp, and Martin E. Marty [New York: New York Public Library / Oxford University Press, 2003], 29).

it does not matter if a place cannot be mapped "so long as [we] can still describe it"[86]—and, I would add, so long as we can still respond "using the things of this world in the manner designed of God, that the places where they occupy may shine as Zion, the redeemed of the Lord."[87]

[86] *Sexing the Cherry* (New York: Grove, 1990), 8.

[87] Revelation to Joseph Smith III, 18 April 1909, *Book of Doctrine and Covenants*, 128:8c.

"Yes, we are a visionary house": The Restoration of Revelation and Dreams by Joseph Smith

MARY JANE WOODGER

IN 1816, SOLOMON CHAMBERLIN received a vision depicting the raising up of a church "after the Apostolic order," with "the same powers, and gifts that were in the days of Christ." When Chamberlin later visited the Smiths, he asked, "Is there anyone here that believes in visions or revelations?" Hyrum Smith replied, "Yes, we are a visionary house." After Chamberlin explained his vision of a restored church, he said, "If you are a visionary house I wish you would make known some of your discoveries, for I think I can bear them."[1] The resulting conversations led to the baptisms of Chamberlin and his wife by Joseph Smith in April 1830.[2]

Interest in the spiritual or religious significance of dreams or visions of the night did not begin in Joseph's day.[3] According to religion and psychology

---

[1] Solomon Chamberlain, manuscript record, "Short Sketch of the Life of Solomon Chamberlain, Written 11 July 1858," LDS Church Archives, ms5886. Larry Porter, *A Study of the Origins of The Church of Jesus Christ of Latter-day Saints in the States of New York and Pennsylvania, 1816–1831: A Dissertation* (Provo, UT: Joseph Fielding Smith Institute for Latter-day Saint History and BYU Studies, 2000), 143–44.

[2] Larry C. Porter, "Solomon Chamberlin's Missing Pamphlet: Dreams, Visions, and Angelic Ministrants," *Brigham Young University Studies* 37, no. 2 (1997–98): 115.

[3] Visions are revelations received while one is awake, and inspired dreams are visions received while one is asleep. For further discussion of the definition of dreams, see James E. Talmage, *Articles of Faith* (Salt Lake City: Deseret Book, 1984), 205; Margaret McConkie Pope, *This Chosen Generation* (Bountiful, UT: Horizon Publishers & Distributors, Inc., 1994), 49–51; Bruce R. McConkie, *Mormon Doctrine* (Salt Lake City: Bookcraft, Inc., 1966), 208.

scholar Kelly Bulkeley at John F. Kennedy University, "The most widespread and longest-standing interest humans have taken in dreams has been in their religious meaning."[4] Indeed, dreams were once seen as religious realities, but they lost some of their religious significance among established religions by way of Enlightenment rationalism or, "an exclusive reliance on human reason alone, and a refusal to allow any weight to be given to divine revelation."[5] According to Oxford University history of theology scholar Alister E. McGrath, Enlightenment rationalism presumed that "human reason [was] perfectly capable of telling us everything we need[ed] to know about the world, ourselves, and God (if there [was] one)," and so "divine revelation [was] an irrelevance, if it exist[ed] at all."[6] Yet, despite the effects of Enlightenment rationalism, historian Richard Bushman[7] observes that, in Joseph Smith's day, visions "were common enough to anger clergymen, who saw them as counterfeit religion, diverting people from the serious business of acknowledging their sins and accepting Christ."[8] Thus, Joseph Smith did not restore a common interest in dreams, but rather, he restored or revived the meaning of dreaming as a real mode of divine communication or revelation both ancient and modern in an organized religious setting, and Joseph accomplished this restoration of dreams by restoring the correct principles of revelation. By restoring revelation, Joseph renewed the life of biblical dreams and visions, and restored the faith in God[9] necessary for many

---

[4] Kelly Bulkeley, *The Wilderness of Dreams: Exploring the Religious Meanings of Dreams in Modern Western Culture* (Albany: State University of New York Press, 1994), 3.

[5] Ira Progoff, "Waking Dream and Living Myth," in *Myths, Dreams, and Religion*, ed. Joseph Campbell (New York: E. P. Dutton & Co., Inc., 1970), 176; Alister E. McGrath, *Christian Theology: An Introduction*, 4th ed. (Malden, MA: Blackwell Publishing, 2007), 144.

[6] McGrath, *Christian Theology*, 143.

[7] Richard Lyman Bushman is Gouverneur Morris Professor of History Emeritus at Columbia University.

[8] Richard Bushman, "Joseph Smith's Many Histories," in *The Worlds of Joseph Smith: A Bicentennial Conference at the Library of Congress*, ed. John Welch (Provo, UT: Brigham Young University Press, 2006), 13.

[9] Joseph Smith taught the following about the faith in God: "Let us here observe, that three things are necessary in order that any rational and intelligent being may exercise faith in God unto life and salvation. First, the idea that he actually exists. Secondly a *correct* idea of his character, perfections, and attributes. Thirdly, an actual knowledge that the course of life which he is pursuing is according to his will. For without an acquaintance with these three important facts, the faith of every rational being must be imperfect and unproductive; but with this understanding it can become perfect and fruitful, abounding in righteousness, unto the praise and glory of God the Father, and the Lord Jesus Christ" (*Lectures on Faith*, comp. N. B. Lundwall [Salt Lake City: N. B. Lundwall, n.d.,], 33).

individuals to once again dream dreams and trust in those dreams as revelation from God.[10]

Revelation Restored

A T THE WORLDS of Joseph Smith Conference held at the Library of Congress in 2005, the themes of restoration and revelation were prevalent in many of the presentations. In his presentation during the Worlds Conference, Richard Bushman noted that to Mormons, at least, Joseph Smith is viewed as a key figure in a long history of apostasy and restoration.[11] At the same conference, Pepperdine University religion scholar Richard Hughes observed that Joseph Smith was not the only restorationist of his time; Alexander Campbell, one of the chief contemporary critics of Smith, was also a restorationist. Hughes described Campbell as "a child of the eighteenth-century Enlightenment," who "had no use for the romantic notion that God might speak to men and women through dreams and revelations. For Campbell, God spoke only through a book that rational people could read and understand in rational ways."[12] Hughes noted other examples of restorationist groups in Joseph Smith's time, including the Shakers and the Oneida Community.

Each of these restorationist communities believed they had a role in restoring the truths of pure Christianity, but the restoration of revelation set Joseph Smith and his followers apart from other restorationists. In their addresses to the Worlds Conference, former Chicago University law professor and LDS apostle Dallin H. Oaks stated that "revelation is the key to the uniqueness of Joseph Smith's message,"[13] and religion and history scholar Jan Shipps[14] explained that through Joseph Smith,

> the heavens were opened and the divine once again spoke in a language that humans could understand. Without the reopening of that conversation, Mormonism would likely be just one more restoration movement that started out, as did the Disciples of Christ, claiming to be the only true Church of

---

[10] Joel 2: 28; Acts 2: 17 (King James Version or KJV). It is interesting to note that the Angel Moroni quoted Joel 2:28 verbatim three times to Joseph Smith (Joseph Smith, "Joseph Smith—History," 1:41–47, Pearl of Great Price, <http://scriptures.lds.org/en/pgp/contents> (accessed on 31 March 2008 [hereafter cited as JSH].)

[11] Bushman, "Histories," 6.

[12] Richard T. Hughes, "Joseph Smith as an American Restorationist," in *The Worlds of Joseph Smith*, 34.

[13] Dallin H. Oaks, "Joseph Smith in a Personal World," in *The Worlds of Joseph Smith*, 153.

[14] Jan Shipps is professor emerita of history and religious studies at Indiana University–Purdue University at Indianapolis and senior research associate for the POLIS Center.

Jesus Christ, but all too quickly took its place on the religious landscape as an idiosyncratic Protestant denomination.[15]

Joseph knew that revelation was essential to his message and mission.[16] As University of Richmond literature and religion scholar Terryl L. Givens observed, Joseph Smith believed that the "cardinal contribution of his calling" was to restore the process of revelation.[17]

In summary, Joseph Smith made many extraordinary claims during his prophetic career, but, as stated by Brigham Young University philosophy of religion scholar David Paulsen, of all Joseph's claims, "none is more fundamental than his claim to direct revelation from God. This claim challenges every variety of Christian thought and, at the same time, grounds all of Joseph's additional claims."[18] One of these additional claims came quite naturally to Joseph Smith—that divinely inspired dreams were indeed the *right* of the Saints.[19]

A Short History of Dreams in America

AMERICA HAD SOME history with dreams (not *the American Dream*) before Joseph Smith. Many Americans believed in the Bible, and as a result, they accepted the Old Testament Israel belief that God revealed his will to his people, and God's mode of revelation could be a dream.[20] The New Testament tells of a similar faith concerning revelation by dreams among Christians.[21] In an article titled "The American Exploration of Dreams and Dreamers," historian Merle Curti notes that Americans brought with them the Old World-biblical view of dreams as a "divine or devilish monitor of things unseen and otherwise

---

[15] Jan Shipps, "Joseph Smith and the Making of a Global Religion," in *The Worlds of Joseph Smith*, 303.

[16] Joseph Smith on 10 March 1844: "The doctrine of revelation far transcends the doctrine of no revelation; for one truth revealed from heaven is worth all the sectarian notions in existence" (Joseph Smith, *History of The Church of Jesus Christ of Latter-day Saints,* 7 vols., ed. B. H. Roberts [Salt Lake City: Church of Jesus Christ of Latter-day Saints, 1932–51], 6:252 [hereafter cited as HC]).

[17] Terryl L. Givens, "Joseph Smith: Prophecy, Process, and Plentitude," in *The Worlds of Joseph Smith*, 56–57.

[18] David L. Paulsen, "Joseph Smith Challenges the Theological World," in *The Worlds of Joseph Smith*, 177.

[19] Joseph Smith, "Copy of a Letter from J. Smith Jr. to Mr. Galland," *Times and Seasons* 1, no 4 (February 1840): 54.

[20] John F Priest, "Myth and Dream in Hebrew Scripture," in *Myths, Dreams, and Religion*, ed. Joseph Campbell (E. P. Dutton & Co., Inc., New York, 1970), 64–65.

[21] Acts 2:17; Matthew 1:20 (KJV).

unknown."[22] For example, early American minister Increase Mather (21 June 1639–23 August 1723) believed that "angels gave warnings and revelations by dreams." Also, Increase Mather's son, the influential minister Cotton Mather (12 February 1663–13 February 1728), derived one of his most popular sermons from a text that he received in a dream. On the other hand, there were many early American clergymen, such as John Winthrop (12 January 1587/8–26 March 1649), who associated dreams with "ravishes of spirit by fits."[23]

Winthrop's skeptical view of dreams anticipated the general skepticism or the ambivalence of many Americans during the late eighteenth and early nineteenth centuries. For example, U.S. Senator William Maclay of Pennsylvania (20 July 1737–16 April 1804) noted in his journal that he had best be "careful and attentive" to his dreams, but he also observed that dreams were "fallacious things." After noting the disturbing content of his recent dreams, Maclay wrote, "I really have little to do, or I would not note all this down."[24] Maclay's ambivalence was perhaps the result of the prevailing social attitudes of his time; some people treated dreams as supernatural, and others treated them as benign, natural occurences. Others revealed their attitude toward dreams with comments such as, "I treat dreams as I would a known liar, who, though he generally tells falsehoods, may sometimes possibly tell the truth."[25] Among educated Americans, rationalism did not allow for revelation, and according to Bushman and Curti, the ministers, newspaper editors, and physicians of Joseph Smith's day and place scorned belief in supernatural gifts. They were persuaded, as was Thomas Paine,[26] that as the Apocrypha reads: "Who so regardeth dreams is like him that catcheth at a shadow and followeth after the wind."[27]

Joseph Smith encountered rationalist skepticism firsthand when he related his First Vision to a Methodist minister. Joseph recorded that the minister "treated my communication not only lightly, but with great contempt, saying it was all of the devil, that there were no such things as visions or revelations in these days; that all such things had ceased with the apostles, and that there would never be any more of them." The minister was not the only one to show contempt toward Joseph's claims, for the telling of his vision produced a "great deal of prejudice

---

[22] Merle Curti, "The American Exploration of Dreams and Dreamers," *Journal of the History of Ideas* 27, no. 3 (1966): 393.

[23] Curti, "Exploration," 394.

[24] William Maclay, *Journal of William Maclay, United States Senator from Pennsylvania, 1789–1791*, ed. Edgar S. Maclay (New York: D. Appleton and Co., 1891), 277, <http://memory.loc.gov/ammem/amlaw/lwmj.html> (accessed on 10 March 2008).

[25] Curti, "Exploration," 396.

[26] Bushman, *Beginnings*, 79; Curti, "Exploration," 397.

[27] Sirach (Apocrypha) 34:2.

against me among professors of religion."[28] According to Bushman, in the minds of clergymen in the early 1800s, the only acceptable form of divine intervention was the "gift of grace ... all else was unholy, unscriptural, and irrational." Yet, many Christians in Joseph Smith's time were looking for the return of spiritual gifts spoken of in the Bible. These Christians were not satisfied with the rational Christianity promoted by the established clergy of their day.[29]

Joseph's Teachings on Dreams

DESCRIBING THEIR FIRST night in Carthage Jail, Dan Jones, a faithful friend and associate of Joseph, records that it was spent in "amusing conversation on various topics." Jones relates that "after prayer, which made Carthage prison into the gate of Heaven for awhile, we lay promiscuously on the floor, the last words spoken were, by the Prophet, 'For the most intelligent dream tonight brethren.'" In the morning Joseph inquired of the others concerning their dreams, and Jones related a dream that Joseph took as foretelling his (Joseph's) imminent death.[30] Joseph taught in an address published in the *Times and Seasons* that divinely inspired dreams are one of various spiritual gifts that may be granted to all worthy disciples of Christ: "We believe that we have a right to revelations, visions, and dreams from God, our heavenly Father; and light and intelligence, through the gift of the Holy Ghost, in the name of Jesus Christ, on all subjects pertaining to our spiritual welfare; if it so be that we keep his commandments, so as to render ourselves worthy in his sight."[31] Joseph believed the Bible to be the word of God, and he believed that the word of God continued in modern times to be revealed to all worthy followers of Christ. Furthermore, dreams as revelation were part of the biblical tradition, and Joseph believed that he was called as a prophet to restore all things—including dreams.[32]

With the restoration of dreams, there had to also be a restoration of the interpretation of dreams, else dreams would have been useless to dreamers. Joseph left one short note in his journal mentioning his interpretive activity: "I read the Book of Mormon, transacted a variety of business in the store and city, and spent the evening in the office with Elders Taylor and Richards, interpreting dreams, &c."[33] Aside from this short note, Joseph provided two seemingly

---

[28] JSH 1:22.

[29] Bushman, *Beginnings*, 79.

[30] Dan Jones, "Letter written to Thomas Bullock on 20 January 1855," *Brigham Young University Studies* 24 no. 1 (Winter 1984): 98.

[31] Joseph Smith, "Copy of a Letter from J. Smith Jr. to Mr. Galland," 54.

[32] Matthew 17: 11(KJV); Doctrine and Covenants 77: 9, 14–15 (LDS; not in CofC editions).

[33] HC 4:501.

random notes on the interpretation of two types of dreams: "To dream of flying signifies prosperity and deliverance from enemies. To dream of swimming in deep water signifies success among many people, and that the word will be accompanied with power."[34] Joseph recorded no dreams of flying, and though he did record dreams of swimming in deep waters, Joseph did not record a particular application of these principles. As for prosperity and deliverance from enemies, Joseph did not prosper financially during his life, but he was delivered many times from his enemies and certainly had missionary success, and his word was accompanied with power. Were these principles of interpretation applicable to all dreams, or were they applicable only to his dreams? Were these statements revealed to Joseph by God, or were they conclusions of his own reason and experience? Joseph's record does not provide an answer to these questions.

Fortunately, Joseph provided additional principles relative to the interpretation of dreams—recognizing that not all dreams or visions were revelatory in nature. He gave specific instruction to his followers applicable to the reception and interpretation of visions or dreams: "When you see a vision, pray for the interpretation; if you get not this, shut it up; there must be certainty in this matter."[35] Joseph's instruction is quite strict—if an individual does not receive divine interpretation of a vision, then he or she should "shut it up." Joseph did not want his followers to be a people that "catcheth at a shadow and followeth after the wind."[36] He wanted his followers to be careful in their reception of all kinds of possible revelation, including dreams.[37] For example, he called Levi Hancock on a mission, but Hancock returned before reaching his field of labor. Joseph "talked plain" to Hancock for not completing his mission, and Hancock accepted responsibility for turning back, saying "I had had a dream that troubled me." Joseph responded: "Don't let that trouble you. I have had dreams as bad as you ever had. You do as I now tell you to and you will come

---

[34] HC 5:254–55. In addition to these short notes in Joseph's record, there are instances recorded in other places where he interpreted the dreams of other people. For example, see Don C. Corbett, *Mary Fielding Smith: Daughter of Britain* (Salt Lake City: Deseret Book Company, 1970), 107.

[35] HC 3:391.

[36] Sirach (Apocrypha) 34:1–8 (KJV).

[37] Joseph Smith: "One great evil is, that men ... imagine that when there is anything like power, revelation, or vision manifested, that it must be of God.... They consider it to be the power of God, and a glorious manifestation from God—a manifestation of what? Is there any intelligence communicated? Are the curtains of heaven withdrawn, or the purposes of God developed?" (HC 4:572).

out all right." Hancock recorded that Joseph then instructed him on how the "Comforter would comfort the mind of man when asleep."[38]

Joseph also taught church leaders not only what they must do, but how they must live to discern the source of a dream. On 2 July 1839, Joseph made some remarks during a meeting with the Council of the Twelve Apostles. In his address, Joseph warned the apostles against pride and many other spiritual dangers, and he taught that "salvation cannot come without revelation; it is vain for anyone to minister without it."[39] Near the end of his address, Joseph taught the Twelve how they must live to recognize and know the source of a dream or a vision.

> In order to have the power to distinguish between truth and error and to interpret properly a dream or vision, one must have a pure heart and a contrite spirit and be living a righteous life. Satan's mission is to deceive, and he can, and does, give revelation to those who permit themselves to fall into his power. "Lying spirits are going forth in the earth. There will be great manifestations of spirits, both false and true."[40]

Joseph taught that to distinguish between a divinely inspired dream and a dream from another source, there were certain requirements. Thus, Joseph taught that like all gospel blessings, receiving the blessings of divinely inspired dreams required righteous living.[41] In summary, Joseph taught that dreams could be divinely inspired, but he recognized that not all dreams were of such a variety. He taught principles that enabled his followers to discern the source of their night visions.

Joseph's Dreams

JOSEPH SMITH WAS raised in a visionary house, and his exposure to dreams in his youth prepared him to exercise faith in all forms of revelation. When Joseph's paternal grandfather heard of the Book of Mormon before his death in 1830, "he said it was true, for he knew that something would turn up in his family that would revolutionize the world."[42] Joseph's mother, Lucy Mack

---

[38] Hyrum L. Andrus and Helen Mae Andrus, comps., *They Knew the Prophet* (Salt Lake City: Bookcraft, 1974), 19.

[39] HC 3:389.

[40] HC 3:391–92.

[41] In LDS Doctrine and Covenants 130:20 (not in CofC editions), Joseph taught that "There is a law, irrevocably decreed in heaven before the foundations of this world, upon which all blessings are predicated—and when we obtain any blessing from God, it is by obedience to that law upon which it is predicated."

[42] George A. Smith, "Joseph Smith's Family—Details of George A. Smith's Own Experience, etc.," *Journal of Discourses*, 26 vols. (London: Latter-day Saints' Book Depot, 1854–86), 5:102.

Smith, recorded a dream that comforted her as she searched for true religion,[43] and Joseph's father, Joseph Smith Sr., received seven inspired dreams.[44] Though Joseph Smith Jr. did not record what effect his family's faith and dreams had on his belief, perhaps his confidence in dreams as divine manifestations was initially founded in the experience and faith of his forefathers.[45] In the words of historian Mark McConkie, "What better place to raise a prophet than in the home of a prophet [and a prophetess]?"[46]

In addition to his family's faith, Joseph Smith had the whole Book of Mormon experience to reinforce his belief in inspired dreams. In Joseph's own record, he says that the angel who appeared to him, first telling him of the Book of Mormon, included in his message a recitation of Joel 2:28–32, wherein Joel prophesies of a day when God will pour out his Spirit on "all flesh" and people will "dream dreams" and "see visions."[47] The angel said "that this [prophecy of Joel] was not yet fulfilled, but was soon to be."[48] The same angel appeared to Joseph four consecutive times in a night and the following day, and during each visit, he quoted Joel 2:28–32 (among other things) and made the same comment concerning the prophecy's imminent fulfillment.[49]

The Book of Mormon itself contains a history or story (depending on one's belief) that supported or expressed Joseph's faith in dreams. For example, the Book of Mormon tells of a prophecy recorded by Joseph the Dreamer from the Old Testament.[50] The prophecy spoke of Joseph Smith Jr. and said that Smith would be "like unto [biblical Joseph]."[51] The Book of Mormon also contains several other nonbiblical examples of divinely inspired dreamers—establishing dreaming as a legitimate form of revelation and serving as a second witness to the revelatory nature of dreams recorded in the Bible.[52] If Joseph invented the

---

[43] Lucy Smith, *The Revised and Enhanced History of Joseph Smith by his Mother* (Salt Lake City: Bookcraft, 1996), 58–60.

[44] Lucy Smith, *Revised and Enhanced History*, 76.

[45] See Richard Lloyd Anderson, "Heritage of a Prophet," *Ensign*, February 1971, 15.

[46] Mark L. McConkie, *The Father of the Prophet: Stories and Insights from the Life of Joseph Smith, Sr.* (Salt Lake City: Bookcraft, 1993), 4.

[47] The recited verse relative to this paper is Joel 2:28: "And it shall come to pass afterward, that I will pour out my spirit upon all flesh; and your sons and your daughters shall prophesy, your old men shall dream dreams, your young men shall see visions."

[48] JSH 1:41.

[49] JSH 1:41–49.

[50] Genesis 37:5; 40:8–9, 16; 41:15, 17, 25; 42:9.

[51] II Nephi 3:15 (LDS; 2:29, CofC).

[52] Lehi recorded many inspired dreams: I Nephi 1:16; 2:1, 2; 3:2; 8:2, 4, 36; 10:2; 15:21 LDS (1:15, 24–26, 60; 2:41, 43, 86; 4:35 CofC); Korihor, an anti-Christ, preached against revelatory

whole story of the Book of Mormon (including the angel's visits), as some have argued, then the many examples of inspired dreams in the Book of Mormon tell us much about his belief in the role of dreams. If Joseph translated the Book of Mormon by the gift and power of God, as he and many others have testified, then certainly this volume of scripture confirmed to Joseph's mind and to the minds of his followers the importance and nature of revelatory dreams.

Despite the tradition of dreams inherited by Joseph from his family and ancient scripture, dreaming was not a primary means for him to receive revelation. Of the many revelations given to Joseph and recorded in the Doctrine and Covenants, not one of them is described as a dream. In fact, the word "dream" is not used once in this particular compilation of canonized revelations.[53] Rather, the revelations received and recorded in the Doctrine and Covenants were received by personal visitations, visions, mechanical devices (e.g., Urim and Thummim[54]), inspiration, and spiritual confirmation.[55]

However, there are records or references to eight dreams attributed to Joseph Smith in the early church records.[56] These dreams are recorded by Joseph Smith, his clerks, or other people who interacted with Joseph in some capacity. In several instances, Joseph's dreams stand alone, with no explanation left by Joseph or the recorder concerning their purpose or interpretation. Yet Joseph viewed dreaming as a legitimate channel of revelation, and this view is evident in his teachings on dreams (discussed previously), and in the fact that Joseph recorded his dreams and used them in his public sermons. His dreams may be loosely categorized as dreams of instruction, prophecy, and comfort. Given the limitations of this paper, not all eight of Joseph's dreams will be discussed; a dream from each category will serve the purpose of showing the importance Joseph afforded to dreams as revelation.

---

dreams in Alma 30:28 LDS, 16:35 CofC; Omer is warned in a dream to depart out of the land in Ether 9:3 LDS, 4:3 CofC.

[53] The Church of Jesus Christ of Latter-day Saints (the LDS or the Mormon Church) considers the Bible, the Book of Mormon, the Doctrine and Covenants, and the Pearl of Great Price to be their standard works or their official canon of scripture.

[54] The angel that visited Joseph and told him of the Book of Mormon offered the following description of the objects accompanying the Book: "Also, that there were two stones in silver bows—and these stones, fastened to a breastplate, constituted what is called the Urim and Thummim—deposited with the plates; and the possession and use of these stones were what constituted 'seers' in ancient or former times; and that God had prepared them for the purpose of translating the book" (JSH 1:35). Joseph later recorded that he used the Urim and Thummim to translate the Book of Mormon (JSH 1:62).

[55] Richard O. Cowan, *The Doctrine and Covenants: Our Modern Scripture* (Provo, UT: Brigham Young University Press, 1969), 3.

[56] Lucy Mack Smith, *History of Joseph Smith by His Mother*, ed. Preston Nibley (Salt Lake City: Bookcraft, 1958), 47–50.

A Dream of Instruction

I N EARLY CHURCH records, there is one reference to a dream by Joseph that instructed him in his ministry. The reference to this dream is brief, and neither Joseph nor his associates describe the dream's content in any other record that we know of. The record of this particular dream seems to indicate that Joseph Smith approached dreams with an attitude that was quite practical and unspectacular. This is not surprising considering the fact that Joseph experienced "visions that roll[ed] like an overflowing surge before [his] mind."[57] On 19 May 1843, Joseph made his only recorded reference to this instructive dream in the following journal entry:

> I borrowed of Orson Hyde fifty dollars, which I paid to Mr. Eric Roades, and which he is either to repay in cash or let me have lumber.
> I roade [sic] out with Mr. Jackson in the afternoon.
> Told Brother Phelps a dream that the history must go ahead before anything else.
> Elder George P. Dykes writes: (a letter reporting mundane/regular missionary activities).[58]

Joseph heeded the instruction given in the dream—giving the history top priority, though he did not elaborate on details such as the dream's timing, or the dream's content. In a journal entry soon after this history-inspiring dream, Joseph recorded that he was approached by his clerk with a complaint about the noise of a school that was disturbing work on the history. Joseph promptly ordered the school to find another place to meet, so the history could go forward. In the same journal entry Joseph wrote that "there are but few subjects that I have felt a greater anxiety about than my history."[59] Was Joseph's dream the cause of his anxiety about his history or was the anxiety the cause of the dream? Maybe the answer is *yes* to both questions, but it is not possible to know for sure based on the available record. However, if Joseph was living according to the principles he taught, then he certainly believed his dream to be inspired, because if he had thought otherwise, he would have *shut it up*.[60]

---

[57] HC 5:362.

[58] HC 5:394.

[59] HC 6:66; Joseph recorded the extent of his obedience to this dream in a journal entry just before his death: "For the last three years I have a record of all my acts and proceedings, for I have kept several good, faithful, and efficient clerks in constant employ: they have accompanied me everywhere, and carefully kept my history, and they have written down what I have done, where I have been, and what I have said" (HC 6:409).

[60] HC 3:391.

A Dream of Prophecy

JOSEPH KNEW OF a conspiracy against his life organized by a group of apostate Mormons in Nauvoo. He published the conspirators' names on 24 March 1844, including Dr. Robert D. Foster,[61] Chauncey L. Higbee, William Law, and Wilson Law.[62] All four conspirators had previously been excommunicated from the church,[63] and all four individuals helped publish the first and only issue of the infamous *Nauvoo Expositor*. The *Expositor* had been declared a nuisance and its press had been destroyed by the city of Nauvoo on 10 June 1844.[64] On 13 June 1844 (two weeks before his martyrdom), Joseph spoke at a meeting of the Saints in which he "related a dream which I had a short time since." In his dream, Joseph was riding in a carriage in Nauvoo with his guardian angel. As they passed the temple, they saw "two large snakes so fast locked together that neither of them had any power." In answer to Joseph's inquiry, the angel explained that "those snakes represent Dr. [Robert D.] Foster and Chauncey L. Higbee. They are your enemies and desire to destroy you; but you see they are so fast locked together that they have no power of themselves to hurt you." In his dream, when Joseph reached the city edge and entered the prairie, his angel was no longer with him, and he was attacked by two men, William and Wilson Law. The Law brothers bound Joseph and threw him into a pit, but soon Joseph heard Wilson screaming for help, and he was able to unloose himself and catch onto the grass on the edge of the pit so that he could see outside of the pit. The following is Joseph's account of what followed in his dream.

> I looked out of the pit and saw Wilson Law at a little distance attacked by ferocious wild beasts, and heard him cry out, "Oh Brother Joseph, come and save me!" I replied, "I cannot, for you have put me into this deep pit." On looking out another way, I saw William Law with outstretched tongue, blue in the face, and the green poison forced out of his mouth caused by the coiling of a large snake around his body. It had also grabbed him by the arm, a little above the elbow, ready to devour him. He cried out in the intensity of his agony, "Oh, Brother Joseph, Brother Joseph, come and save me, or I die!" I also replied to him, "I cannot, William; I would willingly, but you have tied me and put me in this pit, and I am powerless to help you or liberate myself." In a short time after my guide came and said aloud, "Joseph, Joseph, what are you doing there?" I replied, "My enemies fell upon me, bound me and

---

[61] On 25 April 1844, Foster drew a pistol on Joseph and threatened to shoot him in front of Joseph's own house (HC 6:344).

[62] HC 6:272.

[63] Chauncey L. Higbee was cut off or excommunicated from the church on 24 May 1842, and Dr. Foster and the Law Brothers were excommunicated on 18 April 1844 (HC 5:18; 6:341).

[64] HC 6:448.

threw me in." He then took me by the hand, and drew me out of the pit, set me free, and we went away rejoicing.[65]

Joseph believed this dream was inspired, because he did not *shut it up*, but shared it with the church,[66] but whether this dream showed things to come in this life or the next it is difficult to tell from the available record.[67]

There is no record of an interpretation of Joseph's dream. Certainly the Law brothers, Higbee, and Foster had at least an indirect hand in throwing Joseph into a pit (i.e., the grave), by their involvement with the *Expositor*. The publication and subsequent destruction of the *Expositor*[68] stirred up already angry passions that led to Joseph's martyrdom in Carthage, and subsequent warrants were issued for Wilson and William Law for being accessories to Joseph's murder. All four individuals were certainly Joseph's enemies, yet only William was arrested and he was released within a day of his arrest—never standing trial for his involvement in the murders.[69] In a conversation sometime after the martyrdom, Foster acknowledged his part as accessory to the murder, but he also said that he loved the prophet and would have prevented his death if he

---

[65] HC 6:461–62.

[66] HC 3:391.

[67] Brigham Young: "I can tell our beloved brother Christians who have slain the prophets, who have thanked God thinking that Latter-day Saints were wasted away, something that no doubt will mortify them, something to say the least is a matter of deep regret to them; namely that no man or woman in this dispensation will ever enter into the Celestial Kingdom of God, without the consent of Joseph Smith. From the day that the Priesthood was taken from the earth, to the winding up scene of all things, every man or woman must have the certificate of Joseph Smith, Junior, as a passport to their entrance into the mansion where God and Christ are—I with you, and you with me. I cannot go there without his consent. He holds the keys for that kingdom for the last dispensation; and he rules there triumphantly, for he has gained full power and a glorious victory over the power of Satan, while he was yet in the flesh, and was a martyr to his religion and to the name of Christ, which gives him the most perfect victory in the spirit world. He reigns there as supreme a being in his sphere, capacity and calling, as God does in heaven. Many will exclaim, 'O that is very disagreeable! It is preposterous. We cannot bear the thought.' But it is true" (*Journal of Discourses*, 7:289).

[68] Higbee, the Law Brothers, and Foster brought a civil damage action against Nauvoo (presumably seeking reparations for the destroyed press), but the suit was dismissed for lack of prosecution. Also, Oaks and Hill contend that Nauvoo's action against the *Expositor* was a legal action (Dallin H. Oaks and Marvin S. Hill, *Carthage Conspiracy* [Urbana: University of Illinois Press, 1979], 80.

[69] There is little information available about Wilson Law's activities and whereabouts after the martyrdom. William Law established a successful medical practice in Wisconsin and died of natural causes on 12 January 1892. See Lyndon W. Cook, *William Law: biographical essay, Nauvoo diary, correspondence, interview* (Orem, UT: Grandin Book Company, 1994), 71.

had been in Carthage.[70] Of Higbee, there is little known about his involvement in the actual shooting of Joseph or his life after Joseph's death. Not one of these four individuals ever rejoined The Church of Jesus Christ of Latter-day Saints.

A Dream of Comfort

JOSEPH HAD ANOTHER dream just prior to the martyrdom that he related to William W. Phelps and Hyrum Smith on the way to Carthage. In his dream, Joseph and his brother Hyrum were aboard a steamboat in a small bay near an ocean. There was a fire on the boat and the confusion aboard the boat was great. Joseph and Hyrum jumped overboard and tried their faith by walking on water. After putting some distance between themselves and the boat, Joseph and Hyrum looked back and saw the burning boat drift into a town and set it ablaze. Joseph and Hyrum proceeded across the great deep, and soon they heard a human voice. They turned around and discovered that their brother Samuel was following them. Samuel explained that he had joined them because he had been lonely without them. Joseph described the rest of his dream as follows.

> We all started again and in a short time were blest with the first sight of a city whose silver steeples and towers were more beautiful than any that I had ever seen or heard of on earth. It stood as it were upon the western shore of the mighty deep we [were] walking on and its order and glory seemed far beyond the wisdom of man. While we were gazing upon the perfection of the city a small boat launched off from the port and almost as quick as thought came to us in an instant they took us on board and saluted with welcome and with music such as is not of earth. The next scene on landing was more than I can describe. The greetings and the music from a thousand towers and the light of God, himself at the return of three of his sons soothed my soul into quiet and joy that I felt as if I were truly in heaven I gazed upon the splendor. I greeted my friends. I awoke and lo it was a dream.[71]

---

[70] On 3 November 1845, Abraham C. Hodge stated that he had some conversation with Robert D. Foster, who told him his feelings on the subject of Mormonism. He said "Hodge, you are going to the west—I wish I was going among you, but it can't be so, I am the most miserable wretch that the sun shines upon. If I could recall eighteen months of my life I would be willing to sacrifice everything I have upon earth, my wife and child not excepted. I did love Joseph Smith more than any man that ever lived, if I have been present I would have stood between him and death." Hodge inquired, "Why did you do as you have done? You were accessory to his murder." He replied: "I know that, and I have not seen one moment's peace since that time. I know that Mormonism is true, and the thought of meeting (Joseph and Hyrum) at the bar of God is more awful to me than anything else" (HC 7:513).

[71] William W. Phelps, "Joseph Smith's Last Dream," LDS Church Archives, Salt Lake City (punctuation added), quoted in Mark L. McConkie, *Remembering Joseph: Personal Recollections of Those Who Know the Prophet Joseph Smith* (Salt Lake City: Deseret Book, 2003), 390–91.

Joseph's interpretation of this dream is not recorded, and so only guesses can be made of its significance.[72] Joseph did not record the comfort this dream provided as he marched to his death.[73] Perhaps Joseph's dream represented his and Hyrum's imminent deaths (crossing the "great deep"), and if this is the case, then the dream may have also foreshadowed the death of Samuel, who joined Joseph and Hyrum in death (or this "journey") thirty-three days after their martyrdom.[74]

A Result of Revelation Restored: "Yes, We Are a Visionary House."

THE FACT THAT Joseph recorded his dreams and used them in his sermons demonstrates the spiritual significance that he accorded them. Perhaps an even more telling measure of Joseph Smith's restoration of dreams as a legitimate form of revelation can be found in the faith demonstrated by his followers. Emma Smith, Brigham Young, Wilford Woodruff, and many other early church members received what they viewed as revelatory dreams. For example, Emma Smith saw Joseph in a dream after his death, and in her dream Joseph comforted Emma concerning their children who had died.[75] Brigham Young saw Joseph in dreams several times after Joseph's death and received comfort and instruction from him that guided Young's actions as leader of the LDS Church.[76] Also, Wilford Woodruff reported that "after the death of Joseph Smith, I saw and conversed with him many times in my dreams in the night season," and Woodruff believed that Joseph was sent to him in his dreams from

---

[72] Dan Jones recorded a partial interpretation of this dream by Joseph, but he seems to have mixed elements of another of Joseph's dreams in his memory (Jones, "Letter written to Thomas Bullock," 98).

[73] In answer to a question about Joseph's motivation to persevere in the face of great trial and persecution, Elder Henry B. Eyring (an apostle of the LDS Church) said: "For this simple reason that he had dreamed dreams and seen visions. Through the blood and the toil and the tears and the sweat, he had seen the redemption of Israel. It was out there somewhere—dimly, distantly—but it was there. So he kept his shoulder to the wheel until God said his work was finished" (quoted in Sarah Jane Weaver, "Expectations: Today's youth will rise to them," *Church News*, August 2004, 7).

[74] Lucy Smith, *Revised and Enhanced History*, 459.

[75] Alexander Smith retold his mother's dream in an article in the 31 December 1903 *Zion's Ensign* twenty-four years after it happened (Linda King Newell and Valeen Tippetts Avery, *Mormon Enigma: Emma Hale Smith* [New York: Doubleday, 1984], 303).

[76] Brigham Young, *Journal of Discourses*, 18:244–45; Ronald K. Esplin, "Discipleship: Brigham Young and Joseph Smith," in *Joseph Smith: The Prophet, The Man*, ed. Susan Easton Black and Charles D. Tate Jr. (Provo, UT: Religious Studies Center, 1993), 262–64; Glen M. Leonard, *Nauvoo: A Place of Peace, a People of Promise* (Salt Lake City: Deseret Book, 2002), 477.

God to teach him.[77] While only eight of Joseph's dreams were recorded, there are at least twenty-eight dreams (found so far) recorded by prominent followers in which Joseph appeared, and there are hundreds of recorded dreams that demonstrate the faith of Joseph's contemporary followers in the revelatory role of dreams.

In conclusion, though dreams enjoyed some popular support as revelation among individuals largely removed from organized religion in Joseph's day, among the established clergy and educated class of Joseph's day, dreaming was a form of revelation that had an unreliable reputation at best, and a devilish reputation at worst. The cardinal contribution of Joseph Smith was revelation, and Joseph's restoration of revelation included dreams. Even though dreams were not Joseph's primary means of revelation, by restoring revelation, Joseph restored the credibility of revelatory dreams in organized religious settings and in the personal lives of his followers. When Solomon Chamberlin inquired at Joseph Smith's house, "Is there any one here that believes in visions or revelations?" Hyrum's reply was truthful, and even a bit understated—"Yes, we are a visionary house."[78]

---

[77] Wilford Woodruff, "Organization of the First Presidency—Responsibility of the Saints, etc." *Journal of Discourses,* 21:317–18.

[78] Chamberlin, "Sketch" 144.

Life Together: the Path of Most Resistance[1]

As the people were filled with expectation, and all were questioning in their hearts concerning John, whether he might be the Messiah, John answered all of them by saying, "I baptize you with water; but one who is more powerful than I is coming; I am not worthy to untie the thong of his sandals. He will baptize you with the Holy Spirit and fire."... Now when all the people were baptized, and when Jesus also had been baptized and was praying, the heaven was opened, and the Holy Spirit descended upon him in bodily form like a dove. And a voice came from heaven, "You are my Son, the Beloved; with you I am well pleased."

> —Luke 3:15–16, 21–22; Lectionary C
> Gospel reading for the first Sunday after Epiphany

THE FRENCH EXISTENTIALIST and atheist Jean Paul Sartre famously said, *"L'inferne est les autres"*: "Hell is other people." It's not hard to make sense of what Sartre meant. All of us know somebody who has made life hell for us. It is perhaps a little harder to get at the other side of this grim truth: if we dared a self-reflective moment, we might also glimpse the faces of those who have found it hell to be with us. "Hell is other people."

But to Sartre's claim, the second creation story in Genesis offers this counterpoint: "Then the LORD God said, 'It is not good for the human being to be alone'" (Genesis 2:18). To live in joyless isolation—like Scrooge, whom Dickens calls "solitary as an oyster"; to struggle alone; to die alone: unloved,

---

[1] Address delivered on January 11, 2009, to the Community of Christ Seminary convocation, Graceland University, Independence, Missouri.

uncared for, and unmissed— like the poor of India and Africa: is this not a hell that meets and exceeds the pain the other can bring us?

"Hell is other people." "It is not good for the human being to be alone." What shall we do with these two hard-as-flint truths?

The letter arrived late in the summer. I was waiting for it. From the admissions office of the seminary it came, not to announce my acceptance into the M.Div. program (that one had come months before), but to give me that equally important piece of information, my housing assignment. It did not bring good news. My residence for the next year would be "31 Library Place, Princeton, New Jersey." Not the newer Eerdman Hall; not the marvelous pre–Civil War Alexander Hall; not the historic Hodge Hall (named after a famous Presbyterian theologian from the 1800s); they had stuck me in 31 Library Place.

I had toured the campus the previous December, and at a meal one day a group of guys got up and sang a cheeky song inviting the campus to their annual Christmas party. *"Come to the Pits' annual Christmas party, Friday night at 8; fun, and food, and drink that's hearty, come participate."* They were the guys who lived at 31 Library Place, I was told; overflow housing: a three-story, Victorian house on the edge of campus. They called the house "the Pits"—and it was. About fifteen guys lived in it: a stark, water-pipe-banging-in-the-night, food-crumbs-in-the-kitchenette, musty-smelling roach hotel. Woodrow Wilson was rumored to have spent time in this house, but decades earlier, when it was in much better repair. In my December tour of the campus it never once occurred to me that I, as far as I knew the first RLDS person ever to come to Princeton, would be quarantined with a group of other seminary misfits to live their very curious, and very frat-house-like existence. The letter from admissions was telling me, to my horror, that I was being placed in Princeton Theological Seminary's own *animal house.*

I arrived at 31 Library Place late in September of 1979, not quite twenty-three years old. I had been a member of what we then called the RLDS Church for four years. Having spent all of my life in central Michigan, where I even have great-great grandparents buried, I hadn't gotten out much. The trek from Clare, Michigan, to Princeton, New Jersey, was the longest drive I had ever made by myself. Only the burning sense of vocation to the study of theology was strong enough to push me out on this lonely journey toward an unknown end.

I walked up to the ancient front door, sheltered under a massive porch, and rang the bell. A young man with a broad smile and a mass of curly red hair came out and warmly welcomed me. "I'm Steve Tuell," he said, "but everyone calls me Curly, or Curls." He was a United Methodist from West Virginia, a *middler* (in his second year of M.Div. study), who turned out to know a little about our church. We are friends to this day. (He is now a well-known Old Testament scholar whose commentary on Chronicles you'll find in the Westminster/John Knox *Interpretation* series.) That first night Curls, Frank (a Presbyterian from Pittsburgh), Tom (another Methodist, but from Michigan), and I went out for pizza. I didn't know it then, but I was embarking on one of the most transforming journeys of my life: the journey of life together with other Christians.

There were the two Methodists, Curls and Tom, with whom I soon joined forces, to meet in theological combat with the Presbyterians, who outnumbered us. Tom was the first person I had ever met who knew some process theology; because he was from Michigan, I liked him anyway. There was Frank, an occasional cigar smoker and student of Karl Barth's theology, with whom I often argued about sanctifying grace, and also with whom I played catch with a softball. There was Matt from Florida, Steve from Rochester, and Bruce. Bruce was from California, and looked like one of the Beach Boys, one of the first real live Californians I had ever met. There was Conrad, who was from "Long-G-Island," Reformed Church of America. There was Chris, very athletic and rugged, from Maryland, also a Presbyterian. There was Dan, a Lutheran from Minnesota. There was Darwin, an evangelical/Presbyterian of some kind whose parents apparently had a wicked sense of humor when they named him. And though he didn't live in the house, there was Michael, a Methodist and friend of Curly's, who hung around with us. Michael was a former merchant marine or longshoreman turned minister in training, who had never quite abandoned his sailor's tongue and would, with his broad south Jersey accent, shamelessly tell the most racy limericks in the polite company of the campus dining hall, leaving the pious in a state of shock, and me (I confess) laughing so hard I would gasp for oxygen. Finally, there was me. Within a few weeks they all knew "he's not a Mormon," and that I seemed to align theologically with the Methodists, but would listen. They were patient with me, and generous. And in their company I came to shed the idea that I alone had a true call to ministry, and I alone belonged to the one, true church.

What happened among us at 31 Library Place, in this forced experiment of communal living? "Hell is other people"; "it is not good for the human being to be alone." It turns out that Christian spiritual formation takes place around those two truths. Someone once asked a monk what the monks did in the monastery all day long, and he replied, "We fall, and we get up, and we fall, and we get up, and we fall, and we get up." That was our life together. We argued theology a lot, sometimes intensely, but never to the point of breaking fellowship. We helped each other with papers. We watched the news and sat together in shock when the Iranians took over the U.S. embassy in Tehran. We survived the election of Ronald Reagan. We laughed a lot; we yelled at each other. We threw Halloween parties and Christmas parties, and, yes, I stood right there in the dining hall and sang with the guys our cheeky, almost bawdy invitation songs to the rest of the campus.

We deeply loved one another, yet often experienced that other extremity. We complained about our teachers and our assignments. We partied; we played softball; we maintained the Pits's reputation as the seminary's own frat house. We extended each other a lot of grace in the form of breathing space, as we all struggled with the faith questions and doubts that serious study must raise. We listened patiently as Dan the Lutheran began to learn how to chant the Lutheran liturgy (one hoped his future congregation really did believe in salvation by grace alone, or at least had a sense of humor). We wrestled over the ideas of Luther and Calvin and Barth and Tillich, talked about the historical Jesus, the difference between justification and sanctification, and whether the Pittsburgh Steelers were one of the persons of the Trinity. We cheered Frank on as he took his imposing Presbyterian ordination exams. And since we all had assignments in churches on Sundays (I at an RLDS congregation in southern New Jersey), we typically gathered together to talk about our triumphs, our failures, and the *difficult people* in our churches (we never seemed to include ourselves on that list). One Sunday night I came back from church, walked into the house, and heard Curls yell from the living room, "Come on in and have some consecrated host!" The seminary didn't serve meals on Sunday nights, so we all had to fend for ourselves; and Curls and Frank had both brought back fresh bread from their respective churches, bread that had been used for Communion that morning. With theological humor Curly was inviting me to come in and gather together with them around the remains of a Eucharistic meal: one RLDS, one Presbyterian, and one Methodist.

We had a raucous, weekly Bible study, where sometimes, for a few minutes, the testosterone shields would come down, and we would reveal our anxieties to each other. I had never before heard of a lectionary, but I watched as some of the guys wrestled together with weekly texts and weekly sermons. I distinctly remember Frank and Curly arguing about the Transfiguration story. Frank said, "What difference does it make to that little congregation whether Jesus 'glowed'?" Curly replied, "I don't know, but I do know this: there was this woman in one of my churches who was dying of cancer, and even though the Lord didn't heal her, she loved him, and *she* glowed." From these my friends I learned that it's okay to wrestle with texts of scripture, and better to wrestle with them than to discard them.

We were learning together what it meant to be formed not just by our own traditions, but by the wider Christian tradition: to be shaped as *Christians* and as *ministers*, who stood in a vast flowing stream of the Christian church's wisdom, and we were learning how to dip from it. We were learning not only about this tradition, but about letting the Living One at its center, Jesus Christ, shape us. Our confessional differences remained, but they softened and became more like the individual distinguishing marks of members of the same family. When facing the crisis of my grandfather's death early in my second year, I remember telling Chris, the athletic Presbyterian, what was happening, and he knelt right there with me and prayed for me. When I was struggling with whether I even wanted to stay RLDS, I remember confiding my fears in Curly, who gently asked the right question, "Do you think God is calling you out of your denomination?" "No," said I, "I don't think so." He believed me, and then said: "If you ever do find that to be the case, we Methodists would be tickled to have you." In a strange way it helped resolve the crisis because it let me know that I was not alone, and would not be alone, and that there would always be a Christian community somewhere in which to experience Christ in life together. And let me add that these were the guys who surprised me on my birthday in the fall of my second year, announcing that they had secretly arranged to fly my fiancée, Charmaine, out from Michigan the week before Thanksgiving break—to meet them, of course, and receive their scrutiny and blessing, as well as to spend time with me and see us all in our natural habitat. Indeed, it was a kind of zoo field trip for Charmaine, the very Charmaine with whom I love to serve and who suggested to me a short while ago that I ought to tell the story of 31 Library Place in this address.

Princeton's experiment of life together was shut down when 31 Library Place was needed for offices, and when refurbished halls gave more living space for students. I'm glad I spent two years of my three in that old house with those wonderful, irritating, fellow travelers. Our experiment was not as auspicious or as important as Dietrich Bonhoeffer's famous experiment in the 1930s. Unlike his experience, we were not being trained in an underground seminary to be pastors of churches that would choose to resist Hitler. The Princeton police occasionally needed to drive through our parking lot, but the Gestapo did not shut us down. None of us were exiled, jailed, or executed for our resistance to a demonic regime. But we did learn one of the same lessons that Bonhoeffer learned and wrote about in his famous book, *Gemeinsames Leben*, the English translation of which is titled *Life Together*. Christian spirituality is by definition *ecclesial spirituality*; there is no truly Christian spirituality apart from church life—with its agony, its ecstasy, and its various states of boredom and irritation in between.

This is not only one of the great insights of Bonhoeffer; it is a truly great insight of the Community of Christ. Beneath our own unique practices and traditions—camps, reunions, conferences, retreats, community building, and so on—lies this deep instinct that uniquely *Christian* spiritual formation at its most authentic occurs in the gritty rough and tumble of congregational life. Against the enormous cultural forces of individualism that are prying us away from this truth, we really have to pledge ourselves to stand. The word "spiritual" covers a multitude of sins, and thus the times and the moment call us to renew our commitment to *Christian* formation, which by definition is *always* ecclesial.

This kind of radical life together, which we are little by little shaping our own seminary experience around, is the path of most resistance. Why? We really do know. Sartre was partly correct, of course. When we're with others, three things are sure to collide: self-interest, self-love, and self-deception. These are the hard facts of our individual and corporate lives, the substance of what the tradition means by *original sin* (which G. K. Chesterton said was a Christian doctrine for which there was empirical proof). Most of us prefer not to see our capacity for self-love, self-interest, and self-deception, but being in a real Christian community will eventually smoke them out. "It is not good for the human being to be alone," and for many reasons. On the negative side, to be apart from the tough reality of community is to risk giving in to our own false images and nasty ideas. It's not usually communities, or even committees, that write *Mein Kampf.* Hatred of the other is usually nurtured in private, before we spread the virus to others. Thus, God knows we need others to keep watch over us, and that they need us to keep watch over them. Yet on the positive side, it is not good that the human being should be alone, because the very God for whose glory and honor we are called to live *is* communal: in the words of scripture and tradition, God *is* Father, Son, and Holy Spirit. We were created in the image of that God and thus our truest being cannot be fulfilled apart from others.

And so in the scene I began with from Luke's gospel, we must not be surprised to see that Jesus' baptism is not a private experience, but a communal one. He is baptized with *all the people*. He commences his ministry *among*, and not apart from others. He makes common cause with his own people, Israel, even as he sets out on the path that will, for some who come to follow him radically, remake the meaning of God's covenant. And notice at the baptism the communal presence of the three-personed God: the Christ, the Spirit, and the Voice from heaven. Only the divine community can renew the human community. And so God comes in Christ through the Spirit to dwell: in us, with us, among us, for all time. This gift is not for our personal edification alone, but to form us more fully into those who willingly choose again the path of most resistance: to share life together as co-disciples, for the sake of God's coming reign—when at last no creature shall ever again have to fear either the other or being alone.

In that Spirit, in that hope, let us now prepare to approach the table of the Lord to share together in this common meal, in memory of Christ's sacrifice, in renewal of our baptismal vows, in recommitment to the beloved community to which we belong, and in celebration of the *Real Presence of Love* itself among us. Amen.

ABOUT THE AUTHORS

DAVID ANDERSON is a full-time minister for the Community of Christ. He is currently serving as the mission center president and financial officer in the Chesapeake Bay USA Mission Center. He served as a United States Air Force officer for thirty years and has had a wide range of experience in leadership and ethics, both within the church and in the secular world.

ANDREW BOLTON has taught at high school and college level in world religions and peace and justice issues in the UK and more recently as an adjunct at Graceland University and Park University. He has worked for the Community of Christ since 1998 and was ordained to the Council of Twelve Apostles in March 2007. His current responsibilities include supervising the church in Asia, Native American ministries, peace and justice ministries, and the church's annual Peace Colloquy.

ANTHONY J. CHVALA-SMITH serves the Community of Christ as a theologian and Community of Christ Seminary as associate professor of early Christian theology. By training a New Testament scholar and a historical theologian (PhD, Marquette University), he has special interests in the use of the Bible in theology and in Christian spiritual formation. He and his wife, Charmaine, have plans to write a book on the history of Community of Christ theology.

ALONZO L. GASKILL is a former practicing Greek Orthodox who was reared near Independence, Missouri. He converted to Mormonism in 1984 and currently is an assistant professor of church history and doctrine at Brigham Young University. Alonzo is the author of numerous books and articles on the subjects of Mormonism and world religions.

DALE E. LUFFMAN, an appointee of the Community of Christ for nearly thirty years, is a member of the Council of Twelve Apostles. Dr. Luffman serves as an adjunct faculty member for the Community of Christ Seminary, represents the Community of Christ on the Faith and Order Commission of the National Council of Churches of Christ, and is a member of the Academy of Homiletics. A frequent seminar leader and lecturer on topics in theology and church mission, he is also a noted teacher and practitioner of homiletics in the Community of Christ.

WILLIAM D. MORAIN (MD, Harvard) of Lamoni, Iowa, is a retired professor of surgery at Dartmouth Medical School and the former editor of the monthly professional journal *Annals of Plastic Surgery*. He is the author of *The Sword of Laban: Joseph Smith, Jr., and the Dissociated Mind* (American Psychiatric Press, 1998).

JEANNE MURPHEY has an MA in sociology and a focus on abuse issues, with papers published in previous issues of *Restoration Studies*, the *John Whitmer Historical Association Journal*, and the *Theology* series published by Herald House. She is an elder in the Wood River, Illinois, Community of Christ congregation where she currently serves as co-pastor. Jeanne was program chair for the 2008 Restoration Studies Symposium and is incoming JWHA president for 2010.

DONALD E. PITZER, professor emeritus of history and director emeritus of the Center for Communal Studies at the University of Southern Indiana, is a founder and first president of the Communal Studies Association and International Communal Studies Association. He edited and contributed to *America's Communal Utopias* (1997). With early moorings in the Brethren in Christ Church, he has made a lifelong commitment to pursuing peace.

MICHAEL S. RIGGS resides in Philadelphia where he is employed at AECOM Environment as their district manager for Eastern Pennsylvania. His technical discipline is that of public historian. He has previously published in *Restoration Studies IV and VII*, the *John Whitmer Historical Association Journal*, the anthology *The Scattering of the Saints*, and *Mormon Historical Studies*. Riggs is a past president of the John Whitmer Historical Association. He holds an MAR from Park University and has done PhD coursework in history/religious studies at the University of Missouri–Kansas City.

MARK A. SCHERER became Community of Christ World Church historian in 1995. In August 2008, while retaining his responsibilities as church historian, he joined the Community of Christ Seminary faculty by accepting an associate professorship in history with Graceland University. Dr. Scherer is the author of *The Journey of a People: The Era of Restoration, 1820 to 1844*, the first of a proposed three-volume history of the Community of Christ to be published this year. Scherer lives in Independence, Missouri.

WALLACE B. SMITH is a great-grandson of Latter Day Saint founder, Joseph Smith Jr. An MD, he practiced his specialty of ophthalmology in Independence, Missouri, from 1962 to 1976, when he accepted a calling as president-designate of the Reorganized Church of Jesus Christ of Latter Day Saints. After two years he became president of the church. He served in that capacity from 1978 to 1996 when he retired with the title of president-emeritus. Dr. Smith continues to live in Independence where he serves in various volunteer roles in his church, now known as the Community of Christ, and in the community.

G. ST. JOHN STOTT ("GRAHAM") teaches at the Arab American University, Jenin (Palestine), where he is chair of the Modern Languages Department. He is working on a study of how the theology of the Book of Mormon would most probably have been understood in 1830, and the implications of this for ministry today.

CHRYSTAL VANEL is a PhD student in history and sociology of religion at the Sorbonne (Ecole Pratique des Hautes Etudes). He has a BA in history (Sorbonne) and an MA in history and sociology of religion (Sorbonne), his MA thesis being on the Community of Christ. Vanel works as a translator for the Community of Christ.

MARY JANE WOODGER is an associate professor of church history and doctrine at Brigham Young University. Born and raised in American Fork and Salt Lake City, Utah, Dr. Woodger has always had a great love for teaching. Her current research interests include twentieth-century church history, Latter-day Saint women's history, and church education.

INDEX OF ARTICLES, VOLUMES I–X

VOLUME I (1980)

VOLUME II (1983)

VOLUME III (1986)

VOLUME IV (1988)

VOLUME V (1993)

VOLUME VI (1995)

VOLUME IX (2005)

VOLUME X (2009)

Made in the USA